Developing Resilience in Children and Young People

Developing Resilience in Children and Young People: A Practical Guide is the first book to describe the work of professionals using the world's first mentalisation-based mental health education programme – Lundgaard's Resilience Programme. Bringing together accounts from those working with children, young people and parents across many disciplines, this book outlines how they tackle the core issues of self-control, self-esteem and self-confidence with their clients, using the tools and knowledge derived from the programme.

Resilience means being able to handle the challenges of life, especially when life is hard, and The Resilience Programme is unique in its simplicity, efficiency and flexibility. The work presented in the book is based on the fact that mentalising – careful and reflective thinking – often is very helpful when coping with difficult challenges. The chapters in this book provide practical guidance on how to start working with the programme, how to develop resilience in young people, and even how to create resilient communities in a school for children with special needs.

Developing Resilience in Children and Young People is written for those professionals who interact with children and young people on a daily basis, and will become an important book for mental health professionals.

Poul Lundgaard, MD, Senior Physician, has 25 years of experience working in mental health promotion, especially with children, young people and families. He is the founder of The Resilience Programme and is engaged in research building up the evidence base around the programme.

Developing Resilience in Children and Young People

A Practical Guide

Edited by
Poul Lundgaard

Routledge
Taylor & Francis Group

LONDON AND NEW YORK

First published 2018
by Routledge
2 Park Square, Milton Park, Abingdon, Oxon, OX14 4RN

and by Routledge
711 Third Avenue, New York, NY 10017

Routledge is an imprint of the Taylor & Francis Group, an informa business

British Library Cataloguing in Publication Data
A catalogue record for this book is available from the British Library

Library of Congress Cataloging in Publication Data
A catalog record for this book has been requested

ISBN: 978-1-138-23619-6 (hbk)
ISBN: 978-1-138-23620-2 (pbk)
ISBN: 978-1-315-20911-1 (ebk)

Typeset in Times New Roman
by Florence Production Ltd, Stoodleigh, Devon, UK

Contents

Figures

Contributors

Presented in the chapter order of their contributions to the book.

Poul Lundgaard is Chief Physician in the Danish Committee for Health Education and a researcher at the Research Programme for Children's Mental Health, Aarhus University. He is former Manager of the Health Department for Children and Youth in the municipality of Aarhus, Denmark, Municipal Doctor in Silkeborg, Denmark and Manager of the Department of Prevention in the former County of Ringkøbing, Denmark. Poul has 25 years of experience within health promotion and prevention, method development and implementation of research-based knowledge about health.

Susanna de Lima is a Clinical Psychologist with many years of experience in the treatment of vulnerable youth. She has 12 years of experience at the youth centre in the municipality of Aarhus, especially for vulnerable youth with drug abuse issues. Susanna has been part of developing the municipality of Aarhus' model for the treatment of drug abuse for youth under the age of 18. Aside from her work as a practitioner, Susanna works as a coordinator and has ongoing teaching and supervision responsibilities for The Directorate of Social Services, as consultant in relation to the implementation of the substance abuse treatment model in other municipalities, in cooperation with The Directorate of Social Services, among others.

Annalisa Valle has a PhD in psychology and is a Researcher in Developmental Psychology and Educational Psychology at Università Cattolica del Sacro Cuore in Milan, Italy and a member of the Research Unit on Theory of Mind at the Department of Psychology of this university.

Antonella Marchetti has a PhD in psychology and is full Professor of Developmental Psychology and Educational Psychology at Università del Sacro Cuore in Milan, Italy. She is also Head of the Research Unit on Theory of Mind at the Department of Psychology of this university and Coordinator of the PhD Program in Sciences of the Person and of Education of this university.

Davide Massaro has a PhD in psychology. He is Associate Professor of Developmental Psychology and Educational Psychology at Università Cattolica del Sacro Cuore in Milan, Italy, and a member of the Research Unit on Theory of Mind at the Department of Psychology of this university.

Ilaria Castelli has a PhD in psychology and is Associate Professor of Developmental and Educational Psychology at the Department of Humanities and Social Sciences at the Università degli Studi in Bergamo, Italy. She is a member of the Research Unit on Theory of Mind at the Università Cattolica del Sacro Cuore in Milan, Department of Psychology, Italy.

Elisabetta Lombardi is a psychologist and PhD candidate in Sciences of the Person and in Education at the Università Cattolica del Sacro Cuore in Milan, Italy. She is a member of the Research Unit on Theory of Mind at the Università Cattolica del Sacro Cuore in Milan, Department of Psychology, Italy.

Edoardo Alfredo Bracaglia is an honorary fellow in Developmental Psychology and Developmental Psychopathology. He has graduated in psychology.

Francesca Sangiuliano Intra has a PhD in psychology and is a post-doctoral fellow at Don Gnocchi Foundation ONLUS in Milan, Italy. She is a member of the Research Unit on Theory of Mind at the Università Cattolica del Sacro Cuore in Milan, Department of Psychology, Italy.

Heidi Moeller Vestergaard is a Health Visitor with more than 12 years of experience with small children and school children in the municipality of Aarhus, Denmark.

Lene Elmose Broecker has been a Health Visitor for 10 years in the municipality of Aarhus, Denmark. She works with small children and schoolchildren. Since 2011, she has been particularly focused on resilience in relation to interaction, upbringing and obesity.

Peter Skaarup is employed in Hjortshoej Fritidsklub, an after-school club in the village of Hjortshoej, Denmark, as a Pedagogue. Parallel to this, he is teaching resilience in relation to preparedness for education and coping with life in general. His focus is on youth-life among 11–18-year-olds.

Dan Henriksen is educated as a mechanic, a school teacher, a massage therapist, a cranio-sacral therapist, and holds diplomas in psychology and existential psychotherapy as well as mentalisation by Poul Lundgaard in the municipality of Aarhus. He has been employed at Tovshoejskolen, a Danish public school, since 2008.

Lene Steensberg is Educated Cand.Psych. (Candidatus Psychologiae Diploma), and also certified as a teacher. Lene is an Inclusion Supervisor and holds a diploma in leadership. She has many years of experience within learning and development: as a volunteer supervisor for the intellectually disabled and their relatives, in projects for bilingual women, as a facilitator for developmental projects, as a teacher, inclusion supervisor and coordinator for the resource centre at a public school, in the north of Copenhagen, Denmark. She is employed as a Pedagogical Department Manager at Dyvekeskolen, a public school in Copenhagen, Denmark.

Nina Lykke Nielsen qualified as a Pedagogue in 2008 and, since 1 February 2011, she has been employed at the Bispehaven/Fritidshuset Ellekær Playground, Denmark.

Tine Kaarup obtained her certification as a Pedagogue in 2000 and has since been working with vulnerable children and youth. She has been employed as a youth street worker in Aarhus since 1 May 2013. Her focus is particularly on girls' groups in disadvantaged residential areas.

Jeanette Corneliussen has been a qualified Health Visitor since 2001. Jeanette has many years of experience with infants, small children and schoolchildren. She has obtained supplementary training in mentalisation, has experience in working with resilience, for instance in a PTSD-project with bilingual young boys, and has been working as a Process-Manager in a course about inclusion. At the moment, Jeanette is working with early intervention and is taking a diploma in Supervision Methods and Processes.

Tina Brammer Kristensen qualified as a Pedagogue in 2003, and has been working with the criminally institutionalised intellectually disabled (2001–2006) as a Club-Management and Youth-School Coordinator. She is a certification expert and has contributed to the documentation of young people's learning, for instance in relation to resilience. She is employed as an OCN- and Youth-in-Work Coordinator in Gellerup/Toveshøj Nord, Denmark.

Mette Bentzon is Deputy Chief of the clubs and the playground in Gellerup, Denmark. She qualified as a Pedagogue (2003) and has received supplementary education in mentalisation, resilience and coaching communication, etc. She has been working with vulnerable children and young people since 1990 on a voluntary as well as on a professional basis in nurseries, kindergartens, residential areas, schools, after-school clubs and more recently in youth clubs.

Helle Fogtman Welejus has been a Deputy Chief in Toevshoej, Denmark for 6 years. She has undertaken supplementary education in mentalisation, coaching communication and other relevant courses in relation to work within disadvantaged residential areas. Aside from this, she has worked in a children's residential home, in nurseries and with physically and intellectually disabled adults.

Lotte Dalager is a Social Worker and Developmental Consultant and, since 2000, has been teaching staff and youth in the methods from The Resilience Programme. Lotte offers talks and courses in cooperation with The Danish

Committee for Health Education and is an Independent Consultant. http://
lottedalager.dk/

Gritt Graugaard Bonde is educated as a Psychologist. She has many years of
experience with the treatment of vulnerable youth. She has undertaken
supplementary education within mindfulness, for instance by Jon Kabat-Zinn,
and has previously worked with mindfulness with adults. Gritt has been
employed at the youth centre in the municipality of Aarhus, Denmark for
8 years and is responsible for the treatment and diagnosis of youth with complex
psychiatric and psycho-social issues. She also works as a Supervisor and
Teacher.

Joan Dammeyer is a teacher and is employed at Stensagerskolen, a public school
in Denmark with pupils suffering from general learning disabilities, severe
developmental disorders, autism spectrum disorders and multiple disabilities.
She gives courses in resilience for the siblings and parents of intellectually
disabled children and, in addition, she speaks and gives courses in resilience
on behalf of The Danish Committee for Health Education.

Louise Lundgaard holds a professional bachelor's degree in pedagogics. Through
her professional activities, she has worked with neglected children and vulnerable families in exposed conditions. The perspective she uses for care-work is
especially visual and creative, inspired by Theraplay and resilience among
others. She has applied these perspectives in her position as Department Manager at a residential home for children in Greenland as well as in her current
position as a Pedagogical Consultant for refugee families in Denmark.

Mette Haahr was educated as a Pedagogue and holds a diploma in education and
general pedagogics as well as in leadership. She has worked at a residential
home for children in Greenland as a Department Manager and Deputy Chief
(2011–2015).

Johanne Cecilie Andersen holds a Cand.Psych. (Candidatus Psychologiae
Diploma), and is a Work and Organisational Psychologist, Leader of the Human
Resources Department and Work Environment in Guldborgsund Kommune,
a Danish municipality.

Morten Lysdahlgaard holds a Cand.Scient. (Candidatus scientiarum) in Sports.
He has previously worked as a Sports Physiologist for professional teams and
individual athletes. He has also worked as a consultant in the establishment
and support of municipal frameworks for elite sports. Over the past 8 years
he has worked in the domain of people's health, including municipal health
promotion and prevention initiatives.

Acknowledgements

Thank you to all those who have contributed to this book with their wisdom, experiences and personal stories. Warmest gratitude also to all those who, through the years, have worked to bring our knowledge of resilience and mentalising to where it is today. Thank you to our translator team, Kathrine Kjaergaard and Rosa Lisa Lannone. Finally, thank you to Karen Lise Soendergaard Brandt, the book's editor from Klim, Denmark, Joanne Forshaw, Routledge editor for a truly unique collaboration on this book, and to Lisser Lundgaard Bak for invaluable inspiration and cooperation.

Introduction

Poul Lundgaard

This book is written for those who interact with children and adolescents in their everyday lives – professionals, students and teachers. The book is written by a group of professionals who have spent many years supporting the development of resilience in the lives of children and adolescents.

The work of The Resilience Programme stems from the fundamental desire of what we, as parents and occupational professionals, share for our children: the desire for them to have a good life. Naturally, a good life consists of more than good experiences; it's also about going through life safe, healthy and well. Resilience is about our ability to handle life's challenges, big and small, from difficult tasks such as suffering through illness and loss to establishing mutual understandings with others (Zautra, Hall & Murray, 2010). The word *resilience* stems from the Latin *robus*, meaning oak tree. In this context, it is a metaphor for strength and perseverance – our ability to compromise and simultaneously stand firm. Resilience is *not* about being 'hard' and clenching our teeth in order to withstand anything without effect, affect or reaction. To be resilient does not entail never being allowed to get upset, angry or scared – nor does it mean hiding those feelings. Resilience means that when we do encounter tough stuff we know that we can *handle* it. Resilience also means acquiring the ability to reflect upon ourselves and our lives objectively, to judge what is right and what is wrong; for example, having the strength to say 'no' if we are exposed to evident injustices. The concept of resilience is relevant to all, but particularly those who are distinctly challenged due to disability, illness, poverty or marginalisation. When sustaining such hardships, mental resilience opens up our ability to uphold a good quality of life, despite obstructions.

Research in a variety of fields, including psychology, education, neuroscience and sociology, has resulted in a gradual understanding of what resilience means. This includes insights into the contributing factors in the development of resilience as well as how this development can be supported. The concept of resilience can be applied at both the individual and collective level; for example, resilient relationships within familial, educational and even work contexts (see Zautra et al, 2010; Goldstein & Brooks, 2013). And, when supporting the development of resilience, it is often essential to work on both the individual and collective level.

While there are a multitude of factors that affect the development of resilience, there is one in particular that stands out: the ability to *mentalise*, to reflect upon our own thoughts. Supporting a child's ability to reflect may positively influence her/his entire life. Our ability to reflect encompasses the skill to think about our own thoughts and the thoughts of others. Unsurprisingly, it has been proven that this ability is crucial to managing life. *Mentalising* as a concept is further reviewed in Chapter 1.

The background of the mentalising perspective on resilience, which is the theme of this book, is the result of a developmental project conducted by The Department for Children and Youths in the municipality of Aarhus, Denmark, between 2007 and 2010. Based on recognised knowledge from psychology, pedagogy and brain research, a programme was developed, making use of everyday language and imagery, with the knowledge and aim of developing resilience in children and adolescents – in the home, day-care centres, schools and after-school clubs. There was immense interest in the project; initially, 30 occupational professionals were trained to work with resilience, using this approach. These professionals then helped introduce around 4,000 employees of The Department for Children and Youths and a further 4,000 parents to resilience and the so-called 'Thoughts in Mind' material.[1]

The Thoughts in Mind project has provided a foundation for a nationwide research project, led by Aarhus University. Using scientific methods, the aim is to investigate whether the mentalising approach to resilience has value in practice. The research project is financed by the Tryg Foundation and by government funds. It began in 2013 and runs through to 2018. The core of the research project comes from an improved version of the Thoughts in Mind materials, namely, the knowledge and inspiration found in The Resilience Programme, which is freely accessible on the Internet. The Danish version is found at www.robusthed.dk and the English version can be accessed through http://myresilience.org. The research project involves four extensive and controlled studies focusing on: 1) children and adolescents in care; 2) children with ADHD; 3) primary school education; and 4) secondary school education. Moreover, there are other projects being prepared, or which are already under way in Denmark, Greenland, England, Italy and Greece. In these projects, research groups using different methods examine the use and value of The Resilience Programme in relation to a number of highly diverse target groups.[2] Materials for the programme are currently available on the website in three languages: Danish, Greenlandic and English. Even though some of the stories and experiences discussed in this book stem from the Thoughts in Mind project in Aarhus, the programme will be referred to as The Resilience Programme or myresilience.org throughout the book so as to avoid confounding the two. Essentially, these are one and the same programme. The Resilience Programme is simply an extended and edited version of the Thoughts in Mind project.[3]

There are therefore many professionals who have, for many years, worked with resilience using the mentalising perspective, supported by knowledge and inspiration from The Resilience Programme. Among others, this includes healthcare professionals, teachers and educators, social workers, psychologists, family therapists and work environment consultants. They are the representatives from these groups in Denmark, Italy and Greenland who, in this book, use their experiences to demonstrate how to work towards strengthening resilience and the ability to mentalise in children and young people. This book includes practical stories and professional opinions from interactions in everyday life with children, adolescents, parents and co-workers.

The concept of resilience and The Resilience Programme are examined in the first chapter. The end of Chapter 1 explores the tools of the programme; these are referred to throughout the book. In Chapter 2 we go deeper into the theory and research about mentalising and the Theory of Mind concept, illustrated by an interesting school research project. Working with resilience in the lives of children and young people is looked at in Chapters 3 to 5, from meetings between health visitors and families with small children or schoolchildren to interactions between pedagogues/teachers and children of various ages in school and after-school clubs. Naturally, resilience is particularly important for children and adolescents who have distinct challenges in their lives. Therefore, Chapters 6 to 8 focus on ways in which to help children and adolescents with specific needs, such as mental and physical disabilities or social problems. Throughout the book there is a consistent focus on both individual and communal resilience. The final chapter, Chapter 9, looks at the municipal perspective. Children and adolescents spend a significant amount of their daily lives in the presence of professional adults. A positive working environment and resilient communities have significance for both children and adults. The chapter depicts how a local municipality systematically worked to spread the perspective of resilience by implementing it internally, within municipal offices, and extending outwards. When knowledge of resilience and the Thoughts in Mind perspective are to be implemented in organisations, such as schools, solid leadership is vital so that staff see it as a priority. Only in this way can the full advantages of the programme be ensured.

Everyday language and imagery, instead of academic and technical language, is crucial in The Resilience Programme, for two reasons. The first is that we want to be able to communicate with *all* people and *all* professionals, regardless of social or professional backgrounds. The second is that professional language is suitable for communicating with one another professionally, but fails to have any effect on our inner personal lives – everyday language and imagery, however, ignites this. There are probably very few professionals who have felt personally moved by an academic textbook or academic article, whereas the majority of people have been touched by personal conversations with others or by films, literature or music. Work with resilience and the mentalising perspective has a tight professional focus, as is outlined in Chapter 1; however, the entirety of the ideas is conveyed in everyday language and imagery throughout the book.

All contributors to this book have adapted the knowledge and inspiration from The Resilience Programme to the context in which they work – and flexibility is one of the major ideas of the programme. The book is a goldmine of practical ideas and stories from real life. It has been evident over the years that the concept of resilience and The Resilience Programme contribute to mutual understandings and common language when meeting diverse groups of children, youth, parents and professionals as well as in problem solving and cooperation across professions and sectors.

Some readers may wonder why there are no published contributions that illustrate the work of The Resilience Programme in day-care institutions. This is, indeed, a work in progress within many Danish communities; however; its advancement has not yet reached a point at which it is ready to be disseminated. Another area that is not specifically touched upon in this book is autism. The tools of The Resilience Programme are currently being used in a number of institutions working with children, adolescents and adults who fall within the autistic spectrum. There is currently consideration regarding a second book focusing exclusively on the work of resilience with children, adolescents and adults suffering from autism and a third book with a focus on dyslexia and resilience.

Notes

1   Ideas from the Thoughts in Mind project were later published in a chapter of the book *Minding the Child* (Lundgaard Bak, 2012).
2   Updates and overviews can be found at http://myresilience.org.
3   The work to expand and implement The Resilience Programme is now rooted in The Danish Committee for Health. The program is freely accessible on the Internet and license free. The programme is not allowed to be used commercially in any form. To ensure the best possible use of the programme, the committee provides lectures and courses for organisations wishing to implement The Resilience Programme systematically.

References

Goldstein S & Brooks RB (2013) *Handbook of Resilience in Children.* New York: Springer.
Lundgaard Bak P (2012) 'Mentalizing communities for children'. In Midgley N & Vrouva I (eds) *Minding the Child: Mentalization-Based Interventions with Children and Families.* Hove, UK and New York: Routledge.
Zautra AJ, Hall JS & Murray KE (2010) 'Resilience, a new definition of health for people and communities'. In Reich JW, Zautra AJ & Hall JS (eds) *Handbook of Adult Resilience.* New York: Guilford Press.

Chapter 1

What is resilience?

The background of The Resilience Programme

Poul Lundgaard and Susanna de Lima

The development of resilience takes place within interpersonal relations and through an individual's thoughts and feelings. Resilience is therefore about the individual person as well as the relationships one is a part of. There has been a significant increase in research into resilience throughout the past 20 years (Ager, 2013) and there are excellent textbooks and articles about resilience on both the individual and collective levels – including family, school, university and work environments (Zautra, Hall & Murray, 2010).

The concept of resilience overlaps with a multitude of other concepts from the disciplines of mental health and health promotion: coping, managing, handling, self-efficacy and empowerment. Resilience can essentially be referred to as a collection of protective factors (Dray et al, 2015). The American Psychological Association (APA) has identified ten factors that are important in the development of resilience:[1]

- Make connections
- Avoid seeing crises as insurmountable problems
- Accept that change is a part of living
- Move towards your goal
- Take decisive actions
- Look for opportunities for self-discovery
- Nurture a positive view of yourself
- Keep things in perspective
- Maintain a hopeful outlook
- Take care of yourself.

There are individual boundaries for resilience. Resilience is influenced by biological factors, upbringing, life events and living conditions (Zautra et al, 2010). Most people experience resilience in some areas of their lives and vulnerability in others. People do not develop resilience if they are exposed to living conditions that they cannot cope with. On the contrary, they become more vulnerable. It is, of course, a fundamental task, at all levels of society, to help people live within the limits they are able to cope with. Resilience must never be considered as a sort of 'protective coating' that enables people to tolerate anything, such as unreasonable living conditions. Resilience is also about knowing our own limits and, as much as possible, refraining from exposure to situations that are unreasonable or that we do not have the strength to deal with.

Resilience is relevant to at least four life dimensions:

Relationships with other people. As wonderful as it is to spend time with other people – at home, school or work – it can be just as difficult at times. When relations with others are hard, resilience is about being able to keep ourselves together so as not to feel a sort of breaking inside, while also being able to work actively towards fixing situations.

Tasks. As we grow up, our everyday lives are gradually characterised by tasks, on both smaller and larger scales, that need solving. If, as a child, we consistently protest duties and yet undertake them with a 'must do' outlook, this can lead to problems in later life. The ability to complete 'must-do' tasks without reacting emotionally is a vital part of resilience. However, learning to stay away from 'must-do' tasks that could potentially do harm is just as important. The development of resilience in relation to assignments is also about stimulating the motivation to practise.

Temptations. Life is full of temptations – some that are good for us and some that are not. In this regard, resilience is about the ability to say 'no thank you' to the temptations we know are harmful, while withstanding pressures from the outside world or internal cravings.

Suffering. Suffering is an inevitable part of life. One form of suffering is illness. It can require considerable resilience to maintain a good quality of life if we are experiencing chronic suffering.

Another form of suffering is loss. People die around us and relationships do not always last forever. Both friendships and romantic relationships can come to an end. In this regard, resilience is, once again, about the ability to hold ourselves together and get through life as well as possible while things are difficult. At the right time, it is also about the ability to put serious loss in the past and continue in life with a forward-looking perspective. This does not necessarily entail forgetting what happened, but being able to live with it, without being unnecessarily burdened by it.

Lastly, there is a form of suffering that revolves around being different. When we meet a person who is very different from what we are used to, we can become hesitant about how to handle it. This hesitation can, however, for someone who is different, come to be experienced as rejection. It requires significant resilience to be able to handle the hesitations of others simply because of differences.

Essentially, resilience is a fundamental tool to cope with life. Generally, resilience develops organically throughout life, while experiences teach us how to handle challenges in the best possible ways. Multidisciplinary research, however, has provided further extensive insights into the functions of resilience and has presented ideas of ways in which to support its development. The chapters in this book aim to assist in the conversion of this knowledge into practice: how to support the resilience of children and adolescents so that they become better at dealing with the very diverse challenges they will face throughout their lives.

The approach of the book is based on acknowledged research from a number of fields, including psychology, pedagogy and brain research, which has been translated into everyday language and imagery. This collection of knowledge, as well as practical tools, can also be found on www.robusthed.dk and http://myresilience.org (The Resilience Programme). The focus of the websites is on *practical knowledge* and *inspiration* about resilience and thoughtfulness for children, adolescents and adults. Ideas are presented as modules so that people can simply select what is relevant or interesting for a given situation. The modules can, of course, also be assembled into shorter or longer pieces, adaptable to all circumstances. Educational courses that cover all modules can be taught; however, it is more typical to engage with fewer modules that apply to a particular situation. A study from Harvard University (Weisz et al, 2012) concluded that modular-based programmes, in which facets are customised to specific circumstances, are more effective than lesson plans that review curriculum in a fixed order. The Resilience Programme is precisely such a modular programme.

Scientific evaluations of The Resilience Programme indicate that the programme can have positive effects when used by trained staff in schools and youth clubs (see Chapter 2, Valle et al, 2016; Lundgaard Bak et al, 2015), as exemplified by the cases presented in this book, while short introductions in schools and educational institutions are less likely to have substantial effects (Lundgaard Bak, Svendsen & Obel, 2017a). Minimal internet-based intervention with the programme may also have positive effects in groups of vulnerable children and young people taken into care, while minimal intervention does not seem to have any major effects in groups of young adults with ADHD (Lundgaard Bak, Svendsen & Obel, 2017b).

A UK school study evaluating the implementation of The Resilience Programme has ranked programme implementation as 4.00 on a Likert scale of 1–6 (Borlase et al, 2017, submitted for publication). The same study confirms that implementation of The Resilience Programme is subject to the same conditions as implementation of all programmes, for instance leadership commitment.

In order to establish The Resilience Programme as a so-called evidence-based programme, more research has to be conducted by independent researchers.

The Resilience Programme is not reserved for specific groups. It can be used:

- By children, adolescents and adults, both individually and collectively
- For general wellbeing and health promotion and in relation to unique challenges, on both smaller and larger scales

- As an individual programme and/or with any other approach, theoretically and methodologically, because it essentially involves the dissemination of general knowledge about being human – individually and in relationships.

The programme can be used by anyone, directly from the book or the web-pages. However, it is often preceded by an introduction, when used in communities such as day-care centres, schools, educational institutions and workplaces. Introductions can be given by an instructor in one to two hours of lectures and in courses of up to five days' duration.

Over the past few decades there has been a range of efforts to provide vulnerable children and families with good living and learning environments, such as in schools and institutions. Such programmes typically address either individual children and their families or the environments of, for example, the schools they attend (WHO, 2006; Adi et al, 2007a, 2007b; Shucksmith et al, 2007; National Institute for Clinical Excellence, 2008, 2009). Programmes targeted at individuals and families are often used by specially trained staff. As mental health challenges are becoming something of an international epidemic, researchers have contended that there is a need for programmes that extend beyond the highly specialised treatment efforts, which, by nature, can be beneficial for only a very few (Kadzin & Blasé, 2011; Roth & Fonagy, 2006).

The approach presented in this book and on the programme's websites is designed to meet these obstacles, as it can be used at all levels, individually or collectively, and by all people, regardless of their background. The knowledge and inspiration are conveyed in everyday language and imagery, without any complex jargon. As mentioned in the Introduction, there are two reasons for this, the first of which is obvious: everyday language increases accessibility to knowledge for all, in particular for children and adolescents. The second reason is that, while professional language is valuable for communicating precise theoretical and empirical knowledge to experts, everyday language and imagery is imperative when communicating about practicalities or implications in everyday life, especially regarding our emotional life.

The following explains the academic, theoretical and empirical background of the ideas conveyed in this book and The Resilience Programme.

Social learning

Social learning theory, outlined in the 1970s by psychologist Albert Bandura (1977), is a good starting point for the understanding of resilience. Social learning theory forms a background theory for the cognitively oriented knowledge programmes (including many of the so-called evidence-based programmes). All behaviour is, in principle, preceded by thoughts and feelings. Equally, all behaviour leads to an outcome, whether large or small. Behaviour can be a form of communication, such as in a conversation or correspondence, or it can be a practical action.

A choice to engage with or refrain from a certain behaviour in a specific situation is determined by two things:

1 *Expectation of results*: If we expect a positive outcome from engaging in a certain behaviour, there is a higher chance that we will exhibit this behaviour than if there was the expectation of a negative outcome.
2 *Expectation of self-efficacy*: We could be certain that a specific action or behaviour leads to a desired result yet still refrain from engaging, due to a lack of confidence in ability. Self-efficacy is task-specific. It is totally possible to have a high sense of self-efficacy in one area of life and low self-efficacy in another. If we have a high sense of self-efficacy in many areas of life, we are likely to have a high degree of self-confidence and self-worth. Expectations of our own abilities are determined by three factors:

- Personal experiences: If we have previous experiences with specific behaviour leading to positive results, we are more likely to repeat this behaviour. This is also the case for the opposite scenario. If we have previous experiences with negative outcomes from a certain behaviour, we are less likely to repeat it in the future.
- Relevant knowledge: This is helpful in developing our behaviour in specific situations. It is crucial, however, that this knowledge is experienced as personally meaningful. Influential knowledge conveyed by a professional may be particularly relevant, but if it is not perceived as personally meaningful, it is unlikely that it will be used for decisions.
- Confident role models: The people with whom we feel confident can have a significant positive influence on our behaviour. This is naturally the reason why having reliable and confident adults in our childhood is vital in the shaping of our lives.

The Resilience Programme is a collection of knowledge and inspiration that supports all these three background factors so as to develop high self-efficacy. One reason for this is the primary focus on what precedes all behaviour, namely thoughts and feelings.

Mentalisation

Research shows (not surprisingly) that the degree of self-control over our thoughts and feelings has a significant influence on how we cope in life (Moffit et al, 2011; Schlam et al, 2013). In order to keep self-control in thoughts and emotions, the ability to reflect upon our own thoughts is necessary; that is, the ability to thought-read ourselves and modify our thoughts and feelings in case we find them going in an unfavourable direction. Likewise, it is important to be able to modify our behaviour accordingly. This 'double capacity' is called mentalisation. The concept is related to a number of psychological terms and executive functions that embrace Theory of Mind, social cognition and metacognition. It is also related to everyday concepts such as thoughtfulness, empathy, self-knowledge and self-insight. The focus in this book is therefore mentalisation, that is, *the ability to reflect upon our own thoughts as well as the thoughts of others.*

For some people, mentalisation is difficult:

* Small children under the age of 3 or 4: because the brain is not yet developed enough to recognise that invisible events (thoughts) occur within themselves and in other people – events that may be of major importance
* People who are deficient in intelligence: mentalisation is one of the most advanced brain functions. With impaired brain functionality, the conditions for mentalising deteriorate
* People with autism spectrum disorders: reduced mentalisation ability is considered by some researchers to be the basic disability in these types of disorder (Fonagy et al, 2005). People with autism spectrum disorders often find it difficult to read other people and thus have problems with communication and relationships
* People who are on high alert and are stressed, for example, suffering from severe anxiety, post-traumatic stress disorder or ADHD
* All of us: when emotionally excited to such a degree that we are overwhelmed by emotional states. Many have probably experienced how reflection is restrained in such states.

In the company of people who lack mentalising abilities, it is vital that we are able to mentalise – to reflect, keep a cool head and a warm heart so that the situation can be solved in a good way. This can be easier said than done. To be with people who are struggling to mentalise can be wearing in the long run. This may strain our own ability to mentalise. If a child is struggling for a longer period of time, parents can be worn-out and may react inadequately. As a result of having our reflection and mentalising capacities restricted, we start acting differently from how we intend to. Likewise, it is obviously important for professionals to be able to mentalise when helping people who have such challenges.

We do not need to mentalise all the time. Many situations are best solved through routine, without conscious thinking involved. What matters is the ability to mentalise when we need it. Research has shown that mentalising as a competence can be learnt and therefore can become accessible when one needs it. There is a precondition, of course, that we should initially *be able to* mentalise. The capacity to mentalise is limited for people with an emotionally unstable personality structure, such as borderline personality disorder. Research has shown that such individuals improve significantly through intensive mentalisation-based training. In the book, *Minding the Child* (Midgley & Vrouva, 2012), we can read about the research into mentalisation in relation to children, youth, families and schools.

The Resilience Programme is a mentalisation programme focusing on disseminating knowledge about and inspiration regarding how to train ourselves in this ability to reflect – to create a capacity for mentalising. Training ourselves to mentalise is similar to any other type of training:

- We must achieve knowledge about how to do it, and seek inspiration
- We must start the practice with tasks that are not too difficult
- We need to continue, persevere
- We may talk to people we trust if it becomes difficult
- Rewards may be helpful.

The focal point in training is the setting of a direction and a goal. Failure is allowed: we just have to keep trying again and again, and success will eventually come – that is, if the goal is realistic, of course. The small child who is learning to walk does not sit down after a couple of attempts and thereafter conclude that walking is too difficult. Even though the child may cry out of frustration, her/his attempts will not stop until the goal has been achieved. The motivation to practise is instinctive and innate.

For good reasons, we spend a lot of time teaching our children and young people about the mechanisms of the world around them. Yet, it is similarly important to spend time teaching them about mental resilience, imparting knowledge about the mechanisms of the world that exists within them, including the mechanisms of the brain. This can be done by using everyday language, imagery and tools that are simple enough to be understood by children and young people, functioning as a reference to further understandings and new practice. When working with resilience and mentalisation in relation to children and youth in praxis, it is vital not to use professional terms but to stick to imagery that is tied to everyday experiences. Professional language is effective in internal professional communications when many people must obtain a precise understanding of a certain concept. Professional language, however, does not necessarily have a significant effect on anything in our personal lives or our individual, personal understandings. Everyday language and imagery does, however. There are probably very few professionals who have felt personally moved by an academic textbook or academic article, whereas the majority of people have been touched by personal conversations with others or by films, literature or music. The aim of utilising knowledge of the brain when working with resilience and thoughtfulness/ mentalisation is not to enable people to become experts in brain anatomy. Rather, the aim is to offer inspiration to create meaningful ideas about the ways in which the brain operates, thereby prompting action.

In the following, we will describe a number of tools from The Resilience Programme. These tools are presented repeatedly through the praxis stories in this book and will be set in italics throughout:

- *Thought Bubbles*
- Stories
- *Attention – The Brain's Spotlight*

- Knowledge about the brain: The *Thinking Brain* and the *Alarm Centre*
- *Fields of Practice*
- Knowledge about resilient communities.

Thought Bubbles

Thought Bubbles are iconic symbols of our thoughts, known for instance from comic books. Symbols are effective in showing us in simple ways how thoughts and emotions work internally. Placing our thoughts within a *Thought Bubble* by drawing or writing about them and using this as a starting point for speaking about the thoughts helps us examine thoughts from the outside – that is, to mentalise.

In a way you could say that there are two different kind of thoughts.

Useful thoughts   Harmful thoughts

Useful thoughts are not necessarily happy thoughts. It is good to be scared, angry and sad – at the right time and place.

However, if it becomes too much or lasts for too long, it can be harmful.

Things can get pretty bad if you can't find a useful thought.

The worst place is hopelessness – to have the feeling that *nothing* can be done. In extreme situations, this can lead to suicidal thoughts.

If you are struggling with a destructive thought, then it may be worthwhile to stop and think very closely about whether there could be a more useful thought alongside. This may be hard to find if you are faced with very heavy thoughts.

When you do whatever you can to stick to a useful thought (even a small one) repeatedly, that's called practising; gradually it becomes easier. It is like learning to ride a bike – at first it is hard, but when you practise, you eventually learn it.

Figure 1.1 Thought Bubbles

Furthermore, as we talk about a thought through a *Thought Bubble* visualisation, we are prompted to slow down the conversation. Normally the speed of a conversation is high and quickly changing, not allowing us to reflect upon a particular thought before having moved on to the next. In a 'thought-bubble conversation', we create room for reflection and conversation about a specific thought – that is, to train mentalisation. A slower pace is vital when we practise something that may be new.

Stories

Human beings have always told stories, myths and tales as a way to understand and pass on the essentials of life. In modern times, this takes on the form of books, songs, poems, films and plays, but the impulse is the same as always. Storytelling is therefore a natural tool for disseminating knowledge about mentalisation and thoughtfulness at a level of everyday life. As illustrated in the following stories, a metaphorical description of mentalisation is in focus rather than the narrative sequence. The idea behind the stories is to provide people with inspiration on how to act within their brain and build their own meaningful ideas towards solving mental and perhaps also practical and relational challenges.

The following small stories illustrate, in different ways, how knowledge about mentalisation and the brain can be explained and how to practise the ability to mentalise.[2] The stories are frequently utilised in the work of supporting resilience and mentalisation in children and adolescents, which will be used in several chapters of this book.

The story of the House of Thoughts

In a sense, we may say that our thoughts live inside our heads. Imagine that your thoughts live in a house with many rooms where you can wander around and discover them.

When you discover thoughts, you are using the world's finest tool, your attention, which is a kind of spotlight. When you cast light onto a thought, you spot it and discover it. Thereafter you can shift your attention and discover another thought. The *House of Thoughts* has many rooms. One room may be occupied by exciting thoughts and another may be filled with sad, fearsome or angry thoughts. A third room may be inhabited by happy thoughts. From the *House of Thoughts*, your thoughts can call you if they want to be discovered. This may be really exciting and good, but could equally be irritating – especially if the thoughts are annoying and keep knocking, all the time, trying to take your attention. In a situation where you have sad, anxious or angry thoughts that take over and constantly force you into their room, you might end up believing that there are no exciting or happy thoughts to be found anywhere. That's not much fun. However, this is not actually the case at all. All those happy and exciting thoughts are just waiting in other rooms in the *House of Thoughts*, waiting for you to discover them and pay attention to them. Maybe there are even tools to be found in one room that could be used to fix some other thoughts in another room in the house. There may also be thoughts in a room that need to be left in peace, so they won't disturb you too much. If you often go to explore the rooms in the *House of Thoughts* with your attention, it becomes easier to be in charge of your thoughts.

The following is an authentic example illustrating how the story of the *House of Thoughts* can be used as a constructive image and inspiration to solve a problem.

A 10-year-old boy has become afraid of sleeping in his own bed due to recurring nightmares. In a consultation with the boy, his parents and a psychologist, the story of the *House of Thoughts* is read aloud to the boy. In the middle of the reading, it becomes clear that the boy has turned his attention inwards, that he begins to think.

A couple of weeks later, the boy sends this follow-up e-mail:

> So far, I am sleeping well. I have only been sleeping in my own bed and am very happy about it. I hope you will be able to visit us soon so we can speak a bit more about this sleeping thing. There happen to be a few alarming elements in my dreams, but I can make it all good again when I walk out the door, lock it and enter the SLEEP-WELL-room. I wish to always be in the SLEEP-WELL-room when I am supposed to sleep. I hope you are well and will come to visit us.

Through help from the story about the function and nature of thoughts, the boy had constructed a safe mental space through which he became able to sleep well – whenever he decided. This is mentalisation at its clearest. As simple as that, this is what mentalising is all about.

The next story shows what it means to keep practising and being curious about discovery within ourselves.

The story about the boy who shot down a thought

Once upon a time, there was a boy. His mind was filled up by a thought so heavy that he almost couldn't live with it. One day he took a deep breath and then slowly blew the heavy thought out through his mouth. As the heavy thought that used to fill him up now had gone away, he felt a peace in his body and became aware of the normal thoughts that he used to know and that used to be useful to him. However, the heavy thought remained in the air right in front of him and within just a few seconds the thought went back into his mind once again and took up all the space, making him unable to see his own thoughts. Over and over again he tried slowly and carefully to blow the thought out and away and each time he succeeded, but only for a short while. Therefore, one day he shut his eyes, trying to make the thought visible in the air in front of him. And using his gaze he shot his very special arrows at the thought. But to his surprise, he realised that the thought immediately moved, avoiding the arrow. Still, the boy knew that this was an important and dangerous hunt, which was something he knew a lot about, so he kept practising by using his special arrows and saw that he got better and better.

After a while, he had become so much better that he actually hit the heavy thought. And instantly the thought transformed into a memory that he, without using his hands, was able to put into his casket of memories with all the other good and bad memories that are a part of life. From time to time he opened the casket and looked at his memories without them getting dangerous. And the boy told his friends and family about the successful hunt and everyone could see that he had become his old self again, happy and free. And he became a big hunter and storyteller.

Mind party

Imagine having a party inside yourself where your guests are visiting thoughts. Some of these thought-guests might stay for a long time while others just drop in and out. When you discover the arrival of a new thought-guest, you can welcome the guest just by saying aloud 'welcome', to yourself. It's your party, so you want to do your best to make it a good one. Sometimes an unpleasant thought, which you have not invited, visits you. Try speaking kindly to this thought: 'Although I have not invited you, you are welcome as you obviously need to be here, so it's okay right now. I hope you feel better by being here. Just look around, and please excuse me now, for I must also talk to my other guests. Have a nice party.' Our minds are designed in such a way that the best thing to do, if unwanted thoughts and feelings get too much attention, is to leave them alone in a friendly way. Then they will find a way to get better. If unpleasant thoughts and feelings get too much attention, they might grow and become stronger than is desirable.

The big Reward-Factory competition

The brain has a kind of Reward-Factory inside of it. The Reward-Factory makes you feel comfortable. It starts when you experience or receive something you feel in need of. The *Alarm Centre* starts up if you are very hungry, for instance, and it will tell you that you need to find something to eat immediately. When you have eaten, the *Alarm Centre* shuts down and the Reward-Factory starts up and makes you feel satisfied and comfortable. The *Alarm Centre* and the Reward-Factory are not situated in the most intelligent part of the brain. Cheating the *Alarm Centre* into believing that you need something is quite easy, and this sends you out looking for something that you don't really need. The Reward-Factory starts automatically when you have found what you were looking for. The brain is therefore easily persuaded into thinking that you were looking for something important – even though it may be something that you really didn't need. In our society, a major competition about controlling the Reward-Factory in our brains is ongoing. You see it in commercials every day. It is in fact pretty easy to manipulate the brain and thoughts of other people if you touch upon feelings of fear and reward.

The story of a mind train

You probably know how your thoughts come in succession – one after the other. Thoughts are usually linked to one another, like a train with carriages that move together in time towards a destination. When 'I' go by a thought train, 'I' am inside the 'carriages' while the train is moving. It can be hard to grasp, nevertheless the 'I' merges completely with the thoughts while they run – the 'I' and the present thoughts meld together.

If, while thinking of a specific thought, you suddenly decide to think about something else, it's like changing to another train in order to go somewhere else. You can change your thought train so fast that it can feel like magic. When on a certain thought train, it can be difficult to realise that there may be other thought trains on which you would rather be – and if you have entered a wrong thought train, travelling too fast, you may risk ending up somewhere you do not want to be.

This is what happens when there is something you cannot stop thinking about, even though you would rather think about something else; when there is something that you regret or something you want to change in your life, but find it difficult to carry out.

A very different kind of story in The Resilience Programme has the characteristics of guidance. This one is about a so-called progressive relaxation or body scan.

Wellness beads (to be read aloud, very slowly)

Close your eyes and imagine that you have a small wellness bead in every toe and every finger. The small beads rotate slowly, giving you the most comfortable warmth you can imagine.

Slowly let the beads wander upwards, and when they reach your feet and hands, you let them merge together and become bigger beads. These again slowly migrate up through your legs and arms while they rotate, and give you the most pleasant warmth and comfort you can imagine. When the beads reach your body and your head, they continue to rotate slowly and give you comfortable warmth, making you feel relaxed and free within.

When you finish, let the beads be invisible so they may be ready to use the next time you want them.

Attention – The Brain's Spotlight

We think of something most of the time – more or less consciously. The question is, *who* experiences these thoughts? The answer is simple: *I* do. Everybody has an *I* inside. The *I* experiences the world through attention, which is like an invisible spotlight used to discover the world.

Experiences (the *I*'s experiences) from inside our world consist of three parts:

• The world around us (people, nature, things), which we can see, hear, feel, smell and taste
• Our body, which we can feel
• Thoughts and feelings that we experience inside ourselves.

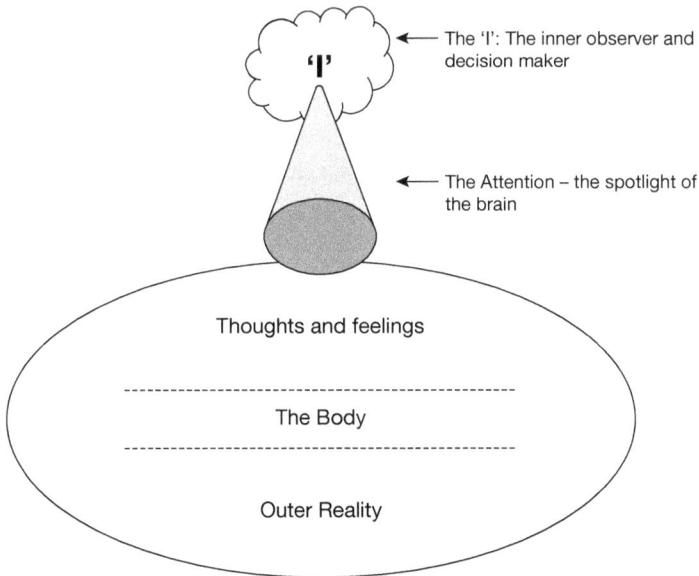

Figure 1.2 Attention – The Brain's Spotlight

Our attention works a bit like the spotlight on a stage: the spotlight highlights what is most important on stage at a given moment. The '*I*' experiences what the attention highlights. The '*I*' is the light operator, the attention is the spotlight, and the stage is the world around and inside each of us.

When we deal with small and big challenges in everyday life, it's useful to be in control of our attention. This enables us to:

- Stay focused on tasks and thoughts that are important, even though we are surrounded by distractions
- Release ourselves from thoughts and feelings that may be disruptive if we stay with them for too long
- 'Scan' our external and internal worlds and discover exciting and important things.

The operative ways of attention can be illustrated through the image of a simple flashlight. Enter a dark room. Turn on the flashlight and hold it in your hand, at the side of your head (like a head torch; Figure 1.3). Turn your head so that the light points towards a specific dot. Freeze the light, your gaze and the dot for a few seconds. Then turn your head, hand, torch and attention to another dot in the room and freeze the light, your gaze and attention at the new dot for a number of seconds. It is the *I* who controls the muscles of your head and hand, the torch and the direction of the light as well as the direction of your gaze and attention – and the moment your attention and the light become focused, this is what the *I* experiences. That means that each of us, right now, decides what *we* experience. Likewise, the *I* can focus attention inwardly and consciously experience thoughts and emotions.

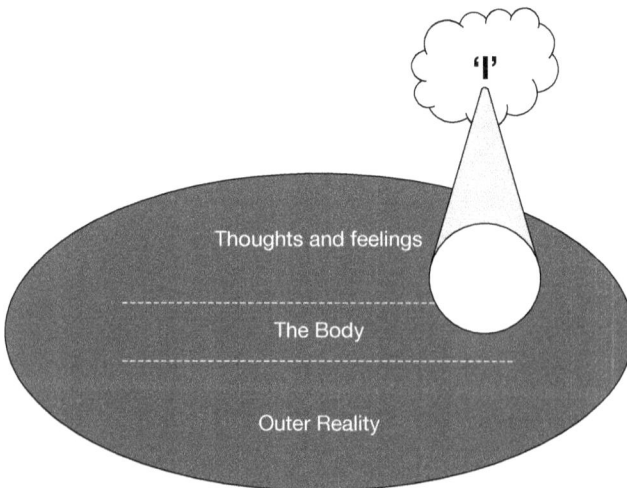

Figure 1.3 Focused attention

When thoughts and emotions attract attention, the '*I*' melts with the thoughts (see *The story of a mind train*). If some thoughts and emotions take power from the '*I*', a kind of self-deception may occur. When absorbed in something of major importance, all other thoughts and emotions vanish. This can compare to the light on a stage: when a strong spotlight highlights a small area of a stage, everything else lies hidden in the dark.

The risk of being in such a situation for a long time is the tendency to interpret everything from the perspective of that single highlighted spot in which you are caught. You become at risk of blindness to other alternatives. Depression and eating disorders may, for instance, imply a distorted self-image as well as being caught in a locked pattern of thoughts. When you are caught in your own 'light', all other perspectives remain in the dark. People may experience having 'seen the light', for instance, through religious, ideological, political, cultural or scientific fundamentalism and, as a result, may suffer from a clouded mind for the rest of their lives where it becomes difficult to experience the world in any other way than what their focus is on.

Issues of self-deception may occur if the *Alarm Centre* or the Reward-Factory of the brain has gained too much power. Fear is an emotion that is potentially dangerous to ourselves as well as to other people. We all have small innocent self-deceptions in our everyday lives. However, a serious self-deception – individual or collective – may cause destructive consequences.

Knowledge about the brain: The *Thinking Brain* and the *Alarm Centre*

Two parts of the brain have decisive influence on our way of thinking and mentalising. We call those the *Thinking Brain* and the *Alarm Centre* (Figure 1.4). The term *Alarm Centre* covers vital structures deep inside the brain, among which is the amygdala. Moreover, the *Thinking Brain* includes the frontal lobes of the brain.

Hyper-sensitivity in the Alarm Centre

Unpleasant and dangerous situations can cause the *Alarm Centre* to be hyper-sensitive. This means that the next time you find yourself in a situation that resembles a 'dangerous situation', the *Alarm Centre* may overreact, with results that give way to fear, anger or sadness – perhaps without any reason at all. It becomes difficult to think rationally. Instead, you may react instinctively to 'survive'. It is obviously good that the *Alarm Centre* takes over by nature when you are facing real danger. If your life is at risk there is no time to consider the pros or cons of taking action. You have to react promptly with either a fight or flight. However, it is not so desirable if the *Thinking Brain* tunes down when there is no imminent danger.

In the centre of the brain is the *Alarm Centre* which checks on dangerous and uncomfortable situations.

We use the frontal part of the brain for thinking. This is our *Thinking Brain*.

Insecurity and guilt activate the *Alarm Centre*. This tunes the *Thinking Brain* down and consequently, it becomes more difficult to think and learn. Fear, anger and sadness can prevail and the body may become sick.

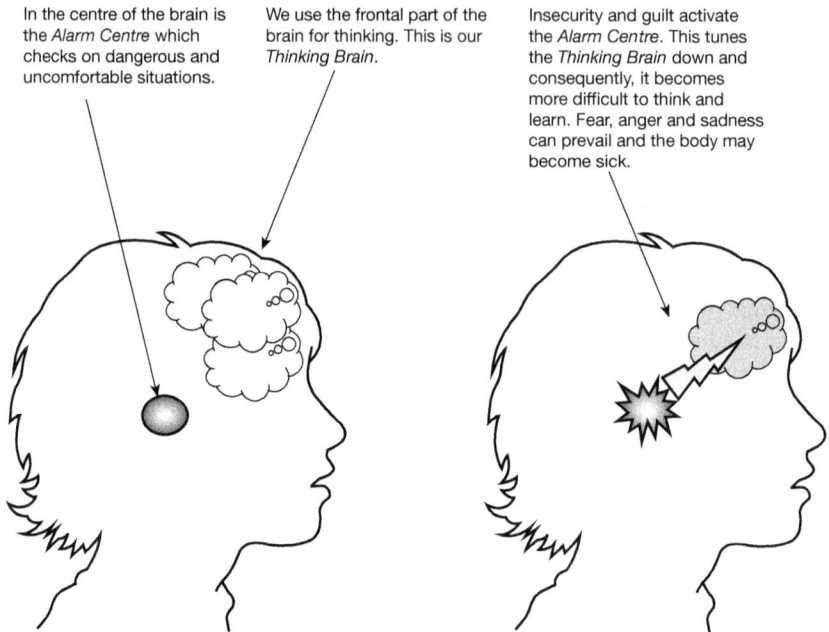

Figure 1.4 The *Thinking Brain* and the *Alarm Centre*

If the *Alarm Centre* has become hyper-sensitive, it may be provoked just by thinking of the uncomfortable. The only thing learnt in situations of alarm is to be on guard in similar situations. You do not become resilient and rather risk becoming more vulnerable. Thoughts about your own psychic and social survival become dominant. Hyper-sensitivity may appear as anger, fear, sadness or reservation. A feeling of defeat and worry activates the *Alarm Centre* and tunes down the *Thinking Brain*, thus making it difficult to understand, learn and remember, even though the brain is completely normal. Many uncomfortable and dangerous situations (trauma, accidents and assaults) increase the risk of hyper-sensitivity of the brain. However, smaller events may in unfortunate cases create hyper-sensitivity in the *Alarm Centre* as well. The most frequent causes of unbalance in the *Alarm Centre* are connected to feelings of insecurity in everyday life; for instance, in your family, at school, at work or in states of stress where the brain is overtaxed.

Excitable children

A worried or agitated child who encounters a calm and understanding adult learns that being in an uncomfortable situation is not dangerous. The child's *Alarm Centre* gradually learns to keep calm while the *Thinking Brain* stays awake and helps the child to be rational and move towards solving situations. Contrarily, should a child be met by a worried or agitated adult in a situation, s/he receives confirmation that interpreting that situation as dangerous is accurate, leading to the development of alertness and hyper-sensitivity. This decreases the child's ability to reflect in situations where that may sometimes be needed. Scolding may likewise activate and intensify reactions in the *Alarm Centre*. The result is anxiety and wariness as well as trouble with learning, remembering and difficulties in understanding the world. When a child is emotionally agitated there is little use for explaining and arguing because the *Thinking Brain*, which we use to make sense of the world, tunes down. The only beneficial way to handle an acute situation is to be calm and provide care and protection until there is enough internal peace to allow the *Thinking Brain* to become reactivated. Not until then will explanations and arguments matter.

If children overprotect themselves or by all best intentions are overprotected by others because of struggles, the consequence may be that their *Alarm Centre* perceives everything as being dangerous, causing them to become even more sensitive. When as a grown-up we encounter an agitated child, for instance a crying child, this will naturally awaken feelings of alarm within – an adult may feel sorry for the child and feel the urge to care and satisfy the child's immediate needs. There can be obvious reasons for doing so. However, this may become problematic if a child is overprotected and realises that an immediate fulfilment of their needs is achieved through a certain behaviour which, in turn, activates adults' *Alarm Centres*. Resilience is very much about the capacity to bear other people's as well as our own emotions without blind reactions. To professionals and parents, it is often easier said than done to keep a cool head and a warm heart when a child is agitated. In situations of little concern, it is important though that a child learns to reflect and be in control of their actions and thoughts – resilience.

It is important also to remember that other people's thoughts are invisible to us. For that reason, misunderstandings that arise between people lead us to believe that the intentions of others are less than good. This may also provoke the *Alarm Centre*. In a case where another person's *Alarm Centre* also becomes triggered, two brains co-exist in high alert – but which one will fight and which one will flee? In situations of alarm it is very soothing to be with somebody who is capable of keeping calm.

The resilient brain

The brain can be trained to have a higher degree of resilience. Providing the *Thinking Brain* and the *Alarm Centre* with appropriate challenges, which are neither too challenging nor too easy, will support the *Thinking Brain* into seizing control of the *Alarm Centre* so that it is not activated without good reason. In this way, resilience is gradually developed. Defining what challenges are appropriate is, of course, individual and dependent on factors such as age, intelligence and personality. Family and school environments have a great influence on all of this, varying from one day to another.

From this perspective, we can conclude that human beings – children, youth and adults, introverts and extroverts alike – who continuously react negatively do not encounter appropriate challenges. When intellectually disabled people react aggressively, it may be because they meet challenges that they cannot cope with. Upon observation, some may consider that what is at hand is a very small challenge. That, however, doesn't change the fact that the individual's high-alert response indicates that, according to their level of function, they have *not* encountered appropriate challenges. Self-confidence and self-worth are developed only through the experience of accomplishing what we were not sure of being able to do. Praise alone does not develop self-confidence or self-worth. Undeserved praise may even cause discouragement (Young-Hoon & Chi-Yue, 2011). This is not to say that praise in daily life is not important when we succeed. It is just as important to receive praise and encouragement when we practise something difficult. Resilience is simultaneously about receiving critique without falling apart and about developing our own critical sense. When, instead of telling each other off, we give each other considerate and respectful critique, there is a good chance that the *Alarm Centre* keeps calm and that such critique can be used to learn something important.

Calming the Alarm Centre

One of the most effective and discreet ways to calm your *Alarm Centre* in an acute situation is to breathe deeply and tranquilly. This method is smart, as it is free, has no side-effects and requires no equipment – and everyone already knows how to do it. People have practised tranquillised breathing everywhere and at all times. Well known, its benefits are reflected in our language, as in 'take a deep breath' or 'count to ten'. The problem is that we do not always have access to that knowledge when we are in a state of alarm. For this reason, it is advantageous to practise tranquil breathing until it becomes automatic and a natural reflex whenever needed. We may call it a kind of mental cleansing, as it is a simple way to wipe out dust and dirt from our minds in daily life.

For children and young people who are troubled to a degree where they are constantly in a state of alarm, and therefore unable to reflect or learn, experience shows that giving them fundamental knowledge about the *Alarm Centre*, and how they can calm themselves by means of breathing, can be a great help, along with support in practising this ability over time.

The stories and our knowledge about the *Alarm Centre* are among the most utilised modules of The Resilience Programme, referred to in several chapters of this book. Sometimes we discover, perhaps surprisingly, that even relatively small children absorb this knowledge. A frequent feedback from professionals and parents who have been introduced to The Resilience Programme is about its simplicity regarding both understanding it and using it. Schoolchildren of all ages, as well as special needs children, have been taught resilience (see examples of this further on in the book). There have been teenagers talking about the pro-gramme to classmates and discussions of it at parent–teacher meetings. Similarly, inspired by the programme, pedagogues in nurseries have been singing songs to very young children who do not yet have the capacity to mentalise. In many ways, this parallels our interactions with newborns, who do not yet understand language – however, by talking to them, all newborns eventually learn. People learn language by hearing language. Likewise, they learn to mentalise by experiencing mentalisation. In a resilience project carried out in an after-school club within a disadvantaged residential area, it has been estimated that The Resilience Programme contributed to a 90 per cent reduction in serious conflicts, as well as halving employee absences. After three years, employees were asked to evaluate The Resilience Programme's actual usefulness in their daily work on a scale from 1–10. The result was that 80 per cent of employees continued to use modules from the programme in their daily work (Lundgaard Bak et al, 2015).

Resilient communities

Knowledge about the *Thinking Brain* and the *Alarm Centre* is also relevant in relation to resilient communities: it is significant that people experience being appreciated. In an insecure community in which people do not feel sure of their worth in terms of who they really are, they are likely to adopt the values and norms of the group in order not to be excluded. The *Alarm Centre* activates and, along with feelings of insecurity, the *Thinking Brain* tunes down. Thus, the capacity for reflection becomes challenged. The *Thinking Brain* is also home to our positive feelings towards others and, as a result, in an insecure community, our ability to identify with and feel compassion towards other people who are excluded from a group is affected. The worst-case scenario is the rising feeling we get from imagining that enemies abound. Many people are ready to pay an extremely high price to gain acceptance in a certain group, including exposing themselves and others to suffering. Those mechanisms are at play in bullying situations and other forms of exclusion – in kindergartens, schools, at work and in the family. Bullying is a group phenomenon – not an individual phenomenon. Both the bully and the bullied react from a position of insecurity. And punishing the bully doesn't always help; it can actually make things worse. When a bully is excluded from a community, for instance through sanctions or punishments, the phenomenon will surface in a different way. The most important thing we can do to prevent and deal with bullying is to spread knowledge about the mechanisms of bullying and actively nurture differences – in all possible facets. Thus, diversity becomes something that is fundamentally valued.

Bullying as a group phenomenon must be separated from situations where a child or young person in a group finds it hard to cope with simply being among peers and outwardly reacts from a sense of alarm, which is in fact prompted by personal factors. In such situations, it may be protective to both the person and the community to move the distressed individual to a safer environment. Occasionally, we may encounter a child who will be sensitive to such a degree that normal, good-natured teasing in a safe environment is experienced as bullying.

Hopefully, resistance to good-natured teasing can be cultivated through the development of resilience. If such efforts fail, the highly sensitive child may require a more protected environment.

Fields of Practice

As mentioned earlier, we may roughly divide thoughts into:

*   Thoughts that may cause us or other people damage
*   Useful thoughts, for instance, thoughts about practical things that support daily life functions. Useful thoughts are not necessarily happy thoughts, though. At the right time and place it is useful to be scared, angry or sad. Useful thoughts may become damaging only if they become too intense or too long lasting.

Mentalisation, thoughtfulness and resilience are essentially about the ability to change focus from damaging thoughts to useful thoughts. This is something we can practise in the same ways as we would practise other things – that is, by doing it often enough and doing it every time we uncover thoughts we know could be damaging. When practising 'thought-relocation' it is very helpful to choose simple, useful and concrete thoughts (see the section above about *Thought Bubbles*).

Practising mentally and practising behaviour are central elements in all cognitive and mentalisation-based therapy. This accounts for the approach presented in this book as well. We have consolidated knowledge about practising into four principles that refer to our knowledge about the functions of the *Thinking Brain* and the *Alarm Centre*, including the principle about appropriate challenges:

*   Protection – but not overprotection – from overwhelming situations: The *Thinking Brain* is able to control the *Alarm Centre* in a way that doesn't activate it without reason, when the *Thinking Brain* and the *Alarm Centre* encounter appropriate challenges – not too challenging, not too easy. Having dealt with a difficult situation, the *Thinking Brain* sends the *Alarm Centre* a message that whatever was at hand was not dangerous. Then, in light of having dealt with difficult situations, we are more likely to face future ones with a calmer mind and a readiness to take on more complexity next time.
*   Use your body to calm the *Alarm Centre*: Practise deep relaxing breathing. It is the most effective method to calm the *Alarm Centre* in acute situations. Be physically active (exercise and get fresh air regularly). This sparks the brain's own pharmacy and creates wellbeing hormones that keep the *Thinking Brain* alert.
*   Practise mental fitness: Speak to people with whom you feel safe about your thoughts and how you may practise your ability to move from thoughts that may be damaging to yourself or others, to useful thoughts (see the section above about *Thought Bubbles* and Figure 1.1).

- Small, safe steps: Are you having to deal with several difficult issues? Start with the most approachable.

In The Resilience Programme, you will find further knowledge and inspiration on how to make your practice successful. From the website,[3] articles can be found on:

- Resilience and praise
- A way to success
- Help someone else
- *Fields of Practice*
- The Mind Game.

The Mind Game (Figure 1.5) is a guide from the Programme you can print on a single sheet of (A4) paper, suitable for drawing-out an overview of a *Field of Practice*.

Giving the brain appropriate challenges is synonymous with the following well-known and often-utilised pedagogical and psychological concepts: small, safe steps, Vygotsky's zone of proximal development[4] and so-called cognitive exposure in vivo. In everyday language, commonly known as 'normal learning', we start with something relatively easy and then proceed to more difficult challenges.

Even though we often refer to thoughts and feelings as being separate, the two are naturally related. We could even say that emotions are the colours of our thoughts. Therefore, in the same way as we can practise being attentive to our thoughts, we can practise attention towards our emotions. Like thoughts, emotions are passing by and changing over time. The ability to feel, describe and acknowledge emotions is important in uncovering what is good and what is less good, respectively. Emotions are part of human life and securing our survival. Fear helps us flee when danger is approaching. Anger can be helpful if we need to set boundaries or fight for something. Emotions can function as a kind of compass, casting light in a certain direction and revealing what is at stake. Just as we can observe thoughts and remind ourselves not to identify with thoughts, we may also learn to observe our emotions and realise that it is not necessary to identify with all of them. We are human beings who experience emotions. If we learn to observe our emotions and be with them without necessarily taking action in all instances, we may train ourselves over time to be less impulsive and therefore more resilient. In an everyday example:

John is 12 years old. He becomes angry when he cannot figure out how his new iPad game is working and immediately reacts with anger, smashing the iPad hard onto the floor. A few seconds later he realises that he has broken it; his anger turns into sadness and being angry with himself because he made it all worse.

The purpose of the Mind-Game is to train your brain in a way that will enhance your ability to take control over your thoughts, and life in general. The game is a reality-game. Make sure you find a great place to put it – somewhere you'll see every day.

Write down what you would like to become better at:

Speak with a friend/mentor about your experiences every day. Your mentor supports you in the process. Write down the name of your mentor:

What you'd like to become better at – your wish, your goal – may be anything, big or small. The goal must be personal, realistic and important – otherwise there is no point. Start with something easy, so as to ensure your success. This builds courage in pursuing bigger goals. However, making it too easy might make the game boring. Examples: Be more at peace within the brain, become better at something concrete, adopt a new lifestyle, etc.

My reward
Write down what you have decided will be your reward – during the process as well as when you reach the goal:

Assess every day
Rate your day with points:
Write this down on a piece of paper, for instance every night at 7pm:

- Mood-points: How do you feel right now? (0-9 points)

- Training-points: How did you perform today? (0-9 points)

- Write, draw or tell your mentor about three valuable thoughts, actions or experiences from your day – big or small.

First step
Write down what you plan to do today as well as in the coming days – make the training fun and easy:

WATCH OUT FOR SIDE-TRACKS

If you become side-tracked, it takes you longer to reach your goal. You might be aware of a time of the day or of a specific place where things get difficult for you.

1. Difficult moments

Note down the times of the day, where you know you are at risk of becoming side-tracked:

2. Difficult settings

Note down any locations you know to be difficult for you:

3. What do I do?

Choose what to do in order to take care of yourself, if you find yourself getting side-tracked:

A. Make an agreement with your mentor on what you will do if you find yourself getting side-tracked
B. Calm down your brain's Alarm Centre (breathe deeply)
C. Listen to music that comforts you
D. Look at a picture that supports you

Write down what you and your mentor have agreed you should do if you find yourself getting side-tracked:

In case you often get side-tracked or that your daily assessment-score is low, change your goal and make your success easier to achieve.

Figure 1.5 The Mind Game

If John could receive guidance about his feelings and how to observe his emotions with restraint, a similar situation could turn out as:

> John is playing with his new game together with a friend. He feels anxious and is becoming irritated and angry about this stupid game. John pauses his iPad and breathes in deeply a couple of times. He shakes his head and tells his friend how he was close to smashing the iPad onto the floor, but refrained from doing so. His anger has already diminished and he chooses to go on with the game.

This example shows how we can learn to hold and deal with emotions without allowing them to take over. It sounds easy, but it requires patience and practice in learning how to handle our emotions in constructive ways. This is the case for adults as well as for children.

People are born with universal core emotions. This means that wherever we were born, we all have similar emotions – it's human. The six core emotions are: anger, joy, sadness, fear, disgust and surprise.

Aside from these core emotions, we have many other often essential emotions. We call them complex emotions, for instance: guilt, shame, pride, gratefulness, envy and jealousy. Complex emotions emerge in relation to other people and include, for instance, social comparisons, which are emotionally based assessments of our own position in relation to written and unwritten norms in the groups to which we belong and the society in which we live.

Fields of Practice in relation to emotions

It is easy to create simple *Fields of Practice* in relation to emotions. The practice of recognising core emotions is a good starting point.

- Do you know the feeling of joy?

  - When did you last experience joy?
  - In which situations do you experience joy?
  - How do other people see that you are happy?
  - Where do you feel the emotion in your body?

- Do you know the feeling of anger?

  - Do you feel the anger in your body – where?
  - In which situations do you become angry?
  - How do other people see that you are angry?
  - What do you do when you are angry?

You can continue this type of questioning by changing one core emotion for another.

Another *Field of Practice* may be to stop and ask yourself a few times a day what you feel, here and now. When doing this exercise, it may be good to remember that you do not need to act upon your emotions in the here and now, but rather register which feeling or feelings pop up:

Step 1   is the practice of being aware of emotions
Step 2   is the practice of finding the conditions underlying the emotion. For instance, by taking deep breaths in order to calm the *Alarm Centre* and then asking yourself what is needed in the here and now (peace, rest, activity, new adventures, food, to see a friend, etc.)
Step 3   is considering which action would be beneficial.

The point of dividing the exercise into steps is to make it easier to practise the ability to recognise and hold emotions without impulsive reactions, thus carving out space to reflect on your needs and, in turn, make a more conscious, and thereby beneficial, choice of action.

A simple and interesting tool, which has been utilised in a couple of the resilience projects described later in this book, is exactly about how to become conscious and how to practise your ability to control your own and other people's emotions and behaviours. The tool consists of a laminated drawing of two remote controls. One remote control has a large button named 'the others' as well as eight smaller buttons, which represent emotions. This remote control illustrates the emotions that other people's behaviours may cause within you. The other remote control has a large button named 'me' as well as eight smaller buttons representing different possible actions.

The remote control to emotions and actions

Working with the remote control supports the movement of thoughts and emotions from 'my action was caused by the others' to understanding and finally mastering 'I am in control!' Having worked with the remote control as a tool, it will sometimes be enough to ask 'who has the remote control?' when anxiety is arising.

Notes

1   www.apa.org/helpcenter/road-resilience.aspx.
2   More stories can be found at The Resilience Programme's websites.
3   Can be found on www.myresilience.org.
4   Lev Vygotsky was a prominent Russian psychologist who lived from 1896 to 1934. Vygotsky formulated the theory of proximal development, which as its core tells how the child, with adult support (or support from a more competent buddy), is able to carry out practical and mental activities which they would not be able to do on their own, leading the child to learn.

References

Adi Y, Killoran A, Janmohamed K, Stewart-Brown S (2007a) Systematic review of the effectiveness of interventions to promote mental wellbeing in children in primary education. Report 1: Universal Approaches: Non-violence related outcomes. National Institute of Clinical Excellence.

Adi Y, McMillan AS, Kiloran A, Stewart-Brown S (2007b) Systematic review of the effectiveness of interventions to promote mental wellbeing in primary schools. Report 3: Universal Approaches with focus on prevention of violence and bullying. National Institute of Clinical Excellence.

Ager A (2012) Annual Research Review: Resilience and child well-being – public policy implications. *Journal of Child Psychology and Psychiatry.* 54(4):488–500.

American Psychological Association (APA) The Road to Resilience. www.apa.org/helpcenter/road-resilience.aspx.

Bandura A (1977) *Social Learning Theory.* Prentice Hall.

Borlase N, Antrobus L, Allen G, Solomon M, Lundgaard Bak P, Kennedy E (2017) Improving mental health and resilience in schools: Challenges associated with the UK implementation of the Danish 'Robust-ED' Resilience Programme, *submitted for publication.*

Dray J, Bowman J, Wolfenden L, Campbell E, Freund M (2015) Systematic review of universal resilience targeting child and adolescent mental health in the school setting. *Systematic Reviews.* 4:186–224.

Fonagy P, Gergely G, Jurist E, Target M (2005) *Affect regulation, Mentalization and the development of the self.* Karnac Books.

Kazdin AE, Blase SL (2011) Rebooting Psychotherapy Research and Practice to reduce the Burden of Mental Illness. *Perspectives on Psychological Science.* 6(1):21–37.

Lundgaard Bak P, Midgley N, Zhu JL, Wistoft K, Obel C (2015) The Resilience Program: Preliminary evaluation of a mentalisation-based education program. *Front Psychol.* 6:753. doi: 10.3389/fpsyg.2015.00753.

Lundgaard Bak P, Svendsen KK, Obel C (2017a) Evaluation of a minimal school intervention with *The Resilience Program* – a mentalization-based health education program, *submitted for publication.*

Lundgaard Bak P, Svendsen KK, Obel C (2017b) Randomized controlled evaluation of an internet-based minimal intervention delivery model for *The Resilience Program* – a mentalization-based health education program, *submitted for publication.*

Midgley N, Vrouva I (eds) (2012) *Minding the Child: Mentalization based interventions with children and families.* Routledge.

Moffitt TE, Arseneault L, Belsky D, Dickson N, Hancox RJ, Harrington H, Houts R, Poulton R, Roberts BW, Ross S, Sears M, Thomson WM, Caspi A (2011) A gradient of childhood self-control predicts health, wealth and public safety. *PNAS.* 108(7):2693–8.

National Institute of Clinical Excellence (2008) Promoting children's social and emotional wellbeing in primary education. National Institute of Clinical Excellence.

National Institute of Clinical Excellence (2009) Promoting young people's social and emotional wellbeing in secondary education. National Institute of Clinical Excellence.

Roth A, Fonagy P (2006) *What works for whom* (2nd ed.). Guilford Press.

Shucksmith J, Summerbell C, Jones S, Whittaker V (2007) Mental wellbeing of children in primary education (targeted/indicated activities). National Institute of Clinical Excellence.

Schlam TR, Wilson NL, Shoda Y, Mischel W, Ayduk O (2013) Preschoolers' delay of gratification predicts their body mass 30 years later. *The Journal of Pediatrics.* 162(2):90–3.

Valle A, Massaro D, Castelli I, Sangiuliano Intra F, Lombardi E, Bracaglia E, Marchetti A (2016) Promoting mentalizing in pupils by acting on teachers: Preliminary Italian evidence of the 'Thought in Mind' project. *Frontiers in Psychology.* 7:1213. doi: 10.3389/fpsyg.2016.01213.

Weisz JR, Chorpita BF, Palinkas LA, Schoenwald SK, Miranda J, Bearman SK, Daleiden EL, Ugueto AM, Ho A, Martin J, Gray J, Alleyne A, Langer DA, Southam-Gerow MA, Gibbons RD (2012) Testing standard and modular designs for psychotherapy treating depression, anxiety, and conduct problems in youth: A randomized effectiveness trial. *Archives of General Psychiatry.* 69(3):274–82.

WHO (2006) What is the evidence on school health promotion in improving health or preventing disease and, specifically, what is the effectiveness of the health promoting schools approach? WHO Europe.

Young-Hoon K, Chi-Yue C (2011) Emotional Costs of Self-Assessments: Both Self-Effacement and Self-Enhancement can lead to Dejection. *Emotion.* 11(5):1096–104.

Zautra AJ, Hall JS, Murray KE (2010) 'Resilience, a new definition of health for people and communities'. In Reich JW, Zautra AJ & Hall JS (eds) *Handbook of adult resilience.* Guilford Press.

Chapter 2

Experiences and results of The Resilience Programme for primary school teachers in Italy

Annalisa Valle, Davide Massaro, Ilaria Castelli,
Francesca Sangiuliano Intra, Elisabetta Lombardi,
Edoardo Alfredo Bracaglia and Antonella Marchetti

Introduction

The concept of mentalization indicates "the process by which we realize that having a mind mediates our experience of the world" (Fonagy, Gergely, Jurist, & Target, 2002, pg. 3). In Fonagy's view (Fonagy, 1991), the concept of mentalization encompasses aspects of two constructs: the psychoanalytic construct of "Reflective Functioning," and the psychological construct of "Theory of Mind." The author bases the concept of mentalization on psychoanalytic work with borderline patients, and contributes to the creation of a mentalization-based treatment (Allen & Fonagy, 2006; Bateman & Fonagy, 2004, 2013), a clinical treatment designed to increase mentalization processes (Allen & Fonagy, 2006; Bateman & Fonagy, 2004; Choi-Kain & Gunderson, 2008; Fonagy & Allison, 2012; Fonagy et al., 2002).

Theory of Mind (ToM), defined as the ability to attribute mental states (intentions, desires, thoughts, and beliefs) to ourselves and to others, and to predict our own and others' behavior on the basis of these mental states (Premack & Woodruff, 1978), is a construct adjacent to mentalization, such that ToM tasks are also considered reliable for the assessment of mentalization (Vrouva & Midgley, 2012). Research demonstrates that this ability mainly develops during childhood (Wimmer & Perner, 1983) and adolescence (Valle, Massaro, Castelli, & Marchetti, 2015), but the more complex aspects also increase in adulthood (Apperly, Samson, & Humphreys, 2009; Sommerville, Bernstein, & Meltzoff, 2013) and continue to change until old age (Cabinio et al., 2015). In light of the socio-constructivist approach, considering that ToM emerges within social interactions through participation in social exchanges (Astington & Olson, 1995; Carpendale & Lewis, 2004), in recent years multiple training programs have been designed to increase ToM abilities, for children exhibiting both atypical and typical development. In the first case, the effectiveness of ToM training has mainly been tested in students with intellectual disability (Adibsereshki, Abdolahzadeh, Karmilo, & Hasanzadeh, 2014) and with autism (Begeer et al., 2011; Fisher & Happé, 2005). In the second case, the literature focuses on ToM training in preschoolers and during the school years. For example, Slaughter and Gopnik (1996), Appleton and Reddy (1996), and Clements, Rustin, and McCallum (2000) created training for children based on the false belief understanding that is effective in ToM development; Ornaghi and colleagues (Grazzani, Ornaghi, Agliati, & Brazzelli, 2016; Grazzani, Ornaghi, & Brockmeier, 2016; Ornaghi, Brockmeier, & Gavazzi, 2011), Lecce and colleagues (Lecce, Bianco, Devine, Hughes, & Banerjee, 2014) and Bianco and colleagues (Bianco, Lecce, & Banerjee, 2016) demonstrated the important role of mental-state conversations in ToM abilities. Specifically, the last study tested improvements in ToM in school-aged children, following Apperly's (2012) hypothesis that in this period children learn to use their understanding and knowledge of mental states in a more flexible and appropriate way than they can in infancy.

Recently, training programs based on the mentalization construct have also been created; in these cases, the aim is to improve the mentalizing abilities of adults/ educators in order to increase mentalizing abilities in children and adolescents. Twemlow and colleagues (2005a, 2005b) tested the Peaceful Schools Program, with the aim of creating mentalizing school communities to reduce violence and bullying. The researchers trained educators to develop a mentalizing attitude: for example, stimulating and supporting their awareness of mental states in difficult moments, intervening in a mentalistic way during violent episodes, and encouraging children to reflect on the mental contents of the participants after bullying episodes. All the above-mentioned practices involve ToM competences. Lundgaard Bak (2012; Lundgaard Bak, Midgley, Zhu, Wistoft, & Obel, 2015) proposed another training program based on the mentalization construct, The Resilience Program, formerly named the "Thought in Mind Project" (TiM Project), an educational application of the concept of mentalization with the aim of creating a mentalizing community. The Resilience Program links mentalization and resilience, and analyzes different aspects of mentalization to promote reflection on and knowledge of our own mind and that of others. Furthermore, The Resilience Program deals with emotion regulation, a mental process considered to be crucial for the application of mentalization competences and the development of resilience.

Based on these constructs and these previous experiences, we designed a Resilience Program project training program for primary school teachers, with the purpose of introducing and explaining the key concepts and methods of The Resilience Program and involving teachers in a direct experience of these methods. Subsequently, we tested the efficacy of this training by evaluating mentalization and ToM abilities in primary school children (Valle et al., 2016).

In this chapter, we present the Resilience training program, based on the suggestions and methods proposed by the original Resilience Program. Next, we discuss our experience of implementing the training program with a group of teachers and present their use in the classroom of the concepts learned. Finally, we provide a summary of the outcomes of this first research evaluating the effect of Resilience Program training on children's mentalization abilities.

The creation of the Resilience training program

Starting from the contents of The Resilience Program (Lundgaard Bak et al., 2015), we designed a training program specifically aimed at primary school teachers. We selected some of the original content and activities of The Resilience Program, adjusted to an Italian context, and created others ad hoc for our training program. We decided to make some adjustments to the original activities in light of the literature discussing cultural differences in ToM and emotion regulation. Regarding ToM, the debate over cultural differences is still open. Some cross-cultural research evidences chronological synchrony in understanding of the false belief in different countries (Callaghan et al., 2005; Oberle, 2009), whereas other studies (see the meta-analysis by Liu, Wellman, Tardif and Sabbagh, 2008) show that Asian children lag behind Western children in their performance on false belief tasks. This timetable difference is discussed with reference to the characteristics of individualistic (Western) and collectivistic (Eastern) cultures, sociocultural and linguistic factors, and children's executive function (Wang, Devine, Wong, & Hughes, 2016). Considering two European countries, Lecce and Hughes (2010) analyzed ToM developmental differences in 5- and 6-year-old British and Italian children, showing that British children seem to outperform Italian ones in false belief tasks. To interpret this result, the authors refer to the "pedagogical experience interpretative hypothesis," which highlights the role of the quality of education in social understanding (C. Hughes et al., 2014; Wang et al., 2016), and discuss the impact of family conversations about mental states, language comprehension, and schooling on children's performance. Although there are still only a few studies and their results are not unanimous, they seem to indicate cross-cultural differences in ToM development, both in countries very far from one another and among European countries.

Regarding cross-cultural studies of the use of emotion regulation strategies, Matsumoto and colleagues (Matsumoto, Yoo, & Fontaine, 2008; Matsumoto, Yoo, & Nakagawa, 2008) found that collectivistic (Eastern) cultures, oriented toward maintaining the social order, exhibit higher scores for emotion suppression when compared with individualistic (Western) cultures, oriented toward obtaining individual affective autonomy and egalitarianism. Haga, Kraft, and Corby (2009) investigated differences among three Western cultures, comparing university students in the United States, Norway, and Australia. Their results showed that US students use suppression strategies more than the other groups, and exhibited more depressed mood and negative affect. Differences in emotion regulation strategies between very similar cultures are also found. Recently, Potthoff and colleagues (2016) compared six European countries (the Netherlands, Hungary, Spain, Italy, Portugal, and Germany), showing that people use the same emotion regulation strategies in different ways: in the northern countries, people use strategies such as rumination, catastrophizing, and other-blaming less than do people in the southern countries, evidencing cultural specificities and different cultural approaches to social adjustment. It is possible to observe this type of difference even in cultural products such as narratives for infants. On the basis of results obtained by Dyer, Shatz, and Wellman (2000) indicating that children's storybooks are important sources of content regarding mental states, Dyer-Seymour, Shatz, Wellman, and Saito (2004) compared the same children's storybooks translated into English and Japanese. Their results indicated a similarity in the use of mental-state language in the two versions of the storybooks (both frequently used mentalistic language and referred to the same mental states), but qualitative analyses revealed that the texts sometimes differed in terms of locations of the terms and use of emotion terms, considered appropriate in only one of the two versions (Shatz, Dyer, Marchetti, & Massaro, 2006). Marchetti, Massaro, Shatz, and Dyer (2005) and Shatz and colleagues (2006) used the same method to investigate cultural differences between original English versions and Italian translations of ten storybooks for children aged 3 to 6. The authors found that in the Italian versions there are more intense emotions, more specific expressions of mental states, and more expressions of social awareness than in the original books. These strands of evidence suggest the existence of differences even between two Western cultures: Italian-speaking people seem to be more interested in and more accustomed to the expression of emotions compared with English-speaking people.

Following these cross-cultural considerations, our adjustments of The Resilience Program activities to the Italian context and our novel activities aim to clarify and improve the emotional and mentalistic contents. Moreover, these adjustments meet the Italian teachers' needs to be trained in emotional management of pupils and classes, which in Italy is considered a very important competence for primary school teachers. In fact, one of the most important goals in schools is the creation of positive relationships between teachers and students, as well as among class-mates, so as to increase children's wellbeing, adjustment, and achievement (Pianta, 1999).

Bringing the Resilience training program to a school

After a presentation on the Resilience training program given to all fifth-grade teachers at a primary school in Milan (in the north of Italy), four teachers, all women, decided to participate in the training, motivated by the desire to learn about the method and acquire some tools to work with their 10-year-old pupils on mentalizing topics.

The main goal of the Resilience training program was to introduce and explain the key concepts involved, and to provide teachers with direct experience of these methods. Moreover, we aimed to support teachers in reflecting together on how to apply The Resilience Program in the classroom with their pupils.

The Resilience training program was implemented in two meetings at the school, each lasting three hours and managed by two researchers. At the end of these meetings, the teachers brought The Resilience Program methods to their class-rooms in whatever ways they liked, meeting the researchers for a supervision twice during the school year. Moreover, teachers could ask for the researchers' support at any time, by contacting them via e-mail or phone.

The first meeting

During the first meeting, the researchers introduced the overall structure of the Resilience training program and the experiential method that the teachers would have to learn. Moreover, they explained the importance of training adults for improving not only their own mentalistic skills, but also those of their pupils. Next, the researchers focused on two concepts relating to brain function that formed the basis of The Resilience Program, the *Thinking Brain* and the *Alarm Center*, and delivered a related activity. They asked teachers to produce some examples of activation of the *Alarm Center* and to indicate some situations that they worried about: for instance, loved ones' accidents or health problems. After this, each teacher made a drawing of her *Alarm Center*: in three drawings, the *Alarm Center* was located within the brain and occupying most of it, while in the fourth drawing the *Alarm Center* was represented as a button in the center of the sheet of paper, surrounded by explanatory comics. Teachers often included question marks, fog, and the word "help." At the end of this activity, the researchers asked the teachers to share and discuss their drawings. In the discussion, it emerged that the symbols used by the teachers represented emotional and cognitive internal states accompanying the activation of the *Alarm Center*, such as fear, confusion, and a desire to escape, and the failure of strategies used to solve a problem. In this way, the group reflected on the consequences of activation of the *Alarm Center*: when this system is "off," the brain can function properly, and the person is calm and can find a solution to a problem; when the *Alarm Center* is "on," the brain is focused only on the alarm, and the person is agitated (frightened and troubled) and does not reflect; thus, he or she is hardly able to find a solution to the problem. As a result, the group agreed on the importance of training the brain to learn to reason, even when the *Alarm Center* is activated.

The second activity aimed to introduce the concept of *Attention: The Brain's Spotlight.* The researchers asked each teacher to build a type of spotlight by rolling up a sheet of paper, and then, one at a time, to use this spotlight to focus their attention on some objects in the room (for example, a window, a table, or a book). Next, the researchers introduced *Thought Bubbles* of various sizes and colors, and teachers wrote one positive or negative emotion or thought in each bubble. They then placed the bubbles on the table and used their spotlights to focus their attention on each bubble. During this experience, the researchers invited the teachers to describe what they were observing and what, in contrast, they could not see through the spotlight: the group reflected on the thoughts and emotions aroused by different bubbles, and on the difficulty of keeping in mind the bubbles lying outside the spotlight. At the end of this activity, the researchers explained that the spotlight is a metaphor for attention, the main tool that allows people to intentionally focus on some entity, to shift their attention from one entity to another, and to concentrate on positive or negative entities. The group identified two types of entities: external entities, belonging to "The world around you," and internal entities, or "Thoughts and feelings that you experience inside yourself" (both as indicated by The Resilience Program). The researchers emphasized that good use of our attention allows us to focus on both external and internal entities, and that training this ability can help when the *Alarm Center* is activated. When this happens, it is important to be able to access internal resources and positive thoughts and emotions in order to control the confusion caused by the alarm and to find appropriate solutions.

The third activity is named "Make the Invisible Visible" and was intended to train teachers in a game that they would be able to use with children in the classroom. The goal of the game is to reflect on the opacity of the mind (Gopnik, 1993) and on the possibility of sharing internal objects with other persons, creating a dialogue to prevent misunderstandings and conflict. The group decided on the topic of the game, "teaching challenges," and wrote it on a "theme bubble" in the middle of a table. The teachers then had two minutes to think about the topic and write a key word in another bubble, after which all the teachers simultaneously placed their *Thought Bubbles* around the "theme bubble" and explained their ideas one at a time. The other teachers were invited to ask questions to better understand the opinions expressed, using phrases such as "Tell us a bit more about . . .," "What do you think is the cause behind . . .?," and "What would it make sense for you to do . . .?" (as indicated by The Resilience Program). Finally, each teacher wrote her new thoughts about the topic on a second bubble and shared these new thoughts with the others. At the end of this activity, the researchers underlined the importance of sharing ideas, opinions, and thoughts to understanding others' points of view and to changing our own internal states. In this exercise, sharing their opinions allowed some teachers to recognize positive aspects of the topic and activated a problem-solving mode of thinking. Moreover, the group reflected on the fact that it may be helpful for children to practice this exercise, because sometimes they find it hard to listen to each other and to recognize the value of others' opinions.

The first meeting ended with a summary of the main topics and concepts discussed.

The second meeting

After a synthesis of the first meeting, researchers introduced the second part of the training program, centered on the concept of resilience. To begin with, the group defined the term "resilience," writing ideas and suggestions about it on a poster: the researchers distinguished between resilience and coping strategies, and focused on the possibility of improving the latter to develop better resilience. Next, the researchers asked each teacher to recall a particularly stressful event and write this on a poster: the events featured were having health problems, being the victim of a car accident, helping a wounded child at school, helping a seriously injured friend, and activation of the fire alarm at school. The teachers thought about everything that they could do to cope with these events and wrote down these thoughts on the same poster. The reactions elicited were of two types: practical reactions aiming to improve the situation (e.g., provide first aid or call for help), and emotional reactions aiming to emotionally support the persons involved. The group reflected on the importance of being prepared for such situations in order to have an appropriate and helpful reaction in case of need, from both the practical and the emotional point of view. If people may increase the practical strategies available to them in different ways, for example by attending a first aid course or participating in exercises, they may also improve their emotional strategies through The Resilience Program training, which aims to build a kind of "toolbox" containing a series of consolidated emotional strategies for dealing with stressful times. With the help of this toolbox, the brain may continue to function even when the *Alarm Center* is activated, and thus the person can deal with the situation easily.

This activity prepared the group to learn new emotional strategies described in The Resilience Program as "Body and Mind" training. The researchers then read *The story of the House of Thoughts* and led a role-playing game: one teacher, the Boss, acted out the part of her own mind, and the other teachers acted out the parts of four Thoughts in the different rooms of the *House of Thoughts*: these Thoughts were sad, scary, happy, and reassuring. The Boss stood in the middle of the room and the Thoughts were located at the four corners. For five minutes, the Thoughts had to persuade the Boss to enter and remain in their own room, and the Boss could freely decide where to go. At the end of this role-playing game, the researchers asked the participants to describe their experience and the emotions aroused. This was a very emotionally intense activity: the Boss was confused by the words of the different Thoughts, and she expressed difficulty with choosing a room because both positive and negative Thoughts had compelling arguments. The Thoughts displayed feelings of happiness and satisfaction when the Boss approached them and feelings of failure and frustration when the Boss moved away; in addition, the teachers who acted out the parts of negative (sad and scary) Thoughts reported a change in their emotional state to a negative mood. The teacher playing the sad Thought struggled to get into the role, and she needed support to handle this task and find good reasons to enhance this negative emotion. Through this experience, she learned that even negative thoughts have a "right of citizenship," that they play an important role in the mind, and that they are worthy of being heard and accepted. In fact, a sad thought can even be helpful, as depicted skillfully in the movie *Inside Out*. In this case, Bing Bong, the protagonist's imaginary friend, anthropomorphizes negative thoughts that are worthy of expression and play an important evolutionary role up to the age of adolescence in becoming aware of a situation. The group understood that knowing of and recognizing all their internal states is the first step toward managing them in every situation, even when the Alarm Center is activated: in this activity, the Boss had to listen to all the Thoughts before settling on the ones most useful to pick out and activate a useful strategy to solve a problem or address a stressful event.

At the end of this activity, the teachers as a group read the other stories of The Resilience Program and devised several ways to introduce them to children in the classroom. In addition to the role-playing game, which would be difficult for younger children, the teachers could imagine drawing the main elements of the eight stories in The Resilience Program, giving physical shape to some of the concepts with building blocks (e.g., to build the Mind Train), or carrying out actions as indicated by a story (e.g., in the case of the Wellness Beads).

The second meeting ended with a summary of the main topics discussed and the delivery of the Italian translation of a manual replicating the content of The Resilience Program website. The researchers invited the teachers to freely access the materials and to choose the stories they considered most useful to their class in view of the types of relationships between their pupils.

Teachers' work with their pupils

At the end of the second meeting, the researchers provided each teacher with a Logbook to record, if they wished, their experiences with the children, indicating the topic, methods, children's reaction, and their evaluation (using a 5-point Likert scale) of the activity presented. Three teachers returned the Logbook containing some activities; overall, these teachers were satisfied with the activities they had conducted with the children.

The most representative activity was organized by the teachers in a team and carried out in three classrooms, over two sessions. The children were frightened because of a piece of bad news that they had heard in the newscast, so the teachers designed a lesson about fear and strategies for dealing with it. In the first session, they read "The story about a boy who shot down a thought" in the classroom and invited the children to participate in a brainstorming exercise to share their personal fears. In the second session, the teachers used the common classroom pedagogical method named "Circle Time," in combination with the *Thought Bubbles* drawn from The Resilience Program: sitting in a circle, the children wrote on the bubbles and discussed the personal experiences that had emerged in the previous session, faced their reactions, and searched together for possible solutions to face their fears. In this activity, the teacher supported the negative emotions that emerged and guided the children to find several solutions in the form of coping strategies to overcome their fear. Moreover, the teachers used this activity to work on compliance with the rules on different topics, from respect for spaces in the classroom to respect for others' turns to speak. Finally, the teachers proposed the "umbrella" as a metaphor for coping strategies to protect ourselvesfrom fear and asked the children to draw their own umbrella. The teachers evaluated all sessions very positively (5 points on the Likert scale) and reported that the children actively participated in all activities, expressed their emotions, and positively discussed their coping strategies.

Among the reasons for their satisfaction, one teacher mentioned the opportunity arising from the Resilience training program to speak about emotion regulation and to help pupils manage a negative emotion such as fear. From our point of view, the teachers used The Resilience Program content in an original, creative, and useful manner, because they integrated The Resilience Program activities into the daily activities of the class. Moreover, they adapted The Resilience Program methods to the pedagogical method they usually applied: for example, they integrated the *Thought Bubbles* into the "Circle Time" activity that the children were already familiar with and responded well to. In this way, The Resilience Program content became a part of the children's everyday lives, and offered a new set of strategies in addition to those already available to deal with their emotions both in and out of school.

Preliminary evidence from Resilience Program training in Italy

One of the teachers who attended the training program, along with her class, participated in a study to verify the effects of The Resilience Program training on children's mentalistic skills (Valle et al., 2016). The hypothesis was that these children would improve their ToM abilities and mentalization style more than a control group in which the teacher did not receive Resilience Program training. The TiM Project training group consisted of 23 pupils (M_{age} = 10.26 years, SD = 3.16 months; 10 boys, 13 girls), and the control group also consisted of 23 pupils (M_{age} = 10.23 years, SD = 5.16 months; 13 boys, 10 girls). The teacher of the control group participated in a non-mentalizing training program that aimed to promote reflection on didactic teaching strategies that may be useful in the classroom. The teachers were enrolled in these training programs at the beginning of the school year; in the same period, children were tested on their ToM and mentalizing competences, and they were re-tested at the end of the school year. During the months of the school year, the teachers could freely use the training program content and take advantage of the researchers' supervision.

All children were individually evaluated through the following tasks: the Mentalizing Task, three false belief tasks, the Strange Stories, and the Reading the Mind in the Eyes Test (Children's Version). The Mentalizing Task (Di Terlizzi, 2010; Sharp, Croudace, & Goodyer, 2007) assesses children's mentalizing attributional styles in everyday life situations. These styles are: overly negative, a cognitive mentalizing bias based on a global, stable, and negative self-attribution of the causes of social situations (typical of children with depressive and anxiety symptoms; Quiggle, Garber, Panak, & Dodge, 1992); overly positive, a cognitive mentalizing bias based on a global, stable, and positive self-attribution of the causes of social situations (typical of aggressive children; David & Kistner, 2000); and rational, a non-self-referent, non-stable interpretation of social situations. Three false belief tasks, two second-order (Astington, Pelletier, & Homer, 2002; Liverta Sempio, Marchetti, Castelli, Lecciso, & Pezzotta, 2005; Sullivan,

Zaitchik, & Tager-Flusberg, 1994) and one third-order (Valle et al., 2015), were used to assess ToM abilities. All these tasks are based on the unexpected transfer paradigm, and they evaluate second- and third-order recursive thinking abilities respectively ("I think that you think that he thinks"; "I think that you think that he thinks that she thinks"). The Strange Stories task (Happé, 1994; Liverta Sempio, Marchetti, & Castelli, 2005) assesses the application of ToM competences in everyday social situations; this task consists of 24 short stories in which the protagonist does or says something strange, followed by questions investigating whether the child refers to characters' mental states to understand the situation. Finally, the Reading the Mind in the Eyes Test (Children's Version; Baron-Cohen, Wheelwright, Hill, Raste, & Plumb, 2001; Castelli, 2010; Liverta Sempio, Marchetti, & Castelli, 2003) tests the affective component of ToM, requiring participants to attribute mental states to people by observing the eye region of the face.

The main results relate to the Mentalizing Task and the third-order false belief task. In the first case, Resilience Program training group children showed an increase in rational attributional style ($F_{1,44}$ = 12.44, p = 0.001) and a decrease in overly positive attributional style ($F_{1,44}$ = 24.24, p = 0.001), compared with children in the control group. With regard to attributional styles in childhood, the literature shows that the critical age for change is 7–11 years old, when a shift from an overly positive attributional style to a rational attributional style occurs (Sharp et al., 2007); in this study, The Resilience Program training group children benefited from the teacher's training, as they reached this stage of development faster than the control group children. A tendency to misperceive others' thoughts, feelings, and intentions seems to be associated with emotional disorders (Ingram, Miranda, & Segal, 1998), symptoms of externalizing disorder (Sharp et al., 2007), and aggression (Baumeister, Smart, & Boden, 1996; Hughes, Cavell, & Gaur, 2001) in childhood, so a mentalizing approach on the part of their teachers can act to protect children from these disorders. The Resilience Program training also impacted performance on the third-order false belief task: children in The Resilience Program training group exhibited significantly better post-test performance compared with that of children in the control group ($F_{1,44}$ = 26.62, p = 0.001). Third-order reasoning represents a very high level of difficulty in ToM competences; this ability increases during adolescence (Valle et al., 2015) and is not completely reached even in adulthood. In the present case, we interpret the presence of a training effect as indicating the efficacy of the teacher's intervention in the pupils' zone of proximal development: 10-year-old children are near to adolescence, and the teacher's mentalizing approach, in which he or she pays specific attention to pupils' mental states and to their understanding of others' mental states in the classroom, seems to help the children to reason about others' minds at an advanced level.

In conclusion, the results suggest that the acquisition of a mentalizing approach by teachers involved in the Resilience training program promoted significant acceleration in the development of their pupils' mentalizing abilities, specifically in relation to their attributional styles and to higher-level ToM reasoning. Future studies with larger samples will confirm this preliminary evidence and assess profitable or fruitful changes in the mentalization of the teachers, as well as that of the children.

Conclusions

In this chapter, we have presented our experience with The Resilience Program, consisting of an adaptation of the Resilience training program for Italian primary school teachers, a training experience with four teachers, and the results of the first research testing the effects of Resilience Program training on children. In conclusion, these experiences show that the administration of a specific training program to adults, the first step for the creation of a mentalizing community, can help children to develop and use their mentalization and ToM abilities. This is particularly important considering that, as suggested by Lundgaard Bak (Lundgaard Bak, 2012; Lundgaard Bak et al., 2015), children with strong mentalization competences show good social adaptation and construct positive interpersonal relationships; moreover, they have a low risk of developing psychopathology (Baumeister et al., 1996) or of manifesting symptoms of behavioral disorders (Sharp et al., 2007).

For the future, we note as a particular aspect of interest the possibility of comparing the results of our Resilience Program training with evidence obtained in other countries from application of The Resilience Program or models inspired by this project.

In this experience, we observed a limitation in the difficulty of organizing supervision meetings with the teachers. Despite the initial interest and enthusiasm, the teachers did not contact the researchers via e-mail or phone during the whole period of the study; any future application of the training program should focus on involvement with this type of supervision, as we think that a stronger link with the researchers could help teachers to improve their mentalization abilities, to reflect on their own progress, and to create many new activities to deliver to pupils in the classroom.

Regarding future research, the positive results suggest another open question: the direct effect of Resilience Program training on adults' competences. In the future, it will be interesting to investigate the impact of this training not only on pupils but also on teachers, as well as the link between children's and teachers' mentalization abilities, considering that mentalization develops through meetings of minds in which people are able to appreciate others' thoughts and think about their feelings.

References

Adibsereshki, N., Abdolahzadeh, M., Karmilo, M., & Hasanzadeh, M. (2014). The effectiveness of theory of mind training on the adaptive behavior of students with intellectual disability. *Journal of Special Education and Rehabilitation*, *15*(1–2), 91–107.

Allen, J. G., & Fonagy, P. (2006). *The Handbook of Mentalization-Based Treatment*: John Wiley & Sons.

Apperly, I. A. (2012). What is "theory of mind"? Concepts, cognitive processes and individual differences. *The Quarterly Journal of Experimental Psychology*, *65*(5), 825–839. doi: 10.1080/17470218.2012.676055

Apperly, I. A., Samson, D., & Humphreys, G. W. (2009). Studies of adults can inform accounts of theory of mind development. *Developmental Psychology*, *45*(1), 190–201. doi: 10.1037/a0014098

Appleton, M., & Reddy, V. (1996). Teaching three year-olds to pass false belief tests: A conversational approach. *Social Development*, *5*(3), 275–291.

Astington, J. W., & Olson, D. R. (1995). The cognitive revolution in children's understanding of mind. *Human Development*, *38*(4–5), 179–189.

Astington, J. W., Pelletier, J., & Homer, B. (2002). Theory of mind and epistemological development: The relation between children's second-order false-belief understanding and their ability to reason about evidence. *New Ideas in Psychology*, *20*(2–3), 131–144. doi: 10.1016/S0732-118X(02)00005-3

Baron-Cohen, S., Wheelwright, S., Hill, J., Raste, Y., & Plumb, I. (2001). The "Reading the Mind in the Eyes" Test Revised Version: A study with normal adults, and adults with Asperger syndrome or high-functioning autism. *Journal of Child Psychology and Psychiatry*, *42*(2), 241–251. doi: 10.1111/1469-7610.00715

Bateman, A., & Fonagy, P. (2004). Mentalization-based treatment of BPD. *Journal of Personality Disorders*, *18*(1), 36–51.

Bateman, A., & Fonagy, P. (2013). Mentalization-based treatment. *Psychoanalytic Inquiry*, *33*(6), 595–613. doi: 10.1080/07351690.2013.835170

Baumeister, R. F., Smart, L., & Boden, J. M. (1996). Relation of threatened egotism to violence and aggression: The dark side of high self-esteem. *Psychological Review*, *103*(1), 5.

Begeer, S., Gevers, C., Clifford, P., Verhoeve, M., Kat, K., Hoddenbach, E., & Boer, F. (2011). Theory of Mind training in children with autism: A randomized controlled trial. *Journal of Autism and Developmental Disorders*, *41*(8), 997–1006.

Bianco, F., Lecce, S., & Banerjee, R. (2016). Conversations about mental states and theory of mind development during middle childhood: A training study. *Journal of Experimental Child Psychology*, *149*, 41–61. doi: http://dx.doi.org/10.1016/j.jecp.2015.11.006

Cabinio, M., Rossetto, F., Blasi, V., Savazzi, F., Castelli, I., Massaro, D., Valle, A., Nemni, R., Clerici, M., Marchetti, A., & Baglio, F. (2015). Mind-reading ability and structural connectivity changes in aging. *Frontiers in Psychology*, *6*, 1808. doi: 10.3389/fpsyg.2015.01808

Callaghan, T., Rochat, P., Lillard, A., Claux, M. L., Odden, H., Itakura, S., Tapanya, S., & Singh, S. (2005). Synchrony in the onset of mental-state reasoning. *Psychological Science*, *16*(5), 378–384. doi:10.1111/j.0956-7976.2005.01544.x

Carpendale, J. I., & Lewis, C. (2004). Constructing an understanding of mind: The development of children's social understanding within social interaction. *Behavioral and Brain Sciences*, *27*, 79–96. doi: 10.1017/S0140525X04000032

Castelli, I. (2010). La comprensione degli stati mentali dallo sguardo. In A. Marchetti & A. Valle (Eds.), *Il bambino e le relazioni sociali. Strumenti per educatori e insegnanti* (pp. 58–82): Milan: Franco Angeli.

Choi-Kain, L. W., & Gunderson, J. G. (2008). Mentalization: Ontogeny, assessment, and application in the treatment of borderline personality disorder. *The American Journal of Psychiatry, 165*(9), 1127–1135. doi: 10.1176/appi.ajp.2008. 07081360

Clements, W. A., Rustin, C. L., & McCallum, S. (2000). Promoting the transition from implicit to explicit understanding: A training study of false belief. *Developmental Science, 3*(1), 81–92.

David, C., & Kistner, J. (2000). Do positive self-perceptions have a "dark side"? Examination of the link between perceptual bias and aggression. *Journal of Abnormal Child Psychology, 28*(4), 327–337. doi: 10.1023/a:1005164925300

Di Terlizzi, E. (2010). Qualità e accuratezza della mentalizzazione nei bambini. In A. Marchetti & A. Valle (Eds.), *Il bambino e le relazioni sociali. Strumenti per Educatori e Insegnanti* (pp. 154–181): Milan: Franco Angeli.

Dyer-Seymour, J. R., Shatz, M., Wellman, H. M., & Saito, M. T. (2004). Mental state expressions in US and Japanese children's books. *International Journal of Behavioral Development, 28*(6), 546–552. doi: doi:10.1080/01650250444000261

Dyer, J. R., Shatz, M., & Wellman, H. M. (2000). Young children's storybooks as a source of mental state information. *Cognitive Development 15*(1), 17–37.

Fisher, N., & Happé, F. (2005). A training study of theory of mind and executive function in children with autistic spectrum disorders. *Journal of Autism and Developmental Disorders, 35*(6), 757–771. doi: 10.1007/s10803-005-0022-9

Fonagy, P. (1991). Thinking about thinking: Some clinical and theoretical considerations in the treatment of a borderline patient. *The International Journal of Psychoanalysis, 72*(4), 639–656.

Fonagy, P., & Allison, E. (2012). What is mentalization? The concept and its foundations in developmental research. In I. Vrouva & N. Midgley (Eds.), *Minding the Child: Mentalization-Based Interventions With Children, Young People and Their Families* (pp. 11–34): Routledge.

Fonagy, P., Gergely, G., Jurist, E., & Target, M. (2002). *Affect Regulation, Mentalization and the Development of the Self*: Karnac Books.

Gopnik, A. (1993). How we know our minds: The illusion of first-person knowledge of intentionality. *Behavioral and Brain Sciences, 16*(1), 1–14. doi: 10.1017/S0140 525X00028636

Grazzani, I., Ornaghi, V., Agliati, A., & Brazzelli, E. (2016). How to foster toddlers' mental-state talk, emotion understanding, and prosocial behavior: A conversation-based intervention at nursery school. *Infancy, 21*(2), 199–227. doi: 10.1111/infa. 12107

Grazzani, I., Ornaghi, V., & Brockmeier, J. (2016). Conversation on mental states at nursery: Promoting social cognition in early childhood. *European Journal of Developmental Psychology, 13*(5), 563–581. doi: 10.1080/17405629.2015.1127803

Haga, S. M., Kraft, P., & Corby, E.-K. (2009). Emotion regulation: Antecedents and well-being outcomes of cognitive reappraisal and expressive suppression in cross-cultural samples. *Journal of Happiness Studies, 10*(3), 271–291. doi: 10.1007/s10902-007-9080-3

Happé, F. G. E. (1994). An advanced test of theory of mind: Understanding of story characters' thoughts and feelings by able autistic, mentally handicapped, and normal children and adults. *Journal of Autism and Developmental Disorders*, *24*(2), 129–154. doi: 10.1007/bf02172093

Hughes, J. N., Cavell, T. A. & Gaur, P. (2001). A positive view of peer acceptance in aggressive youth risk for future peer acceptance. *Journal of School Psychology*, *39*, 239–252. doi: doi.org/10.1016/S0022-4405(01)00067-X

Hughes, C., Devine, R. T., Ensor, R., Koyasu, M., Mizokawa, A., & Lecce, S. (2014). Lost in translation? Comparing British, Japanese, and Italian children's theory-of-mind performance. *Child Development Research*, *2014*, 1–10. doi: 10.1155/2014/893492

Ingram, R. E., Miranda, J., & Segal, Z. V. (1998). *Cognitive Vulnerability to Depression*: Guilford Press.

Lecce, S., Bianco, F., Devine, R. T., Hughes, C., & Banerjee, R. (2014). Promoting theory of mind during middle childhood: A training program. *Journal of Experimental Child Psychology*, *126*, 52–67. doi: 10.1016/j.jecp.2014.03.002

Lecce, S., & Hughes, C. (2010). "The Italian job?": Comparing theory of mind performance in British and Italian children. *British Journal of Developmental Psychology*, *28*(4), 747–766.

Liu, D., Wellman, H. M., Tardif, T., & Sabbagh, M. A. (2008). Theory of mind development in Chinese children: A meta-analysis of false-belief understanding across cultures and languages. *Developmental Psychology*, *44*(2), 523–531. doi: 10.1037/0012-1649.44.2.523

Liverta Sempio, O., Marchetti, A., & Castelli, I. (2003). *Test degli Occhi-versione Bambini (TOB)*. Unità di Ricerca sulla Teoria della Mente, Dipartimento di Psicologia, Università Cattolica del Sacro Cuore. Milan.

Liverta Sempio, O., Marchetti, A., & Castelli, I. (2005). *Traduzione italiana delle Strane Storie e delle Storie fisiche*. Unità di Ricerca sulla Teoria della Mente, Dipartimento di Psicologia, Università Cattolica del Sacro Cuore. Milan.

Liverta Sempio, O., Marchetti, A., Castelli, I., Lecciso, F., & Pezzotta, C. (Eds.). (2005). *Mentalizzazione e competenza sociale. La comprensione della falsa credenza nello sviluppo normale e patologico*: Franco Angeli.

Lundgaard Bak, P. (2012). "Thoughts in mind": Promoting mentalizing communities for children. In I. Vrouva & N. Migdley (Eds.), *Minding the Child: Mentalization-Based Interventions With Children, Young People and Their Families* (pp. 202–218): Routledge.

Lundgaard Bak, P., Midgley, N., Zhu, J. L., Wistoft, K., & Obel, C. (2015). The Resilience Program: Preliminary evaluation of a mentalization-based education program. *Frontiers in Psychology*, *6*, 753. doi: 10.3389/fpsyg.2015.00753

Marchetti, A., Massaro, D., Shatz, M., & Dyer, J. (2005). C'era una volta un pensiero. La letteratura per l'infanzia come fonte di conoscenza sugli stati mentali. In O. Liverta Sempio, A. Marchetti & F. Lecciso (Eds.), *Teoria della mente tra normalità e patologia* (pp. 37–68): Cortina.

Matsumoto, D., Yoo, S. H., & Fontaine, J. (2008). Mapping expressive differences around the world. *Journal of Cross-Cultural Psychology*, *39*(1), 55–74. doi: 10. 1177/0022022107311854

Matsumoto, D., Yoo, S. H., & Nakagawa, S. (2008). Culture, emotion regulation, and adjustment. *Journal of Personality and Social Psychology*, *94*(6), 925–937. doi: 10.1037/0022-3514.94.6.925

Oberle, E. (2009). The development of theory of mind reasoning in Micronesian children. *Journal of Cognition and Culture*, *9*(1), 39–56.

Ornaghi, V., Brockmeier, J., & Gavazzi, I. (2011). The role of language games in children's understanding of mental states: A training study. *Journal of Cognition and Development*, *12*(2), 239–259. doi: 10.1080/15248372.2011.563487

Pianta, R. C. (1999). *Enhancing Relationships Between Children and Teachers*. American Psychological Association.

Potthoff, S., Garnefski, N., Miklósi, M., Ubbiali, A., Domínguez-Sánchez, F. J., Martins, E. C., Witthöft, M., & Kraaij, V. (2016). Cognitive emotion regulation and psychopathology across cultures: A comparison between six European countries. *Personality and Individual Differences*, *98*, 218–224. doi: 10.1016/j.paid.2016.04.022

Premack, D., & Woodruff, G. (1978). Does the chimpanzee have a theory of mind? *Behavioral and Brain Sciences*, *1*(4), 515–526.

Quiggle, N. L., Garber, J., Panak, W. F., & Dodge, K. A. (1992). Social information processing in aggressive and depressed children. *Child Development*, *63*(6), 1305–1320. doi: 10.1111/j.1467-8624.1992.tb01696.x

Sharp, C., Croudace, T. J., & Goodyer, I. M. (2007). Biased mentalizing in children aged seven to 11: Latent class confirmation of response styles to social scenarios and associations with psychopathology. *Social Development*, *16*(1), 181–202. doi: 10.1111/j.1467-9507.2007.00378.x

Shatz, M., Dyer, J., Marchetti, A., & Massaro, D. (2006). Culture and mental states: A comparison of English and Italian versions of children's books. In A. Antonietti, O. Liverta Sempio & A. Marchetti (Eds.), *Theory of Mind and Language in Developmental Contexts* (pp. 93–106): Springer.

Slaughter, V., & Gopnik, A. (1996). Conceptual coherence in the child's theory of mind: Training children to understand belief. *Child Development*, *67*(6), 2967–2988. doi: 10.1111/j.1467-8624.1996.tb01898.x

Sommerville, J. A., Bernstein, D. M., & Meltzoff, A. N. (2013). Measuring beliefs in centimeters: Private knowledge biases preschoolers' and adults' representation of others' beliefs. *Child Development*, *84*(6), 1846–1854. doi: 10.1111/cdev.12110

Sullivan, K., Zaitchik, D., & Tager-Flusberg, H. (1994). Preschoolers can attribute second-order beliefs. *Developmental Psychology*, *30*(3), 395. doi: 10.1037/0012-1649.30.3.395

Twemlow, S. W., Fonagy, P., & Sacco, F. C. (2005a). A developmental approach to mentalizing communities: I. A model for social change. *Bulletin of the Menninger Clinic*, *69*(4), 265–281. doi: 10.1521/bumc.2005.69.4.265

Twemlow, S. W., Fonagy, P., & Sacco, F. C. (2005b). A developmental approach to mentalizing communities: II. The Peaceful Schools experiment. *Bulletin of the Menninger Clinic*, *69*(4), 282–304. doi: 10.1521/bumc.2005.69.4.282

Valle, A., Massaro, D., Castelli, I., & Marchetti, A. (2015). Theory of mind development in adolescence and early adulthood: The growing complexity of recursive thinking ability. *Europe's Journal of Psychology*, *11*(1), 112–124. doi: 10.5964/ejop.v11i1.829

Valle, A., Massaro, D., Castelli, I., Sangiuliano Intra, F., Lombardi, E., Bracaglia, E., & Marchetti, A. (2016). Promoting mentalizing in pupils by acting on teachers: Preliminary Italian evidence of the "Thought in Mind" project. *Frontiers in Psychology*, *7*, 1213. doi: 10.3389/fpsyg.2016.01213

Vrouva, I., & Midgley, N. (2012). *Minding the Child: Mentalization-Based Interventions With Children, Young People and Their Families*: Routledge.

Wang, Z., Devine, R. T., Wong, K. K., & Hughes, C. (2016). Theory of mind and executive function during middle childhood across cultures. *Journal of Experimental Child Psychology, 149*, 6–22. doi: 10.1016/j.jecp.2015.09.028

Wimmer, H., & Perner, J. (1983). Beliefs about beliefs: Representation and constraining function of wrong beliefs in young children's understanding of deception. *Cognition 13*(1), 103–128. doi: 10.1016/0010-0277(83)90004-5

Chapter 3

Stories and valuable questions
Experiences from health care

Heidi Moeller Vestergaard and
Lene Elmose Broecker

A SMALL STORY AND A GOOD QUESTION

Heidi Moeller Vestergaard

In my work as a health visitor, I occasionally meet new parents, who may be in an emotionally vulnerable situation because they must deal with all the new challenges of parenthood. I experience a great demand for help and support in handling all the new thoughts and feelings that naturally occur when one becomes a parent. In my work as a health visitor, I also meet children and young people of all ages, who may feel so challenged that it affects their wellbeing and health. At school, the so-called health talks help to uncover a child's view of personal health, both physically and mentally. Here, The Resilience Programme has been particularly useful in focusing on the mental health of young people, giving them knowledge and insight into what is happening in the brain and how to exercise control of their attention, thoughts and feelings.

Knowledge about resilience and mentalisation is useful when, as a professional, we must gain insight into what is at stake for the person being cared for. The professional knowledge and approach to care provides very good opportunities for people to express their thoughts and feelings and develop a mental surplus that translates into actions.

The Resilience Programme in school health care

A girl in the 9th grade came for a health consultation, which included measurements of her height and weight. The girl had previously had an eating disorder, and it turned out that the disorder still dominated her life. She revealed that her sad thoughts had been overtaking her life and that she feared waking up at 20 years of age and regretting that she had wasted her youth. I considered how I, as a health visitor, could help her get better. Initially, I recognised the problem and that it was hard for her to spend so much energy on the negative and sad thoughts involving the possibility of her wasting her youth.

As we talked, I thought about the story of the *Mind Party*, and I considered whether it would be appropriate to read the story for her. I decided to try.

Immediately after reading, she exclaimed, surprised and happy: 'It's exactly how I experience it!' Clearly, the story made sense to her. I was very impressed that the story had such an immediate impact. The girl used her energy to avoid all the negative, sad thoughts, which had meant so much to her that they ended up being all-consuming. I took her immediate reaction as an expression of relief – she recognised herself in the story and also valued my professional recognition of her and of her challenges. In my position as a professional, I did not set out to make myself an expert, but by reading the story of the *Mind Party* I recognised her challenges, and met her where she was at. I could not take away her problem, but she felt 'seen' and understood, and experienced that it would be possible to regain some control over her thoughts. The story helped her become aware that she had choices. Suddenly she could see these unwelcome thoughts as uninvited guests who would come in, but that she could consciously choose not to pay any attention. The story gave the problem a readily understandable expression that she could relate to and recall whenever needed.

I got confirmation that the story and conversation we shared had a positive impact when her parents later phoned me and told me that their daughter had, for the first time ever, been happy when she came home from a talk with a health visitor.

Experiences with mentalisation in a family with a newborn child

As a health visitor, you sometimes encounter very complex problems that place great demands on your ability to mentalise.

I once visited a newborn's parents who, when I had previously visited, had quarrelled. In my follow-up visit, when I had come to weigh the child, I had prepared to ask the parents about their situation by means of mentalising questions that could open up new thoughts and thoughtfulness. I decided that I would try to help the couple shift from being very emotional to being able to talk and listen to one another. Mentalising questions can also be called curiosity questions, for example:

- Tell me a little more about . . .
- What can the explanation be for . . .
- What do you think we can do . . . right now . . . later . . .
- What can make sense for you . . ./for you to try . . .

During my home visit, the couple began quarrelling again. The conflict was about the mother accusing the father of controlling her. She felt that when he came home after work, he would always ask her about when the child had eaten, how much, etc. The mother felt very provoked by his questions – a recurring theme in their quarrels.

I asked the first question to the mother, 'What do you think about what he says?', and she answered, 'It pisses me off that he's going to check me all the time!'

I then asked the father, 'What do you think about what she thinks about what you think?' and he answered, 'I know that this is what she thinks, but I only ask because she is the one who knows the child's routine and I have not been home so I do not know where we are in today's programme. She is also better than me at reading when the little one is going to eat and sleep.'

I then asked the mother, 'What do you think about that?', to which she replied, 'That makes me happy.'

I experienced for the first time that there were pauses and thoughtfulness in their conversations – a reflective dialogue without accusations and persecutions. They talked to each other and really listened. It ended with them laughing a bit at themselves, and they had been very touched to discover that the other's intentions had always been about recognising the other.

Working based on mentalisation does not necessarily entail telling or teaching about mentalisation. For example, we do not need to convey knowledge about the *Thinking Brain* or the brain's *Alarm Centre*. It may be just as effective to ask mentalising questions. At the same time, as professionals, we can use our knowledge of what is happening in the brain in order to understand what is happening within the people involved. In the case presented above, the brain's *Alarm Centre* had taken over the parents. The fact that I consciously asked for their thoughts and, not least, their thoughts about the thoughts of the other, prompted them to rest and made them slowly come back to the *Thinking Brain*. They gave each other space to talk and could use their thoughtful reflections about what they were so emotionally engaged in. The mentalising questions opened a process where the parents listened actively to one another in a very present and loving way. They became curious to know each other's thoughts and feelings. To me, as a professional, it was an experience where I did not have to solve their problems, but where I could act as a catalyst for a process where the couple could become better at listening to one another. They became aware that they were often worried because they felt unsafe and vulnerable, which made it difficult for them to endure criticism.

The knowledge and insight I have gained about resilience and mentalisation has made it easier for me to discover when a so-called mentalisation collapse occurs in conversations; not only for parents and children, but also for me as a professional. It has strengthened me personally and professionally. To succeed in getting others to act with care, to me, is the whole essence of successful health care – both for new parents and schoolchildren.

THE HEALTH VISITOR'S ROLE

Lene Elmose Broecker

As a health visitor, you meet all kinds of families. In many families, everything works well. Other families have complex problems, and then, as a professional, it is sometimes hard to keep your head clear. Your attention may move rapidly from one issue to another as more and more problems become apparent in a visit. As a professional, you also risk losing sight. It is a constant battle to keep your focus and concentration when you work with complex health care issues, and it is incredibly important to be aware of this. I have enjoyed using *Attention – The Brain's Spotlight* as a tool to sharpen my own attention.

Thinking about my thoughts and feelings as well as others' helps keep me more aware, focused, present and attentive as a professional. When I have felt emotional or very distressed, I have visualised the *Thinking Brain* and the brain's *Alarm Centre*, concentrating on bringing myself to rest. Here, breathing exercises as well as attention to the story of the *House of Thoughts* and the story of the *Mind Party* have been a great help. My knowledge about mentalisation and resilience has made me a stronger, more skilled and more present health visitor and colleague. I have gained a greater understanding of family dynamics and feel better equipped for my work.

Teaching a resilience and mentalising course for parents

For three years I have taught a course for parents of overweight preschool children: 'Fat for fight'. Parents who attend come from various social and ethnic backgrounds. In this course, I have talked about resilience and mentalisation in simple ways. Among other things, I have talked about:

- What happens in the brain when we are troubled and have thoughts that dominate too much. For example, the child's urge for food or the parents' immediate urge to meet the child's demands
- What we need when we are uneasy (peace, care and protection)
- What parents can do to support their children in building resilience (adapt to sleep, appropriate challenges, perseverance, stability and attention).

As a professional, I know that it is extremely important to convey knowledge in a careful manner. Parents with overweight children are often filled with contradictory feelings: on the one hand, they feel guilty for the child's situation. On the other hand, they feel it's a shame for the child. They experience urges to meet their children's demands, which seem urgent, and are most often related to food. I find that parents have a great benefit in gaining knowledge of how the brain works. It helps them understand what happens to both themselves and their children, for example in conflict situations. A mother in the course once said, 'Now I can better understand why we see no progress.' Another mother said she would practise thinking differently so that she would not get so full of 'I'm-feeling-sorry' thoughts, and therefore give in to her child. She would try to stand firm and be more consistent in relation to what her child eats. The attention that these parents have on their own thoughts and feelings and on their children's thoughts and feelings helps them become more resilient parents.

Experiences with resilience and thoughtfulness in infant health care

Most parents, from time to time, experience doubts about how to cope with challenges in relation to their children's wellbeing and behaviour. In my work in families with small children, I have greatly benefited from using mentalising questions. I find that parents achieve a greater peace of mind and understanding of their own situation by curiously exploring what is difficult, for example, with troubled children or children who do not want to sleep. Parents get in touch with their own thoughts and feelings, as well as the child's, which is a prerequisite for being able to see opportunities for action. In my work with parents and children, I show pictures of the *Thinking Brain* and the brain's *Alarm Centre*, explaining what happens to us as humans when we become challenged. And, I also use the story of the *House of Thoughts* and the *Mind Party*, as well as breathing exercises that help calm the brain's *Alarm Centre*, while promoting greater attention. For most parents, this makes sense. However, I have also experienced parents who need to have many examples and concrete 'opportunity images' in order to use the ideas of resilience. Not everyone can formulate thoughts and feelings in certain situations. For example, an opportunity window may be to set a specific scenario, where I have very simple and specific questions that open up a space for parents to talk about and think about what's happening in a situation. Examples of questions related to a newborn who cries a lot and is unhappy may be: 'What do you do when the child cries?', 'What happens to the child?', 'What do you feel about the situation?', 'Could there be an opportunity that you could . . .?', 'Could it be that the child needs . . .?', 'Could it be that you need . . .?'

In terms of postpartum depression or after-birth anxiety, the mentalisation tools can be used by mothers to help them achieve greater peace of mind. For example, a mother with many worrying thoughts benefited from the images of the *Thinking Brain* and the brain's *Alarm Centre*. We talked about what it was like to be on high alert and what she could do to bring about more peace of mind and move back towards the *Thinking Brain.* The mother felt that knowing what really goes on in the brain helped calm her. It became obvious to her how important it was for her to have a little time for herself, every day; for example, a quarter of an hour, where she could go for a walk alone.

Chapter 4

Resilience at school

Peter Skaarup, Dan Henriksen, and Lene Steensberg

THE FIRST EXPERIENCES: RESILIENCE FOR SCHOOLS AND CHILDREN'S GROUPS

Peter Skaarup

Course one – Teaching within the classroom

The starting point of this course was a workshop on resilience in children and youth in which I had participated. At the onset of having to apply my new knowledge on resilience in practice, I was nervous and insecure about teaching resilience. I felt there was a huge difference between receiving knowledge versus preparing a course for 23 young people. How would they accept me? Would I be able to keep the overview in this new context? I am a pedagogue, not a teacher. Eventually, through reflection, I became more at peace with the challenge. I prepared myself mentally, a structure was formed and I moved into a more rational approach in which my focus turned to the preparation of materials for these expectant young people.

The school's management allocated nine hours throughout the course of a nine-week period for a course on resilience, for pupils in grades 7, 8 and 9. They were introduced to:

- the *Thinking Brain* and the brain's *Alarm Centre*
- *Attention – the Brain's Spotlight*
- factors that influence thoughts, body and brain
- setting objectives
- breathing exercises that bring peace to the body
- communicating to others what it means to be resilient.

The starting point was the modules from The Resilience Programme. Along the way, pupils were given the opportunity to fill out a notebook with exercises, and document their learning. Pupils who completed the notebook were given a certificate for their participation. The teaching should be provided in small steps, for instance by resolving assignments using the notebook throughout the nine units of the course. The course units had a diverse content and were arranged in a coherent progression in which we worked with 'memory-tracks', weaving the individual units together.

Initially I spent a lot of time explaining the basics of resilience. I presented knowledge and tools from The Resilience Programme and supplemented this with video. It was very teacher centred and the pupils had to exert themselves in order to hold their concentration. Later, when the material became more familiar, I could start improvising and let go of this very meticulous teaching style. Pupils harnessed their focus through group work and their own reflections on various solutions to situations of conflict. Over time, I succeeded in placing more learning responsibility onto the pupils, for instance by having them initiate and verbalise their reflections.

The visual aspect

As the course progressed, my teaching became more visual by using wall sheets, colour photos with big letters, etc. The pupils did not receive material and instead I printed and laminated the *Thinking Brain* and the brain's *Alarm Centre* and placed them on the classroom's blackboard. After briefly introducing the tools, the pupils had to come up with their inputs, thus expressing emotions and thoughts that they experienced in various states. I noted their answers up at the front of the class directly on the image of the brain. In this way, I managed to involve most of the class. When one pupil came up with an answer, I asked another to deepen this answer and vice versa. An open reflection with room for perspectives was established in this way in the class. By use of a torch, which could help focus on a single point, casting darkness on the rest, the image of attention being the *I*'s spotlight became more concrete to the pupils. Several of them came to the blackboard and illustrated the torch exercise, which showed them how attention, and therefore also the teaching, may be disturbed by, for instance, mobile phones, chatting and noise.

Teaching methods and motivation

Various teaching and learning methods, for instance drama, were applied to support the teaching. The class was divided into groups, each having a theme such as bullying or criticism. They would then present an example where the *Thinking Brain* would be functioning to solve a conflict as well as an example in which the brain's *Alarm Centre* could have the power to the point of disaster. After the dramatic presentation of each group, the class jointly spoke about their suggested solutions. This was again for the purpose of reflection and for widening per-spectives. Cooperative learning as a teaching method was applied as well. The method is effective in creating active learning as the pupils are given various active roles: one pupil would be reading the story of the *House of Thoughts* while another would be taking minutes, a third would be taking notes and a fourth would be sharing the narrative with the rest of the class. Similarly, I used the method in an exercise where I had laminated small cards of questions regarding resilience. Pupils had to form pairs, ask one another the questions from the cards they would have in their hands, answer the questions and then swap one another's question cards, forming new pairs and starting again. It was a dynamic way of becoming acquainted with resilience that worked very well.

In order to activate and motivate pupils in the most effective way, disseminated knowledge must be related to everyday life. The pupils should regard it as meaningful to them. If people experience themselves as being resilient, viewing resilience as natural, and thus typically approach daily life with positivity, it may be difficult to understand why teaching resilience is relevant at all. I experienced some 'resilient' pupils backing out of the sessions on resilience, instead turning their attention to other activities, such as preparation for exams or other school-related work. It seemed that they viewed resilience as a given and had become bored. Other 'resilient' pupils chose to participate actively. One perspective that may have motivated them is the opportunity to further practise the advantages of resilience. They may have wanted to practise their awareness of the brain's *Alarm Centre*, so that in tense situations, such as their upcoming exams, they could prevent their minds from going blank. Some pupils were naturally very actively participating in the teaching. They could relate to concepts such as the brain's *Alarm Centre*. They recognised this state of mind and were very curious about learning the ways in which they could move themselves out of the brain's *Alarm Centre* and return to the *Thinking Brain*. The experience of having a drifting and impulsive attention span was recognisable for some as well, whereas others did not relate to that experience or self-understanding.

Teaching methods and activities that demand physical activity and individual exposure may require adaptations to the size of the class, and grade. A breathing exercise with deep breathing to calm the brain's *Alarm Centre* did not, for instance, work for all pupils in this course. The class was too big and it was difficult and embarrassing for some of them to engage themselves in this way. A lot of giggling and playful behaviour came out of it, and instead, I chose an exercise in which you gradually tense certain parts of your body for five to ten seconds and then relax through deep breathing. This exercise made participation easy for the pupils. It may seem strange at first that simple deep and relaxing breathing is barrier breaking. However, it can be new and privacy challenging to undertake such an exercise with others around. In many cases it is obviously better to just explain the technique and why its benefits are so decisive without practising the actual exercise within the classroom setting. In other contexts, it may be an appropriate challenge, even though the experience is perceived as somehow barrier breaking in the beginning. See the narrative of praxis from a club-playground later in this chapter as well.

As mentioned above, the young people were given the opportunity to obtain a written certificate of their participation in the resilience course, and this seemed to be motivating for some. On the other hand, already resilient pupils who had backed out did not receive a certificate, which seems a bit paradoxical, given that they are indeed resilient.

The pupils experiencing general challenges in school also had a hard time concentrating on the teaching, and it required constant effort to keep their attention. Some ended up with a certificate and some did not. Overall, my experience was that these pupils found documenting their learning in a notebook to be dry and boring. These exercises actually stopped their learning. It was exactly what they already struggled with in school. In this situation, it could have been better to drop the documentation part and focus entirely on the verbal and visual parts, which motivated these pupils to a higher degree.

The learning environment

Resilience requires individuals to be present and reflective; something that is easiest to acquire in calm and secure surroundings. I often have experienced the learning environment as being full of disturbances, which distract attention. In some classes, I encountered a dominating culture where pupils consistently came late to class. Many could not keep their mobile phones and tablets in their bags and they therefore had a hard time staying attentive during class. At times, there was a lot of noise from the corridors and once in a while it happened that a pupil from another class would poke her/his head in the doorway to deliver a message to a classmate or just make some fun. Classroom furnishing also played a role. Some were arranged in a horseshoe layout and others in small groups. Clusters of four were very beneficial for group work, but could encourage disturbances when I was teaching and the pupils were not fully concentrating. Adjoining rooms, especially those that could be opened through partitions, were very sound sensitive. If for instance a movie was being played in a room connecting to the one I was in, it could be heard and disturbed the teaching. At times, I experienced a lot of mess in the classrooms. Paper would lie about on the floors and tables and chairs could be out of place. My total impression was that there were generally a lot of auditory and visual disturbances that made it difficult to engage in reflective and deep learning.

Class size and composition also had a great influence. I was teaching up to 23 pupils at once, in what is known as the 'periphery times' in Denmark (early morning or late afternoon), where the pupils' collective concentration is low, imposing challenges. A kind of hierarchy was also dominating within classes, sometimes making it problematic or anxiety provoking for some pupils. This prevented them from actively contributing their reflections or solutions in class; they seemed to be restricted by their peers.

It is fundamental that both pupils and the school support the course and secure a learning environment shaped by continuity and trust. This course was arranged as a process in which each class was a natural continuation from the previous one. The pupils should not be regularly absent, as they will then benefit less from the teaching and perhaps gradually lose motivation.

Course two – Resilience course in a group

After a meeting with the pedagogical leader and a class teacher, the decision was taken to start a resilience course for seven boys in grade 8. They had been declared 'not equipped for further education' and struggled with coping in class due to diverse challenges. We agreed upon five two-hour lessons. The overall objective was to support the youngsters in their efforts to improve their coping skills at school and help them acquire a higher degree of readiness for progressing in their education. We also agreed that the pupils should individually formulate a personal goal for themselves at the outset of the course, which would be shared with their regular classroom teacher. In turn, their teacher could help support them in achieving their goal throughout the five-week resilience course, and beyond.

The teaching would take place in the after-school club that was located just beside the school. The change of context was intentional, in an effort to provide a quiet space suitable for deeper learning processes while strengthening a sense of comfort in more leisurely surroundings. It was important for me to create a relaxed learning environment from the beginning. The room had good lighting and a good indoor climate. I had arranged a longer table along with bean-bag chairs in which the boys could lounge. The walls were decorated with quite a few wall sheets, visualising aspects from The Resilience Programme through phrases and images. I made sure that fresh fruit and water were made available in every class.

The seven boys had diverse challenges, such as ADHD or challenges of a social, family-based kind, which made it hard for them to cope in school. Indeed, I had met with a group of challenged as well as challenging boys. What became immediately obvious, and was present throughout the whole course, were the power dynamics within the group. They could generate a lot of noise together and they could prompt anxiety within one another in a very short period of time, egging one another on. A common challenge seemed to be a lack of self- and impulse-control. There was a lot of façade I had to break through.

My professional starting point was to meet the boys at eye-level. I was ready to change the course as we went along, even though I was equipped with a teaching plan. I made it clear that their choices and behaviours influenced the degree to which the course would be rewarding for them. Scolding was not part of my teaching. Telling-off and punishment activate the brain's *Alarm Centre*, even in a resilience course, and this would not be of use to me nor to them. I had to meet them appreciatively and open-mindedly and build my teaching upon the positive elements that each could contribute.

Teaching resilience to pupils in grades 7 and 9 gave me valuable experiences. The connection between theoretical background knowledge and the pupils' own pool of experiences is vital. What is optimal is to draw from a topic the youngsters relate to easily. This helps them more easily connect their reflections about resilience to something they find meaningful. The seven boys in this group were struggling at school. School therefore became the first topic in an exercise of cooperative learning. They would come together in pairs and ask questions about school – questions I had prepared in advance. This exercise encouraged reflection. It also got them to move about the room, which became a good starting point. Using the school as my main theme, I easily drew connections between it and concepts from The Resilience Programme. Step by step, elements such as concentration, awareness in the classroom, the brain's *Alarm Centre* and drifting attention were explored in relation to their influences on daily life at school and a coherent school experience. We examined the influence of sleep, diet and exercise as well as their influence on blood sugar levels and learning. All related to the challenges that school pupils were familiar with.

At the beginning of each teaching session, I placed importance on spending time to 'land' in the room together. Because of this, we began with a relaxation exercise. I used a muscle-relaxing exercise, where we tense parts of the body and then relax afterwards, suitable for the boys. They experienced the exercise as both fun and relevant because the focus was on tightening their muscles – something they could easily relate to.

Beforehand I had planned how the five lessons should develop, what the pupils would learn and how. It became clear pretty fast that I had to correct quite a bit on the way, because it turned out that the boys had a lot to contribute. Some of their preoccupations related to experiences of prejudice and a lack of respect from teachers at school. It became my task to find ways to integrate this into the topics of resilience. The ability to be together with other people in a constructive way, without the necessity for good chemistry, is part of what being resilient implies. Also, what one contributes while meeting another is mirrored in the other's behaviour and their perceptions. Respect must be reciprocal. This was helpful to open up reflections and suggestions of what the boys could do to be more recognised and 'seen' in a more positive light at school: they should try to do certain things differently in order not to activate the brain's *Alarm Centre*. They could try to be prepared for school, be rested, be curious about the teaching, try to regulate their behaviour and be more participating in class, be more conscious and step back from the impulses that constantly disturbed their attention. In practising this, the teacher would possibly take them more seriously and treat them more respectfully in the future, thereby creating better days at school. The concepts they had learnt from the theoretical part of the resilience course were useful for them. They enabled them to verbalise their immediate experiences concerning the lack of respect they felt, and also gain the ability to project some potential actions they could take in light of this, in the future. It would, of course, take time and require practice.

A certain amount of self-insight is required to face our challenges. It was my experience that some of the boys found it hard to link their trials with the idea of setting a personal goal, especially when the starting point was rooted in their feeling of lack of respect from their surroundings. Only a few of them managed to set a personal goal initially. As the course evolved and they became more reflective, self-insights eventually arose in most of them. They started to understand and verbalise what they could do themselves. It was especially interesting to hear them trying to describe their own attention processes and how they could actually start practising a higher degree of awareness and step back from the disturbances that caused them to react impulsively all the time.

Overall, the course with the seven boys was positive. They had exposed some of the challenges they were experiencing in school, and the concepts of resilience helped them create understandings and new ways in which to act. They got to learn about the relationship that exists between the *Thinking Brain* and the brain's *Alarm Centre*, attention, sleep, diet, rest and other factors that influence how we cope with life. Serious challenges such as ADHD and parents having alcohol or other drug abuse problems certainly influence, to a great extent, how a young person copes and how much resilience is developed in their early years. My experience tells me that these factors must be taken into account when we plan a course in resilience. We need to be ready to correct and adjust along the way. Unfortunately, one of the boys was so challenged at home that he was not able to participate fully in some of the sessions, yet he attended, stayed still and observed. Considerations regarding whether he and his family needed professional help came about. Overall, this particular example highlights that the course had its limitations, as did the course's setting.

Teaching the course over a five-week period is indeed a short time in relation to reaching a personal goal. I still know that the young participants at least opened up to self-understanding and reflection. The experience from the two courses indicates that children and adolescents with special needs have a greater output from practising resilience in smaller groups, as is the case with other methods.

EXPERIENCES WITH RESILIENCE IN A SOCIALLY DISADVANTAGED SCHOOL

Dan Henriksen

This section contains descriptions of, and reflections based on, teachings in mentalisation and resilience with different pupils of various grades in one-to-one situations, in groups and in classrooms. Special focus is placed on the development of intrapersonal and interpersonal competences through work with resilience and mentalisation.

The significance of attention

I know I am about to start an exercise, an exercise where I practise using my body.

> I know that I simply direct my attention, my imagination, and that I try to rule my mind. The first thing I imagine is having a pellet in my thumb. It is nicely soft, comfortably warm, completely fine and round. It slowly turns and when I notice carefully, I feel a warmth in my thumb, and also very relaxed.

This is one of several relaxing exercises that pupils are introduced to in the teachings of resilience. The purpose of the exercise is to offer experience and insight into what happens when we make use of the *Brain's Spotlight* and our thoughts in different ways. It is an exercise where we learn to relax by directing the attention and focus into the body. The interesting thing is how our thoughts, emotions and sensations are ruled by where our attention points to in a given moment. However, in everyday life, this is not conscious. By being aware of the possibility to direct our attention and gain access to different thoughts, emotions and sensations, the opportunity opens up for us to choose how we see ourselves, others and the surrounding world in that moment. For most people, it is an expanding experience of the self when they use the mind and attention in a specific way to sense the body in a pleasant, relaxed state. After some practice, the pupils expressed that it feels like being able to control something within – namely our attention. In a similar activity, where we shift the direction of attention between positive and negative thoughts, a similar awareness arises.

As in every other kind of learning, this also rests on beginning with and establishing a praxis routine. The thought about, focus towards and the decision to act in new ways, starting to bring these into reality, must be practised again and again. A praxis is shaped and defined by the pupils and the teacher collaboratively. It is essential that a pupil's own motivation to act be reinforced in everyday life, defined and guided by the content and goal of the practice. Constructing a *Field of Practice* is often fun and creates insights into our individual thoughts about the initiation part, obstacles that will arise, and the objectives – it is pure mentalisation in practice.

Learning environment and language

It is interesting to look at the environments we create around groups of children and young people and around the individual child and youngster when we work with the ability to mentalise and be resilient.

What kind of language and which values do I prioritise ideally and concretely? How do I form a safe learning environment and how do I motivate another person to be willing to learn? What words and phrases activate the brain's *Alarm Centre* and which activate the Reward-Factory? How do we move from language and theoretical knowledge to the creation of motivating imagery within a child? In short, how does everyday life and school become interesting, action oriented and competence giving for each child?

The interest is, of course, directed towards children in general but especially towards children who grow up in resource-deficient environments, who may therefore be negatively predisposed and struggling either with performance in school, socially, or both.

The child who is prepared to learn will naturally grab onto everything within scope. This child will be resilient in relation to withstanding and overcoming resistance, all while growing and developing – precisely due to challenges.

I therefore refer here to the children and adolescents who need to be lifted and helped in moving on from a frozen learning process where energy and engagement are very low. A readiness to learn is absolutely dependent on an individual's care to create peace, safety and security. The question is how one, as a professional, initiates this. One way to work with this is through a sharpened awareness of our language. Let me illustrate with an example. On a trip with a small group of pupils I witnessed a teacher say something that was well meant but that, in the end, turned out to be demotivating: 'So well done! You were the best of all!' It was clearly intended as and received as praise. And praise is undoubtedly good at face value. Why then should I be critical of what was said? Firstly, this was said in the presence of all other pupils. Secondly, there is no way to treat what was said as objective truth. My experience was that everyone had contributed on that day with exemplary effort and that they all could, depending on a given benchmark, be seen as 'the best'. Thirdly, the pupils could have interpreted from the statement that the point was to become the best, to become 'number 1' in the group, as an elevated position in relation to their peers. When we reward something, we value it as being good but verbalise it as being the best, and as a result, we may unintentionally be advocating a culture of competition. There is a paradox in the cultivation of a competition and winner culture – that the consequence delineates 'losers'; and often, there are more losers than winners. I believe competition has its place; however, highlighting competition in learning situations creates an unnecessary focus on the social positioning of winners and losers, which will cause at least as much insecurity as it will security. In the long run, a deeper lack of trust and meaning in relation to an individual's self-image and effort may develop.

I guess this event marked me so deeply because of the reactions I noticed in the other pupils. Initially they drew back and stopped what they were preoccupied with for a moment – sharing food and drinks, relaxing and feeling good after having completed their task. Their effort had now been evaluated and one of them was singled out as being the best. The rest were not mentioned and, because of this, their whole attitude, concentration, willingness to cooperate and contribute came to be devalued. I experienced how the praising of one pupil as being the best was followed by every other pupil feeling less successful, despite them having actually done their best. Instead, the praise could have been expressed as: 'It looked like you did your very best', or, 'You were active nearly all the time,' or, 'You looked very focused.' In these examples, effort is acknowledged and praised instead of performance or comparative results. In other words, the attitude towards a task becomes the centre of attention. This attitude develops into a value that may rule how future tasks are addressed. The values we verbalise in daily life should point towards an individual sense of self-worth and self-confidence and they should also support the dynamics between the attitudes we adopt when facing a task and the competence we source in order to solve it.

In relation to others, we are constantly required as individuals to adjust to the frames and rules of a context. At the same time, our experience may be an individual longing and sense for self-care. We all experience a continual shifting between self-care and our individual existence on the one hand and breaking out of that self-image through definitions provided by other people on the other. In my professional work it has become central, starting from the concepts of the *Thinking Brain*, the brain's *Alarm Centre* and the Reward-Factory, to be aware of each and every pupil's reaction. Depending on the context, I then choose words, phrases and language that can promote learning, the pupils' desire for learning, and their ownership of the learning process.

Resilience in praxis

Albert is in the 3rd grade. He has been attending this school for a couple of months and visited me for dialogue sessions because of continuous clashes with his maths teacher. Albert would react aggressively, speak slightingly and use obnoxious language, as he had also done with several pupils, and a decision was made to take action. I had been assigned a function at the school where I had been granted time to speak with pupils individually as well as in groups. I met with Albert for dialogues, once per week over the course of eight weeks, for 20–30 minutes per session.

There was no doubt that Albert tried and struggled to keep on track in and out of class. At his previous school he was constantly in conflict with teachers as well as his peers. He often fled his school and viewed the whole school setting as a place where he was not allowed to be himself and where he was constantly being chased. Given this context, it was not necessary to investigate the exact reason underlying his conflict with the maths teacher. What was important was to note that the situation had developed in a negative way and had become precarious for Albert. It became clear pretty fast that Albert did not see himself as co-responsible for the development of the situation and he was also not very receptive towards changing his attitude and behaviour.

At the beginning of our dialogues I told him about the *I* and the attention towards thoughts that we, at any given time, find significant. We drew *Thought Bubbles* and placed both positive, negative and neutral thoughts within them. We spoke about reactions in the body when we focus on different thoughts, about our core emotions and how we appear when we are caught up in emotions. I showed him images to illustrate different emotions, facial expressions and body language, and also to point out and speak about what preoccupies us in life, which can be quite airy-fairy and hard to put into words. Can we, for instance, always control our thoughts and feelings? We quickly agreed that this is not always the case. Albert understood everything and could repeat back what we had spoken about; however, it seemed not to relate to him. His behaviour revealed that what he learnt through our sessions did not matter to him, even though he would be responding positively and encouragingly when we met. It was obvious that he would come to me because he had to. We spoke about *The story of a mind train*, drew *Thought Bubbles* and practised relaxation exercises. I had a sense, though, that he held it all at a distance. At some point, Albert spoke about a conflict he had encountered on a recent trip with the class. It reminded me of an episode from my own childhood where I had become both furious and sad and had acted in a way that I regretted afterwards, once I had calmed. I shared this with Albert. While I was speaking, he sat still and listened with a distant gaze. Suddenly he burst out saying, 'But then I'm just like everyone else.' It seemed to be a turning point. From this moment, things started making sense to him in new ways, speaking about thoughts and how we individually can decide what we want. His behaviour in school remained agitated, impulsive and physical. Still, his perspective in his encounters with others was slowly changing and he began understanding his role in both good and bad situations in school.

Benjamin was in 3rd grade. He had an intense temper with very reactive behaviour. He seemed discouraged at the same time and showed no initiative in class, nor at school breaks. Benjamin's teacher and pedagogue were worried about his lack of participation in class activities, and about his negative and overall evasive behaviour. To try to help, arrangements were made where Benjamin would attend another school with his parents, twice per week, for remedial learning. He also came to me for dialogue sessions once a week, for a period of time. At first, these sessions were one-on-one, and later, we held group sessions with his peers.

The first time Benjamin visited me, we started speaking about the reason for it. He listened attentively but did not say much. I told him about the concepts from The Resilience Programme and we used a great deal of time to draw out *Thought Bubbles*, writing out thoughts and drawing them out. The first drawings he created were about his family and things that he wanted. At that point, Benjamin expressed something that later turned out to be significant: 'When I know what I am supposed to do, I feel light.' We drew this thought out in a *Thought Bubble* and as a balloon with text and colours.

At our next meeting, we spoke again about Benjamin's need to know what he was supposed to do and what would happen to him. Out of the blue he told me that the day before, while running at the back of the sports class, suddenly he had decided to run at the front. And then he did it. I asked him: 'Do you know that in that moment, you made a decision?' He looked at me as if I had just said something inconceivable. He did not realise that he had made a decision. This opened a conversation about the options available to him, which would help direct his attention, take decisions on his own and be able to follow what he's really wanting to be better at. He immediately started setting objectives for reading. He had learnt that if he could both think and act upon his thoughts, his self-image and worldview could change.

Courses within classrooms

At some point, I was given a certain number of hours at school to use, for example, for presentations and supervision for colleagues, and courses for pupils about how to handle daily life challenges in practical ways. I primarily was guest lecturing in middle grade classes where the social and/or learning environment was deemed challenging. Interest from pupils was surprisingly strong, and hours flew by due to the high degree of engagement and activity.

Prior to lectures, I would send out some brief information to classroom teachers in relation to the content of a two- to four-hour course.

Dear . . .

The content and the duration of the teaching is arranged as a two- to four-hour course.

The intention of the course is to cast light on an issue that everyone struggles to deal with; namely, governing our thoughts. What can we do to be better at that which we want to become better at? How must I/can I relate to being at school, having to learn something new every day? What do I do when it is difficult for me to be in class? How do I speak to others when they are angry or sad, or when I am angry or sad myself? As a starting point, we will focus on understanding how the brain works in relation to our surroundings, body, thoughts and feelings. We will use The Resilience Programme as our foundation and emphasise:

* Images of the brain. How is the brain built and how does it work? Here, we focus on the *Thinking Brain*, the brain's *Alarm Centre* and the Reward-Factory
* *The I* – who experiences the world? The *Attention – the Brain's Spotlight*. Where is my attention directed? To what can I direct my attention?
* *Thought Bubbles*. Practise with *Thought Bubbles*. Positive, negative and neural thoughts
* Breathing. When can breathing be supportive? How do I become aware of my breathing?
* Working with an objective (*Field of Practice*). What do I want? Where am I going? What obstacles do I see? Can I get support from someone or something?

I would like to motivate the pupils to continue working with resilience and their ability to mentalise. We will form a support group and then motivate two to three pupils from each class to work on a weekly basis with, 'How do I become better equipped for school?', 'How do I become better at learning something new?', 'Can I do something to feel good in my breaks?', 'If I was supposed to teach younger children, how would I go about it?'

Best regards,
Dan Henriksen

The engagement, interest and activity were, as mentioned, high, and several pupils reached out, enquiring afterwards in relation to the theory as well as the practical ways in which we can approach challenges. Unfortunately, systematic measurements of the effects on the learning environments and conflicts were never carried out. After a couple of months, there was, however, a renewed demand for some hours of teaching about resilience and mentalising. That leads me to believe that there was both a positive effect from, and trust built into, the quality of the materials. Likewise, it became clear that a continuous effort is necessary whenever the aim is to change habits on an individual level and in relation to social patterns.

Second grade (2.A)

After the summer holidays, I started teaching Danish to a second-grade class. In the previous year, when they were in grade 1, these pupils had experienced a very high rotation in teachers. The class had been described as being problematic; too much trouble and noise, internal conflicts and violence, grim language among pupils as well as towards the teachers. Nevertheless, the students could also concentrate on their work at times, especially in mathematics. I started the school year by prioritising extra time in class with the maths teacher – in his lessons. My motivation was to experience this group of pupils in an environment with a teacher they had already been with throughout grade 1, where there was a reciprocally positive relationship between the teacher and the pupils. The class was rich with learning and was equally rewarding, giving me some insight into the class culture and what the students responded to positively. It became apparent that clear and direct guidance combined with high variation in the teaching, and a mixture of short sequences of teaching, enriched with physical activities, created the conditions for a suitable learning space for these pupils. As in most classes, there were immense differences between the pupils' academic and social strengths and challenges, and the variation of activities the maths teacher offered somehow addressed each of the pupils' mental and physical needs for consideration and acknowledgement.

Parallel to the teaching in Danish where I mixed blackboard teaching with individual and group-oriented exercises, I created various exercises in resilience primarily with the aim of generating conditions for a safe and motivating learning environment. In the team of teachers, we talked about the effects of being direct and precise in our choice of objectives and feedback in relation to the learning environment – also towards each other as colleagues. The social environment and the learning culture we wished to create should be supported by an awareness towards and controlling of the immediate effects on pupils' choices, engagement and subsequent actions. In the beginning, this required great attention to shifts in the rhythm and focus of content throughout lessons.

Teaching and mind trains

How do we initiate teaching in and dialogue about thoughts in the 2nd grade? In order to keep explanations and dialogues simple and relevant, I always root my starting point in an actual situation. An actual situation is an opportunity to investigate the reasons that underlie our own individual and collective reasons for doing something in a specific way. Actual situations are relevant and motivating. My starting point is to use a variety of situations that may help elucidate the fact that we always have thoughts that lead to the decisions we take from moment to moment. Throughout the course of about two weeks, we work in short intermissions with the questions: 'What are thoughts?' and 'who experiences the thoughts?' *The story of a mind train* can kick-start a discussion about where the train goes and in which compartment a pupil chooses to place her/himself. The train can also represent a subject or a lesson where each compartment represents a specific attitude towards a subject or exercise we are about to initiate.

For instance:

- Do you choose to be in compartment 1, where you will try to cooperate and work in a concentrated way?
- Do you choose to be in compartment 2, where you *may* try to cooperate and work in a concentrated way?
- Do you choose to be in compartment 3, where you will definitely not want to do anything?

In this exercise, pupils suddenly realise a variety of options available to them and it becomes clear to them how different choices lead to different consequences.

A torch is also useful in showing how *Attention – the Brain's Spotlight* can move between the outer world, the body, thoughts and emotions. Many pupils experience the new concepts they engage with in their work with resilience as confusing. It helps to visualise each one and make each one concrete. It is entirely possible that pupils learn about attention in such a way, that they understand how it is actually possible to direct our attention and our thoughts. In these exercises, pupils drew out their own *Thought Bubbles* with positive thoughts, which were then put up on the board. The drawings were highly important to the pupils. They were happy to see the drawings on display and to talk about them afterwards in class. A reward that can be meaningful for individuals is also motivating and leads to continuity within an activity and other, similar, activities. The drawings were then left on display in the classroom for a long period of time, and more were added.

Experience and collaborative learning

We learn through language, together with and from the people and the surroundings we are a part of. I am always relating to something and I am part of a context that influences the pupils I meet and teach. I am therefore always responsible.

The questions that concern me are, 'How do I want to care for this responsibility?', 'Which cultures and environments will I be part of shaping and how do I, in praxis, partake in supporting the underlying values of these cultures and environments?' Research into mentalising confirms that learning and development towards wellbeing and health for individuals and groups flourishes best in predominately positive and acknowledging environments.

My experience is that the work done with resilience and mentalising is a professional, as well as a personal, journey of development. It makes no sense to teach and inform about strength, flexibility, awareness and control of social and learning behaviours if we are not at the same time demonstrating and living out these intentions in our own performance. I have to do what I say in order to be seen as trustworthy. We have to source our own surplus of energy and find the appropriate resources to be used that will enable meaningful connections between academic objectives, pupils' competences, learning aims and expectations.

LUXURY ISSUE? NO, IT'S NOT

Lene Steensberg

I would like to invite the reader behind the scenes of an ordinary public school in which The Resilience Programme is being implemented on all levels of the school. I will describe the challenges we meet in our daily work and how we bring in the resilience way of thinking as a tool to work towards the development of resilient pupils, resilient communities and resilient cooperation between our school and families. Our experiences at school with The Resilience Programme cover specific exercises with individual pupils, presentations about resilience to classes followed by class exercises, as well as presentations at parent meetings and at school board meetings. We arranged a pedagogical afternoon for the teachers where the subject was resilience for adults, with a focus on work–life balance. In this section, I will describe how resilience can be implemented at all levels in a school, and at the same time I will point out actual areas in which resilience is on the school's agenda.

Our school – our opportunities and challenges

Our school is a public school within a resource-rich district. The school is located in the so-called green area in the north of Copenhagen. The school's employees are professionally skilled and very much engaged, the parents belong to the upper middle class and most of the school's pupils come to school well dressed and well prepared, full of experiences from their safe family lives, exciting holidays, sports and leisure activities. From outside, we seem to be close to the ideal school. Some may be tempted to think that joy runs out into every corner at this place and that the school's employees have something that could seem a bit of an easy job, compared with other schools that are located in more disadvantaged areas. However, if you were to dig a bit further, it becomes apparent that we have our challenges in everyday life as well, and that work with resilience is appropriate here too – we do not encounter only rich people's problems. Challenges with fear and hyper-sensitivity[1] are very real for many of the pupils at this school and worry preoccupies some parents accordingly. Challenging for us, the individual pupil, class communities and in terms of learning capacity is when children are anxious in their daily life situations or are not able to cope with ordinary challenges. Sometimes children express their worry, nervousness or hyper-sensitivity. Sometimes the parents are the ones who send a message to the teachers and pedagogues, asking for special considerations to be granted to their children at school. The examples are multifarious: a boy from middle school who needs support getting to the staircase as he fears passing the higher grades' classroom doors; one who is afraid of being left without an adult in the room while in the company of peers; girls who do not show up in school because they have been arguing with their friend or because the friend played with someone else the day before; ordinary children's play or physical horseplay that a child cannot handle emotionally. We have pupils who asked permission to skip sports during menstruation, or due to a football match the day before, or sleepiness. We have pupils who are sad or nervous because of parental health issues, children who burst into tears because they are afraid of failing, and upper school pupils who are physically influenced by nervousness in relation to their impending leaving examinations.

We do, of course, have a large group of children and adolescents who handle everyday life challenges in school easily. It strikes me, however, that we do have daily episodes where pupils cannot cope with ordinary challenges or requirements. Not because they refuse, but because fear or sensitivity obstructs everyday life, restricting these pupils and impacting their classmates who feel cautious or predisposed to anxiety. All of this influences the academic learning opportunities as well. Teachers struggle to handle situations where pupils become fearful, and this sometimes takes the focus away from the rest of the class.

Just as anxiety and sensitivity preoccupy some children, worry preoccupies some of the parent groups. Parents are worried about whether their children are learning enough, whether their children have enough friends or whether they have the 'right' buddies. Parents are worried about whether the school makes use of the newest teaching methods, whether their children receive enough attention from teachers, whether the class is thriving and whether the communication between the school and home is sufficient to keep them informed about activities at school. Such worries stem from being preoccupied with children growing up to have a good life – and all parents will recognise this as an absolute priority for their children. At our school, parental involvement sometimes slides into worry, which is something that impedes the development of a resilient school community and a child's chances to develop individual resilience. Teachers receive emails from worried parents on a daily basis and many clarifications take place over the phone and in 'emergency meetings' involving teachers, pedagogues, inclusion supervisors, psychologists, management, parents and their children. Sometimes this obviously concerns pupils who are particularly challenged, for instance in cases where children are suffering from a serious physical illness, attention-disturbances and so on. It is not only this group of pupils and parents, though, who request special arrangements and action-plans in everyday school life. Normal and well-functioning parents are also preoccupied with well-intentioned worry on their children's behalf. And normal, well-functioning and often academically skilled children and adolescents can also turn fearful about common everyday life situations.

We value the dialogue with all parents at our school. A constant awareness and a continuous development of a trustworthy cooperation between schools and parents are highly prioritised by both management and staff. Still, the dialogue with parents about their worries is starting to overtake teachers' and pedagogues' working life, shifting our focus away from the academic and social learning environments. Therefore, it is in everyone's interest that we look more closely at how we handle worries, fearfulness and sensitivity within our schools.

Resilience and systemic methods

Teachers and pedagogues are continuously inspired by – or have imposed upon them – new methods and approaches for teaching in general, and more specifically for pupils. For this reason, I was originally curious about whether resilience was just another method in the vast collection of methods or whether resilience could be related to other methods we are already working with. We have several method-ologies already in place at the school, directly connected to our municipal strategies, which focus on visible learning, inclusion and, not least, a systematic view into issues surrounding children and adolescents (Nordahl, 2012). In praxis, this implies analysing the circumstances around an issue: planning the teaching, relations between the children in a class, an individual child's intentions of action, etc. Throughout the municipality, we work with a systemic method called SAL (Systemic Analysis of the Learning environment). When challenges arise in relation to a particular child's learning and wellbeing or in relation to the learning environment of an entire class, we analyse the child's relationships or the learning environment in order to discover openings for actions that are have not yet been unveiled. When something is not working optimally in school for one or more pupils, we take a 360-degree look so as to observe and perceive our pupils and ourselves as part of a wider system.

Aside from the systemic approach, I am academically interested in narrative approaches to children with difficulties as well as developmental work in general. In this context, a narrative approach implies that we, as professionals, are curious about the stories and narratives created by children and their peers, individually and in groups. Within the narrative approach, we do not look for rights or wrongs, truths or falsities. On the contrary, we are interested in the stories that are created around a single child, for instance. Especially in working with stories that have a child 'locked-in', impeding that child's learning opportunities or behaviour in learning situations, it is relevant to examine more closely the dominant stories of that child so as to elucidate possible new orientations towards new opportunities and actions. The narrative perspective opens the possibility to create new stories about ourselves and about each other (Bro, Løw & Svanholt, 2009).

The resilience approach has come to be an approach for children with difficulties, befitting the systemic and narrative perspectives that are already a part of my work. There is no discord between The Resilience Programme and the other tools and approaches we use in our work with wellbeing and learning. Actually, resilience and our other perspectives supplement one another. This has been a prerequisite for my further curiosity in relation to developing and implementing resilience here, at the school. The work with resilience at our school was prompted by a lecture given by Poul Lundgaard on the subject, and by a curiosity as to whether we could use it as more than just an interesting input. In contrast to schools with more visible challenges, we are just an ordinary good school in a financially rich area – still struggling with our own challenges. Two years since that first lecture at our school, which piqued my curiosity about developing the resilience approach within the school's frames, resilience has become a central action point – here presented in headlines:

- Management
    - Resilience is written into the school agreement
    - The school board's management and employees have been given a lecture on resilience
    - Resilience is integrated into the function of the coordinator/inclusion supervisor
- Staff

    Resilience is on the agenda at department meetings and is a main theme

- Resource Centre
    - Staff here have worked with resilience during a thematic development day
    - Staff have been working with case studies and have received supervision in their work with resilience
    - Staff make use of resilience in their work with problem solving
- Class
    - Resilience has been included in weekly lessons about class wellbeing and in a course known as 'perform better'
- Parents
    - Lectures to parents about resilience have been provided

- The school board has informed parents about the work with resilience they are undertaking at school
- Resilience is part of school–parent conversations

- Individual (pupil)

  - Resilience is part of conversations with pupils
  - Short movies from www.robusthed.dk are used to support conversations.

The resilient way of thinking is spread over many levels and within many cooperative relations at the school and, in the long run, my guess is that this will create opportunities for resilience to become not only a pedagogical tool, but part of a mindset that spreads to all the school's relations. On the management level, settings are in place for implementing resilience:

- Resilience is described in the school agreement as a focus area
- Functions for coordinating the resource centre and inclusion supervision are being prioritised, along with the implementation
- Lectures on resilience and inclusion are part of the school board's strategy seminars.
- Development meetings for staff include resilience
- There are follow-up lectures for pedagogues and teachers on resilience, as well as 'where are we at?' staff meetings
- There are lessons in class wellbeing for all grades that create opportunities for us to work with resilience on a class level
- There are work–life balance development days for teachers where resilience is in focus.

The organisational framework is thereby set to ensure that resilience can unfold and develop in our school context. However, the setting is not enough. It is important that resilience is driven in practice as well as on a reflexive level. This level takes place to a very high degree in the resource centre, where resource teachers, pedagogues, psychologists and inclusion supervisors are represented. In the resource centre, a group of resource teachers and pedagogues examine resilience through case studies. In this forum, we have worked with specific challenges from everyday life, finding ways to act within The Resilience Programme. This work has resulted in praxis experiences that are ready to be implemented in classes, with the pupils.

In the spring, the resource centre arranged their yearly development day. The subject of this year was resilience. The day involved three sub-subjects:

- Resilience in early, middle and upper school classes
- Parental cooperation and resilience
- Connections between resilience and other methods.

Each sub-subject began with an academic lecture followed by group work on how to transfer knowledge into praxis. Every group briefly presented their work and reflections, and then we opened the dialogue and questions to all. The aim of the day was to equip resource teachers to work with the resilience approach within their classes and at parents' meetings. In this school year, some of the resource teachers have initiated specific resilience workshops for pupils in their classes. Within the resource centre, we intend to continue working with exemplary resilience workshops directed at pupils of all grades, just as we will continuously work with exemplary workshops in parent meetings. All teachers and pedagogues may immediately start lecturing on and using exercises of The Resilience Programme. However, through the work with exemplary workshops, we integrate the resilience way of thinking into methods that are coherent with the other methods the school is already using. We then integrate that into our school's specific conditions – potentials and challenges.

Resilience and parental cooperation

Parents are increasingly playing a role in the cooperative link between school and home – and so are their worries. Many parents with normal and well-functioning children contact the school's teachers and pedagogues about worries they have about their children or about the relationships their children are having at the school. Dialogues between the school and home are therefore starting to take up a lot of space in schools – in time and in consciousness. It is my experience that the insistence on dialogue that is prompted by parental worries is a contributing factor to teachers and pedagogues experiencing fatigue. All parents know the feeling of wishing the very best for their child. The question is, though: What is the best for our children? Is it best when children go through childhood and school years in the easiest possible way, where conflicts and challenges are minimal? Or is it best that our children are allowed to experience for themselves the good and the bad? Answering is not simple; there is great complexity in choosing the right balance.

At our school, we have both active and well-intentioned parents who support our children's school life and learning by being engaged in the school and sharing their surplus energy. Our challenge, however, is that parental engagement is not always appropriately offered, from the school's perspective. I may even be able to go as far as to say that parental involvement is one of the biggest challenges at our school. Engagement develops into parental worry about whether their child is provided with suitable challenges in class, whether the teaching methods are optimal for the child and whether the child's classmates' behaviour and actions support the child's developmental opportunities, etc. This focus of worry may cause an individual child to become more vulnerable and partly creates the grounds for vulnerable class communities – the exact opposite of what parents as well as professionals wish for. Perhaps as a school we have not been capable enough in transmitting how parents could actually support class wellbeing and the learning environment in classes. Or, maybe it's that relationships with the school and parental approaches have changed in recent years, demanding of us, as a school, to be clearer about good ways in which parents can support their children throughout their school years. Indeed, we can be clearer about the benefits of parental engagement in children's school life, which also promotes strong attendance records and active participation in all school activities throughout the school year. We can emphasise the importance of fundamental confidence building in our children, in knowing that they are capable, seeing themselves as part of a class and learning community, where openness and curiosity, academically and socially, become natural. We can also be more precise in communicating that present knowledge about learning and children's development informs us of the fact that parents best support their school-aged children when they provide them with the space to live out their own experiences. These include all learning experiences – including when things get difficult, experiences of falling out with friends, reunifications, experiences of saying 'never mind' when something unintended happens, experiences of being rejected and thereby moving on to new opportunities. Children must go through numerous experiences throughout their school years, and sometimes these will be painful, sad or difficult. However, only through all of these everyday challenges, at a child's level, can the individual child learn and develop into a whole being.

There are, of course, situations – at our school as well – where children should not experience things on their own, but where adults must intervene. As professionals, we are able to evaluate when such a situation arises. Likewise, parents should once in a while consider whether specific situations require special intervention and contact with their child's teachers or a classmate's parents. Concerning the small challenges in everyday life at school, I deem parental involvement as best invested behind the scenes – this suggests that parents should show their belief in a child's capability, that they listen, comfort, help the child to see other perspectives and support the child in finding highlights in daily life. In other words, they are backing the child in her/his learning to handle all the different situations we all meet along the way.

As a means for transmitting the message about resilience to parents, we have introduced special initiatives. At the school board's strategy day, I was invited to speak about resilience and inclusion. Along with management and staff representatives, the school board includes parent and pupil representatives. Presenting resilience was especially aimed at equipping the parents with knowledge related to which challenges we face, as a school, concerning resilience, and how we implement resilience at the school. The parent representatives are closest to the other parents at our school and they play a significant role when it comes to spreading the word at parent meetings about our focus on resilience. Following my presentation on resilience, the parent representatives were invited to take a closer look at the concrete ways in which the school works with resilience, at the challenges we experience as a school, and at our parent–school cooperation:

- Fear and hyper-sensitivity
- Matching expectations in relation to school–home cooperation
- Parental involvement that is well intended but sometimes gets out of hand
- Building confidence in how the school works professionally with class wellbeing.

I went through the challenges we encounter at our school when parental engagement takes a turn towards worry. I made a point of presenting to the parents that their worry, however well intentioned in solving their children's everyday challenges, fosters insecurity in the children and influences classrooms and the general school's learning community. I mentioned how resource demanding this becomes for our teachers, especially when they deal with long e-mail correspondences concerning parental worries. E-mail correspondence may take up several hours of a teacher's work-life – every little worry, for every child, takes up a lot of time in fact. E-mail correspondence is not only time-consuming for our teachers, it's also wearing. School and parents have, in my opinion, a common interest in collaborating closely in a focused effort, but with different roles in the collaboration. The following was also presented at the school's strategy seminar:

- A stimulating learning environment must exist
- A foundation for class wellbeing must be established
- We must be able to look at cases from different perspectives
- Pupils must encounter resilient adults
- Pupils must become as resilient as possible
- Teachers and pedagogues must keep their motivation up
- Teachers and pedagogues must spend their time on the right priority.

The school board has become knowledgeable about resilience, The Resilience Programme and the school's initiatives concerning resilience at the various organisational levels. We continue to further collaboration concerning resilience as a continuous process that develops between the school and its parents – hopefully as ongoing dialogue in homes, at parent meetings and in a school board context.

A more direct initiative in relation to resilience and collaboration with parents has taken place at parent meetings. Throughout the last year I have repeatedly been invited to speak about resilience at parent meetings – both in general, and more specifically about the role of parents. I have recently been asked to speak at a parent meeting for a middle school class. Teachers and parents had previously asked me to use real-life scenarios in order to better illustrate points about resilience. They wanted cases that illustrated the challenges of our reality so that they, as parents, might, through brief recommendations, handle the challenging situations of everyday life in the best and most resilient way possible. One of the cases that was presented at the parent meeting tells Olivia's story, and how she cries herself to sleep every night. She is sad, and she explains that she feels left out and rejected by the other girls. In contrast, teachers experience her as a girl who actively participates in her learning and thrives in her classes. Olivia is friends with two other girls and participates just as much as everyone else in school. Olivia can somehow appear to be reserved as well – a bit quiet and withdrawn at times.

A guide to being a resilient parent in this situation could include:

- Keeping calm – Olivia needs to be able to mirror herself in peaceful adults
- Listening – this shows Olivia that you have an interest in her
- Acknowledging – focus on the fact that her worries may be more common than she realises: 'I can hear it has been difficult for you today. How do you think the others feel – do they also find it hard with friendships sometimes?'
- Showing opportunities for action: 'What can you do to participate more in the game tomorrow?'
- Shifting attention: 'Tell me about something that was good today.'
- Trusting – that Olivia will handle the challenges of the day to come.

Before the parent meeting I had considered whether my recommendations were too action oriented. When presenting the story at the parent meeting, I made the point that the recommendations I was sharing were mere examples, and that parental support to our own child *could* look like this, seen from a resilience perspective. The parent meeting was a great success. The parents were presented with two cases they could mirror, and find inspiration from. They received a professional view on adult support for their own children in coping with the realities of everyday school life, and at the same time, they learnt how to create a framework that would enable children to feel safe and trusting. The parents also received materials that would help keep conversations about modern parenting ongoing.

Since then, I have prepared more cases to be used as examples that parents could mirror. It is my experience that such case-based presentations at parent meetings are useful for prompting dialogue about the ways in which we can support individual resilience, and resilient class communities more broadly. Also, it is quite useful to start with examples of frequently experienced school challenges.

In public schools, we are trained to instruct individual pupils and classes through a learning perspective; however, when it comes to parent groups, we are perhaps a bit inexperienced. Following the parent meeting, I see good prospects in continuing on this track because I got confirmation that my action-oriented approach for parents who wish to support their children in becoming resilient was working. We have a group of parents who are very keen to cooperate, and the cases and action-instructions resonated with them and were deemed useful.

As school professionals, we must dare to walk in this direction more in the future. That is, we must strive to be clear about how parents can best support their children's school life in a broad sense – for the benefit of our children, their relationships to others and for the learning community that exists in our classrooms.

Individual sessions in resilience

In the following, two courses are described in which I, as an inclusion supervisor, have had individual conversations with pupils. Both courses involved work that took place in close dialogue with the pupils' teachers. Likewise, ongoing dialogue with the children's parents was essential for the success of the course. In these two specific cases, the parents had initially been very worried about their child's learning at school and their general wellbeing. In both cases, the parents had, among other things, expressed that their child is extra sensitive or hyper-sensitive. It is my estimation that the parents had described their concerns about extra sensitivity to us in an attempt to help us, as professionals, handle each child's challenges. In praxis, verbalisations like these have a tendency to produce tunnel vision, such as: the child is especially sensitive, manifesting in these ways, and we are therefore expected to be cautious in our demands at school to that specific child, while also being expected to ensure that the surroundings (and other children) show extra consideration towards the child.

It may seem logical at first to alter a child's surroundings when a child is categorised as being hyper-sensitive. Yet, I am convinced that we can best care for the individual child by supporting her/him in coping with the realities as they are. Naturally, the amount a person can cope with before the brain's *Alarm Centre* becomes fully activated and the *Thinking Brain* shuts down is individual – for children and adults alike. As a school, we can support parents by being clearer about what works and maintaining an open and curious approach to collaborations between the school and homes.

The story about Philip

Philip is in grade 5 and does not function so well in class. He cannot concentrate academically, he becomes intensely preoccupied by things that are not related to his lessons and thereby is disruptive in class. The teachers deem him as need orientated – he sticks to an idea and will not let go of it. When Philip is not able to follow the class, he criticises his surroundings aggressively. Afterwards, he typically is not able to recall the episode, relate to what happened or to what others tell him about their experience. The teachers feel challenged in their efforts to create a framework for Philip's learning and they experience how his classmates start to pull away from him because of his often unbalanced reactions. Philip's parents have become worried about his lack of a social life.

Before I met Philip, several meetings had taken place involving teachers, parents, management and me, as an inclusion supervisor, in order to examine the challenges that revolve around him. We worked together in order to reach a shared understanding of what the focus points and action plan should be. The first time I met Philip I told him about the challenges that the teachers expressed and the learning objectives that the adults deemed relevant for him, namely to:

- Learn to stick to a situation, remember and reflect upon a given event
- Learn to see his own part in situations
- Learn to control his needs and reactions (how he is affected) in situations
- Learn to receive general instructions
- Learn to readjust.

Philip's immediate comment was, 'What nonsense!', followed by a deep sigh. In hindsight, he might have been partly right. These aims are first and foremost formulated from an adult perspective and they are relatively abstract.

I spent the first four to five sessions with Philip listening to him tell his story about school life, social life and about the powerlessness he felt in relation to his teachers. His teachers have been powerless because his behaviour is sometimes incomprehensible to them. Initially, conversations with Philip did not come easy. He is a child of few words and short sentences. I showed him drawings of the *Thinking Brain* and the brain's *Alarm Centre* as something that might feel more concrete, that he might be able to relate to. Still, I remained tentative because Philip did not really show a need to work with the above-mentioned learning objectives, except for what he called: 'Learning to control his temper'. Together, we watched the short movies from The Resilience Programme about the *Thinking Brain*, the brain's *Alarm Centre* and the *Brain's Spotlight*.

We spoke about what arises when the brain's *Alarm Centre* is activated in Philip and his *Thinking Brain* tunes down. We used *Thought Bubbles* to practise focus, and categorised them into green *Thought Bubbles*, which represented useful or nice thoughts, black *Thought Bubbles*, which were damaging or sad thoughts, and white *Thought Bubbles*, which were his neutral thoughts. We trained his capacity to focus throughout a couple of sessions. We drew the three types of *Thought Bubbles* out on paper. He would choose a thought and then place his finger on the type of *Thought Bubble* that best represented the thought he was having. I timed Philip, and he would tell me when his thoughts shifted from one *Thought Bubble* to another. We drew out a diagram on paper and wrote down the time intervals. At first, these were very short, showing Philip that his focus was transient and that he was only able to stick with a thought for a short period of time. After a few trials, it came to be somewhat of a sport, to be able to keep focusing for a longer period of time. The diagram and my timings became something tangible that showed Philip how he could improve his ability to focus – that he is, so to speak – able to learn how. In other instances, we practised how he should shift focus from one type of thought to another when asked. He would explicitly look and point at the *Thought Bubble* he would choose for himself when I said: 'Shift thoughts'.

Paralleling my sessions with Philip, his teachers provided me with descriptions of daily life situations where Philip wasn't successful. One day, a teacher explained that a recurring problem is Philip's constant need to eat, and how he would often talk about food or his stomach. I had simultaneously noticed myself, that in our weekly meetings (just before the lunch break), Philip kept quite a lot of attention on the hour, saying: 'I have to get to class in time for lunch.' His urge for food and his lack of ability to hold off a need was something tangible I would use to open a new line of dialogue with Philip.

I brought The Resilience Programme's *Thought Bubbles* for the occasion, and Philip was tuned into the idea right away. Together we filled out the green and black *Thought Bubbles* – in the green ones, we wrote useful and good thoughts about food and in the black ones, we wrote out the damaging or less useful thoughts about food. Philip had, especially in the beginning, a great amount of input for the green *Thought Bubbles* because, as he put it: 'I just become so happy when thinking about food. Food is the best thing I know.' Over time, Philip discovered that thoughts about food might actually belong in both the green and the black *Thought Bubbles*. The fact that food so extensively preoccupied his thoughts was not necessarily good. In working through the exercise of focus shifting, Philip became conscious of the fact that when his focus was directed towards one element, his awareness actually narrowed in relation to other aspects. He became conscious that he might actually be missing out on something else, when he focused too intently or too often on food.

In our subsequent sessions, Philip practised extending his focus. For instance, I presented Philip with an exercise, telling him that it would last five minutes and that he should set the timer on his mobile phone. My instructions were that his attention should be focused on the exercise until time lapsed. In addition, we agreed that he would refrain from speaking about food or hunger throughout the exercise. We trained with this exercise for a total of five to six weeks and Philip greatly improved his ability to focus for longer periods of time on one specific exercise. At the same time, Philip significantly improved his ability to shut off his thoughts about food. In one of our last sessions, he never even mentioned food, despite my omitting the reminder that he should not think about food during the focus exercise. Our work even extended into the lunch break. I told Philip that we were done for that day and that he had not mentioned food, hunger or eating even once, and that, by the way, the lunch break had already started. Philip had become significantly better at thinking about things other than food. At the same time, the teachers experienced that his ability to control emotional outbursts had also improved and that he was better at focusing on the learning and shifting his focus from ideas he was known to fixate on in the past. He was no longer easily angered and was also no longer aggressive, as he once was. His increased ability to generally control his own capacity for focus, and more specifically in relation to thoughts revolving around food, had influenced Philip's ability to control his thoughts and feelings in the classroom – to his own benefit and to the benefit of his classmates and teachers as well.

It is still useful for Philip to receive extra support in structuring his everyday life at school. However, from an adult's perspective he had greatly improved from where he started. Prior to our sessions, there had been weekly episodes in which Philip would, in one way or another, act out in class, interrupting lessons regularly with outbursts. Teachers essentially had a negative narrative about Philip.

Following our sessions and work with resilience, Philip himself had expressed that he had become much better at handling everyday school life and that he was becoming less irritated.

In my post-reflection on my time with Philip, I was reminded about something I had already learnt: that development is more fun and easier when it makes sense to the person who's in need of growth. Philip's development in holding his focus and controlling his thoughts, and emotions, really intensified when the work came to relate to something that mattered to him – namely, food. The Resilience Programme's approach and exercises have worked as useful and concrete tools, in combination with other tools, just as it had worked well in complementing our school's systemic and narrative frameworks.

The story of Laura

The first time I met Laura, she was in 4th grade and often involved in verbal and physical conflicts with girls her age. Many pointed to Laura as the root cause in conflicts. Statements such as 'Laura always kicks', 'Laura bites', 'Laura always becomes angry' were common when speaking about her – for pupils, parents and teachers. Laura's relationships were conflict-ridden, especially with one of her friends, a girl her age. In this specific case, her friend's parents were also quarrelling behind closed doors, and prevented Laura from visiting their home – the friend's parents had the opinion that Laura was a bad acquaintance for their child.

When I met Laura for the first time, she appeared to be a girl who was almost constantly on high alert, expecting new accusations, feeling insecure with herself and towards others and dealing with feelings of being left out. In the beginning, my effort was put into listening to Laura's story, not so as to judge what was true or false, but to try to understand Laura's perspective and how she was coping in the world she was experiencing. At the same time, my aim was to build Laura's confidence in me. Through this, it would be possible for me to help her see various new sides of life and find new ways of handling life. In our initial phase together, we practised breathing exercises every time we met. Laura chose one that she found most helpful and we agreed that she would practise every morning and evening – just before getting out of bed and just before she fell sleep. In this same period, I encouraged Laura to be curious about what happens just prior to her anger rising, and just prior to that anger bursting out of her system. Laura discovered that her breathing quickened and that her body tensed before anger set in. After practising with her breathing for a month, Laura could start applying the breathing techniques in difficult situations at school. When her breathing quickened and she could feel her body tense, this was Laura's signal that anger was on its way. The breathing exercises became automatic for her, and she was able to utilise them to control her anger, which would otherwise have taken control.

The number of schoolyard conflicts involving Laura decreased dramatically in this period. There were, however, a few relapses where Laura resorted to her old behaviour patterns, where anger or frustration took control, and fingers were pointed to Laura yet again. Both the school and Laura's parents have been very keen on quashing her relapses altogether.

Laura and I investigated new possibilities through the Mind Game from The Resilience Programme. The Mind Game is a simple and manageable model that helps to create *Fields of Practice* to reach a goal.[2] Laura expressed that she was keen on trying the Mind Game, if I could manage to convince her parents that she could be rewarded (through some type of agreement) when she eventually reached her goal.

She had long wished for a special, and expensive, computer drawing programme. We filled out the Mind Game together: goal, timeframe, difficult times throughout a day, rewards when successful, etc. She mentioned, of her own volition, that her mother should be her supervisor and support along the way. Laura's goal was to stop calls from the school to her house concerning bad behaviour throughout a period of a little less than two months – this includes any conflict; not just those Laura may acknowledge, but also conflicts she may not be aware of but which nevertheless cause others to experience distress. This was quite a challenge for a 4th-grade girl, even with me in the background to support and conduct exercises with her, helping her see situations from other people's perspectives. Laura brought the Mind Game papers back home to her parents, enthusiastically presented them with her action plan and, not least, her wish for the drawing programme as the reward. Her parents accepted the agreement and we began. I asked Laura what she would do if she were to fail. To that, she answered, 'It will be a success. I never thought I would get that computer program. It is my greatest wish. And then it is also super nice that I will not have to feel guilty every time there's a conflict.' The computer program was the most important thing for her, and the added bonus was to stay out of conflicts. From an adult's perspective, these priorities would be reversed, but what's important is that the reward mattered to Laura.

Laura has her computer program today. After half a year of us having sessions once per week, we started having monthly follow-up meetings, and today my only role is to greet her when we see each other in the school hallways. Today, Laura performs well in her classes, both academically and socially. She is not an angel, fortunately, but fingers no longer point in her direction in times of conflict. Laura has learnt to avoid conflicts and has become better at socialising with children of her age in a positive way.

The additional bonus is how important the Mind Game had been for Laura's parents. They were very busy keeping on track with Laura's school-days and felt a lot of pressure stemming from Laura's constantly being at the centre of conflicts. Throughout the short two months in which we used the Mind Game, Laura's mother sensed her level of worry dramatically decrease. Through the Mind Game she was able to have five minutes of focused conversation with Laura, daily, and ask about her actual experiences and ways of coping throughout each day. Laura's mother gained new insight into the fact that her daughter was bravely fighting through her objectives, and was doing a great job. Her mother let go of her worries and since then, Laura gets to experience a mother who trusts in her ability to handle the challenges of the day.

We are still in the process

In this chapter, I have described how we can, at an ordinary local public school, implement the resilience approaches at all organisational levels, in a way that supplements and supports other pedagogical and didactical approaches. We are not a resilience school, but the resilience way is becoming one of the tools we have in our toolbox, that is complementary to the other tools we use. It is a tool we are confident in applying and use when relevant. It's also a tool we will continuously reflect upon.

In the collaboration between children, adolescents, parents, teachers and pedagogues, the resilience approach makes sense in an ordinary public school like ours. There can hardly be any other organisation where so much is at stake, and where so many perspectives are at play, as can be found in a public school. This can be challenging, and requires all stakeholders to be able to mentalise. When I speak about resilience in the various parts of our school, when I practise with a class or a single pupil, or when I speak about the resilience perspective in meetings with parents, my aim is to offer it as a concrete tool that can empower us to cope with everyday life's challenges. Like the methods we also make use of in our school context, the systemic approaches for instance, The Resilience Programme can be used to build a framework for the learning community we wish to establish in our classes.

Through teaching resilience in our classes and by organising and speaking at workshops about resilience with our parent groups, we pass on, relatively easily, simple workable strategies that help people handle, in a concrete way, teenage life or parental hardships, for instance. We empower people to stand up to challenges while learning in general.

Notes

1   The term 'hyper-sensitive', distinct from the medically used 'hypersensitivity' diagnosis, has come to be a popular term people use to describe sensitivity that is especially nervous, profound and complex, exhibited in challenging situations in daily life, with other people or when facing requirements and solving tasks. The term refers to someone who easily feels pressured and stressed, reacting both emotionally and physically. It is a topic that is well explored on the Internet and in self-help books.
2   See also the section about *Fields of Practice* in Chapter 1.

References

Bro, K, Løw, O & Svanholt, J (eds.) (2009) Psykologiske perspektiver på intervention – i pædagogiske kontekster. Dansk Psykologisk Forlag.
Nordahl, T (2012) Eleven som aktør. Fokus på elevens læring og handlinger i skolen. Hans Reitzels Forlag.

Chapter 5

Being like the others

Resilience for children and adolescents in club activities[1]

Nina Lykke Nielsen, Tine Kaarup, Jeanette Corneliussen, Tina Brammer Kristensen, Mette Bentzon, Helle Fogtman Welejus, and Lotte Dalager

RESILIENCE IN A SOCIALLY DISADVANTAGED AREA I

Nina Lykke Nielsen

After participating in several courses for pedagogues and other professionals about resilience, I thought that this knowledge would be able to help some of the children and adolescents who visited the pedagogically managed playground, in which I work. It could potentially help them become more conscious about their thoughts and feelings and lead them through conflicts in a more positive way – perhaps also help them concentrate better in school. In the spring of 2014, I carried out a resilience course for the first time with eight 7th-grade boys and girls. The course spanned eight sessions: once per week, at a specific time. If the children showed up and participated actively for a given number of sessions, they could obtain a certificate. As further motivation for them to participate, I had planned a trip to Copenhagen at the end of the course.

The participants and their goals

This group of eight youths, who were offered this course, frequently came to the playground. They knew each other because they were from the same class, from the school nearby. They were a tight group and trusted me. Furthermore, they wanted to learn, and were happy to discuss, generally curious. Several of them had special challenges. One of the boys from the group had experienced violence through most of his childhood, including neglect and abuse. He sometimes had a hard time controlling his temper and was often involved in fights. One girl lived with her ailing single mother and a younger brother. In the periods when her mother was ill, the girl was responsible for the household. This caused her difficulties in concentrating at school. She thought about her mother all the time and worried about her. She also had other challenges. In general, the children in this group struggled with concentration at school, were impulsive and often involved in conflicts.

Challenges

Each participant was given a folder in which they could keep the different exercises and stories from one session to the next. They were supposed to bring this folder to every session. Already in our second session, however, half of the group had forgotten their folder. This prompted me to take the decision that I would take care of the folders myself until the course was over, at which point they could take them. It became clear to me, pretty quickly, that I had too many participants. The level of conflict in their class was high, with the result that we spent too much time catching up on the conflicts stemming from school. Initially I felt frustrated because I could not follow the programme I had spent a lot of time preparing. My feelings weren't so constructive, though, and the pupils became frustrated as well. I came to understand that they viewed me as their teacher's representative because they thought she had asked me to offer the course to them, due to the many problems they were experiencing in class. This obviously caused insecurity in the group. They doubted my intentions and whether there was a hidden agenda. I opened a dialogue about this and decided to explain why I had specifically chosen them as participants. That seemed to calm them down a bit.

Adjusting the course

Early along in the course, it became necessary to put my own plans aside and set a more adult-driven framework than I had originally intended. In this way, it became possible to include materials and exercises that suited the needs I thought the group required. Aside from this, I decided to divide the group into two, which turned out to be a positive move. In one group, they became very serious and earnest in their way of approaching the exercises, whereas the other group had a hard time concentrating, either because of internal conflicts or due to too much clowning around. I still succeeded in catching their attention once in a while. Among other things, they became interested in how we experience situations in various ways. For example, in an activity about conflicts, I had asked them to move around the room, pretending to be the various people involved within the conflict we were discussing, in order to perceive the conflict from various perspectives. This worked well. We also spoke about the previous experiences people carry around with them, and how these may influence what they experience in a given moment. One of the boys later told me, proudly, how he had stood up in class when the topic of conflicts came about, and that he had drawn out one of our figures from our sessions onto the class's blackboard while explaining to the rest of the class and their teacher how the figure and his new knowledge could be used.

I ended each session with a breathing exercise. This was hard for several of them in the beginning, especially when they had experienced conflicts at school. However, they quickly began to feel safe in the exercise and would ask me, 'When are we going to relax?' As a part of the exercise, I would also take their pulse.

First, they were asked to jump for two minutes to see how high they could raise their heart rate. After the relaxation exercise, we measured their pulse again to see how low it could fall. Several of them were excited about this.

Ending

There were four out of the eight who participated steadily and received the certificate. I still decided to take all eight on the trip to Copenhagen as they all had legitimate reasons as to why they were not able to participate fully throughout the whole course. They were also told that they would be welcome to participate in any future courses, should they so wish.

This was the first course based on The Resilience Programme that was carried out in this particular residential area. The course became a learning experience for me, and I gained both positive and negative insights. It became necessary to adjust The Resilience Programme, and after this adjustment it is my impression that everybody got something positive out of it. The experiences of this course made us plan yet another one; this time, with two teachers and fewer participants.

RESILIENCE IN A SOCIALLY DISADVANTAGED RESIDENTIAL AREA II

Tine Kaarup and Nina Lykke Nielsen

The experiences from the first course as described above caused us – an employee from a local playground and an outreach worker from the local area – to plan another course. We benefited a lot from the experiences we had in the first course, and we included important elements, such as preparatory visits with our participants' parents. We were also more prepared in terms of formulating tangible objectives that considered individual needs, and then worked very concretely with these objectives throughout the course, eventually using them for evaluation purposes.

The course lasted seven weeks, with sessions once per week. We had a classroom available in an after-school club where we could pin our posters and images up on the wall. We had chosen four girls from grade 6 for this time around. The aim was to equip the girls with tools to draw from, to help them cope with the challenges they meet in the very socially disadvantaged area in which they live. Before starting, we visited their homes and told their parents more about the course. We told them that it was important for us that they support their daughters and remind them to come to each of the sessions. We also explained why the course should be of such high priority. We were well received, and the parents found it interesting.

At the beginning of the course we had an individual conversation with each of the participants so as to define each girl's personal goals. To make the goals more concrete, we had five dialogue-cards divided into categories of life: school, home, leisure time, friends, me. Every card had a colour that corresponded to one of five rows on a bead frame. This system was used to prompt the girls to illustrate, using a scale from 1 to 10, how they felt in the different areas of their lives. Using this system, it became easier for the girls to find concrete objectives within each category of their lives, and value what was most important to focus on from moment to moment. We wrote down where they were on the scale in order to be able to note any shifts at the final evaluation.

The teaching focused on an overall subject from session to session. The framework included considerations for the start, location, method and the end of a session, which were all similar each time. We tried to create a nice atmosphere in the room, serving fruit, biscuits and juice, as the participants would come to the sessions directly from school. A couple of hours before the teaching started, we sent out text messages to the girls, reminding them of their appointment. Before starting we visualised where we could place ourselves on a 'Brain-Alarm-System-Barometer', an exercise we also participated in together with the girls. The aim was to give everybody an understanding of the differences in our meeting points at the start of the session and how each of us might have entered the room with different moods, depending on the experiences we had encountered throughout our individual days. Another fixed point in the programme was ending the session with breathing exercises where the girls completely relaxed, something they became better at doing as the course progressed. As in the first session, they received a folder in which they could save information concerning the various exercises, papers, stories etc. Experience from the previous course had shown that the children often lost or forgot their folders. For this reason, we kept the folders with us, until the end of the course.

We went through the theory about the *Thinking Brain* and the brain's *Alarm Centre* and made an exercise where they wrote down, on an image of a brain, what could help them in situations where they felt themselves in alarm mode. They were asked to do exercises at home where they should pay attention to their personal brain's state of alarm and to the potential state of alarm in others: 'What happened?', 'What did you do?' It turned out that the girls took these home exercises very seriously. They eagerly told us about all the situations throughout their week where the brain's *Alarm Centre* had been activated, the conflicts they had observed and the conflicts they had been a part of themselves.

In order to visualise how attention can be sharpened, each participant received a torch. In the first exercise, they were just to sit still, watch and reflect. When a thought came to their mind, they were to turn the torch towards their head, and when their attention was diverted from something that occurred around them, they should point the torch outward. Following this, they were given sheets with *Thought Bubbles*: a green one for a nice thought, a black one for an annoying thought and a white one for a neutral thought. When they discovered and evaluated the characteristics of their own thoughts, they were to point a finger to the *Thought Bubble* with the colour that best represented their thought. Eventually, they were to see whether they could stick to a specific thought or not. It was a difficult task, but the girls liked it nevertheless. They could not resist involving one other in their thoughts all the time. Following this, they were assigned to monitor, in their regular classes, when their attention shifted, whether they could get it back on track or not, when it was difficult and when it was easier. Subsequently, they recounted their experiences with this exercise in our sessions. One girl in particular had taken it very seriously and could tell in which lessons she found it easy and in which lessons it was difficult. She expressed how she could not keep her attention when she was sitting beside a specific girl and, consequently, she had asked the teacher to be allowed to sit somewhere else.

We read about the story of the Reward-Factory as well and made an exercise afterwards where we spoke about what was good for the brain, body and thoughts, and what was bad. We had a huge poster with a picture of a man who had a vertical line drawn through him, dividing him in half. On one side, he was depicted as fresh and healthy, and on the other side, in the opposite way. The girls were asked to write down, on Post-It notes, what could influence the brain, body and thoughts, and then they were asked to place their Post-Its on the poster. They grasped all the aspects of the activity and enjoyed the exercise. We were surprised to see how much they knew.

Two of the girls were friends and could practise different goals with one other. Annie had the goal that she should be better at saying 'no' to friends. Beatrice had set herself the goal of becoming better at accepting 'no' as an answer. She found it difficult to hear her mother say 'no', and then realised that she also found it hard to hear 'no' from her friends. Having this as a starting point, the girls could train towards their goals, especially at school. For instance, one day when Beatrice wanted Annie to follow her to the cafeteria and Annie didn't feel like going, she said 'no'. Beatrice didn't accept her 'no' and kept trying to persuade her anyway. Annie thought about her goal and stuck to her 'no'. Then Beatrice realised that even though she had always managed to persuade Annie in the past, she was perhaps putting too much pressure on her and should accept Annie's 'no'. The girls came to the next session and were proud of how they had both worked towards their goals in that situation. Another of the girls set as her goal that she would concentrate better in school. She expressed how she was easily distracted by sounds or if anything happened outside the window. She was also often lost in her own thoughts and pondered a lot about things. The girl adopted the attention-and-torch exercise and explained how she could use the method to keep her focus on tasks at school. At the conclusion of the course, she expressed that she clearly had become better at concentrating but also that she was nervous that she would forget how to apply the new methods after some time and fall back into her old behaviours. This made us come up with the idea of arranging a shorter version of the course, as a follow-up. The participants received a certificate, evidencing their learning in a ceremony where the Alderman for Children and Youth handed them their certificates. And they also received a rose and a t-shirt. Their parents were invited and took part in celebrating the occasion. We then ended the course with a trip to a cottage. This was, among other reasons, meant to spark interest and motivate participation in the course. It was also an opportunity for us to share in the completion of the resilience course in an environment where we could enjoy ourselves, relax and talk about our experiences.

DREAMS FOR THE FUTURE

Jeanette Corneliussen

- What are your dreams for the future?
- What is needed to make them come true?
- What do you think would be useful to learn beforehand?
- Do you sometimes do something that you regret afterwards?
- In a group, it is important to learn to control our thoughts, emotions and temper. Does this make sense to you?

The questions above were some of the appetisers we were hoping could help motivate 10–14-year-old boys from this socially disadvantaged area to participate in a series of group sessions on resilience. At the outset, all of the club children's parents were invited to a meeting where they were informed about the aims and the content of the proposed group sessions, so as to get them to agree with and support the boys' participation.

In all, each group of boys and pedagogues from the club met for six sessions each. In this way, a kind of simultaneous training of the pedagogues, who usually spend time together with the boys, took place. They could then follow up with what they were learning in their daily lives and even transmit some of that to non-participating children and colleagues. The children's participation was voluntary, as part of an after-school youth club, and the sessions took place in their free time. This required some informational and motivational preparation and posed some challenges in maintaining attendance and adherence to some of the key features. The boys were of different ages, and of different ethnic and linguistic backgrounds. We attempted to exploit this pedagogically and worked with the boys' group dynamics so that these could be viewed in a positive light. Some of the more popular boys were invited first and, later on, as soon as we succeeded in spreading some positive stories about the group's work, more followed. Backed by management, we pinned laminated images of the *Thinking Brain* and the brain's *Alarm Centre* on the clubhouse walls. Through this, the participants developed a shared language that was used in daily pedagogical work.

Stories from group sessions

We sat around a table, enjoying cups of tea. I started by talking to the boys about our attention and used a torch as a visual tool to introduce *Attention – the Brain's Spotlight*. I showed them laminated *Thought Bubbles* as well. We spoke about which elements were able to hold or break our focus in daily life. The boys asked a lot of questions, commented and shared stories. I had noticed that confidence and interest were building up as we went along. We experimented with enhancing awareness, focusing, listening and learning how to be present and appreciative when others are speaking. This was difficult for some of the boys, though. Sometimes, things from outside our room would draw their attention away. In those moments, some of them had to stand up and walk around a bit, and others became irritated while waiting to speak. However, these became opportunities for us to connect our dialogue to what took place in the here and now:

- Do you feel what happens in your body?
- At this exact moment, what are you thinking about?
- Why can it be difficult to concentrate – where are your thoughts going?

We did an exercise with one of the boys who wished to time himself to see how long he could resist checking his messages. 'I'm addicted', he said. He found it difficult and we spoke about possible actions he could take, and others offered their ideas too. In the end, we spoke about why it is vital to be able to keep focusing, and how it is the first step towards fulfilling someone's dream of, for instance, educating themselves to become a doctor or a mechanic. We also spoke about the possibility of strengthening attention through training, by taking time to see how long someone succeeds in not checking their phone – and then repeating the exercise again and again.

In the second session, I told them about our *Thinking Brain* and the brain's *Alarm Centre*. How do we react – with fight or flight? What do we need when the brain's *Alarm Centre* is activated? I again used visual material in the form of laminated images. From there, the dialogue shifted to where we began talking about kindness – especially unexpected kindness. We explored what this could mean, as kindness is shared between people, and that kindness can help reassure people who find themselves in a state of alarm. Several of the boys related examples from their own lives. We talked about the special 'love-hormone', oxytocin, which contributes to us feeling connected to one another with feelings of belonging. We agreed that between that session and the next, the boys should take notice of explicit kindness that arises in unexpected situations.

In the next session, the pedagogues began with the follow-up: 'How did it go with the (unexpected) kindness – the spreading of oxytocin?' Everybody smiled, laughed and came with examples. One of the stories they shared was when Benny had given one of the pedagogues a warm welcome. He had not seen her for a few days, was glad to see her, and expressed this openly. She became happy, and Benny himself felt warmth and happiness throughout his body. Since then, the club has kept a focus on kindness in general and how they may spread this positive energy around the club. The adults in the club had expressed that they sensed a change in the club's atmosphere and acknowledged that the boys had played a significant role in this.

A short movie from The Resilience Programme about bullying and the brain's *Alarm Centre* was shown to illustrate and repeat several of the elements we had discussed: attention, the brain's alarm, safe and unsafe communities, language, etc. Some said afterwards that they recognised the emotions depicted by the movie's children. The movie prompted a valuable step towards a good dialogue about how the boys, each in his own way, had experienced either being a bully, being bullied or being in conflict in one way or another. To bully and to be bullied may be two sides of the same coin – prompted by a strong desire to be part of a community. For a period of time, Adrian told us that he had been part of a group of friends who were stealing. In order to be part of this group he had started to steal and to mock those who hadn't the courage to dare, even though he was aware that such behaviour was wrong of him. In the end, he had been helped to break from the group by one of his older cousins, who had been to juvenile prison. It was my general impression that the boys struggled to feel and express what they sensed. The term 'annoyed' was often a word they used, also when referring to feelings I could discern as anger, worry or sadness. It was also my clear impression that some emotions were harder for them to express than others within the existing culture of the club; for instance, sadness. Dialogues relating to something else, for example movies or laminated images of the brain, were very useful in breaking these taboos. When referencing knowledge and research for these taboo emotions, it helped generalise things for the boys and thereby made them easier for the boys to talk about.

The stories and narratives had the same effect. The boys were encouraged to draw or write out their own versions of the *House of Thoughts* on a piece of paper and, starting from there, put some questions into words, such as, 'How do I feel when I am in the *Thinking Brain*?', 'What interests me?', 'How do I feel when I am in the brain's *Alarm Centre*?', 'What can I do myself?', 'How may adults or others help me?' This was utilised pedagogically in individual conversations that were arranged between the boys and their contact-pedagogues, and as a means to speak about strategies for help and self-help.

The stories helped the boys visualise their emotions. For example, *The story of a mind train* resonated well with a couple of the boys. Martin was a highly skilled football player, just like his older brothers, who unfortunately had to stop what could have been promising football careers because they couldn't control their tempers. Spontaneously, Martin shared an episode he experienced at a football match, where he had succeeded in tempering his emotions, 'before they took over'. One of the opponents ran beside him and started to bother him by shouting provocations. Martin felt how he became 'annoyed' and how his emotions, 'were on the rise and I thought to myself, "I need calm down"'. He described how he tried to breathe deeply and managed to think, 'If I hit this guy, he will hit me back. My friends will back me and his will back him, and then we'll all be in trouble.' I asked him what he did then, and to my pleasant surprise he answered, 'Not a damn thing! We just kept playing.' Martin could recall and talk about his thoughts and feelings after the match (which his team won, by the way) and about his inner victory. Football meant a lot to him and he had experienced the regret of impulsive reactions many times before, where the trainer and co-players had become angry with him because he had been given red cards and had been kicked out of the matches. In the episode he described, he was very happy and proud of himself. When we were speaking about resilience in the group, we included this and other examples from the boys' everyday lives, and these could help demonstrate how, through training their attention, people can indeed improve on governing thoughts and emotions. It became cool for the boys to be able to control themselves and it was nice to see them patting each other on the back whenever they succeeded.

Fields of Practice

We also worked with the ability to set realistic objectives. It is important to be persistent in practising towards these goals, eventually with adult support; to be continuously practising, even when we meet challenges or obstacles and go astray. It is vital to be able to focus, return, continue to practise and hopefully reach our goal. The most important prerequisite to doing this is the motivation for our future dreams. For this reason, it is critical to speak about a young person's goal as something that makes sense to the individual. Success comes easiest when a young person is supported in setting simple, concrete, manageable and time-limited objectives. It may be a good idea to work with intermediate objectives as well, in order to widen their chances for success. When we reach our intermediate objectives, we get the energy and courage to work towards an even greater target. It is also important to state that making mistakes is both okay and unavoidable – to go astray.

As a group, we drew roads on a canvas on the floor – one road towards a goal and one leading away from it.[2] We implemented an activity using the body; while standing and also walking on the canvas, the boys were asked to speak about the roads they were on. On the goal-oriented road, they sensed and expressed feelings associated with being on the road towards their goal, and the same was done on the road leading away. One of the boys realised that he was not yet ready to work with the objective he had chosen for himself, which was to stop smoking hash. He spoke about how he had fallen back into smoking, despite his aim to stop, and that he experienced both happiness and cravings when he stood on the road going away from his goal. In this way, it became clear to both of us that he was not sufficiently motivated towards his goal – yet.

Ending

The staff and management of the club could observe how the atmosphere of the club had changed during our sessions. A shared language was established – with words for what had been difficult to describe beforehand. There was a lot less need for intervention and significantly fewer reports of incidences were made.

Funding was found to offer all pedagogues an opportunity to train in mentalising, and today they continue to work enthusiastically with and seek to find new and optimal formulations for teaching resilience. From our experiences in the project described above, the work with resilience has been integrated in the everyday life of the after-school and youth-club framework in the area. In the next section, we will go deeper into how this is being achieved by a coordinator and two deputy chiefs in the residential area.

RESILIENCE: 'ONLY FOR PAKIS?'

Tina Brammer Kristensen, Mette Bentzon, and
Helle Fogtman Welejus

In our clubs and club-playgrounds, which are located in a socially disadvantaged residential area with residents from 70 different nationalities, we have worked with thoughtfulness, mentalisation and resilience in groups of children and teenagers between the ages of 10 and 18, since early 2011. The playground is freely open to all children and youth in the local area, whereas the club requires registration. All in all, we have around 150 registered members between the ages of 10 and 17.

The shared outdoor spaces are designed with considerations for ideas of empowerment, focusing on community in order to make it a gathering place in the area for all children – small and large, youths and adults. The idea of empowerment is expressed through activities for and together with the area's residents. We support associations that arrange activities for children and lend the premises out at no cost, requiring only a helping hand, as the form of repayment, in the free annual summer activities put on for the area's youth. We work with the area's social capital, for instance by engaging adults in activities and giving them responsibilities. Through a strong partnership between our closest collaborator and the local football association, we join forces and involve adults who are looking to make a contribution towards the betterment of the area and its people. New energy is infused when grown-ups, who might otherwise have little to do, come out of their homes, participate and engage with other adults in coordinating activities for the youth. Precisely in an area like ours, where we lack grown-ups (around half the residents of the area are under the age of 21), this makes a difference, both to our children and teenagers, as well as to their parents. With this in mind, we designed our playground as a community space for all youth and adults, where everybody can play. Even after the pedagogical staff leave, both the club and the playground are left open for all to use. Also, the clubs and the playground frequently host various cultural activities and parties with positive aims, such as those focusing on citizenship.

The club-playground is a club and playground-offering that is available to all children and youth who live and attend school in the municipality. The after-school and youth club have a total of around 120 registered members, with the addition of 5th and 6th grade pupils who come from the local school every week, as a part of their all-day school teaching curriculum. The club-playground is situated near the neighbourhood's school, in an area surrounded by a lot of natural beauty. The physical space of the club is suited for physical activities, as well as activities that may require a quiet environment, indoor and outdoor. Our outdoor facilities include bikes our children can borrow, a BMX-track, a game field, moon cars, an electronic playground, a fireplace and shelters for overnight stays. We offer activities such as bike rides, swimming, taking care of animals and horseback riding through trails for those who come with their own horses, etc.

Targeting PTSD

The starting point, which resulted in resilience being a permanent and integrated part of our pedagogical work, was a methodological development project that came under the Social Ministry's initiative: 'Reinforced social and prevention efforts for challenged residential areas' (described in the first part of this chapter). The clubs were selected as one of the project's institutions. The target group was to be boys from families impacted by trauma, between the ages of 10 and 14 years. The initiative was divided into three areas: dissemination of knowledge about PTSD to the boys, their parents and other adults in their surroundings, physical activity as well as resilience (mentalising). The goal was to test methods that might help the boys gain more peace and thereby enhance their quality of life and future opportunities, while improving their chances to complete whatever they set out to do.

Throughout the project, which was undertaken in the first half of 2011, all staff received training in resilience. Following this, there was side-by-side-learning in praxis with our youngsters, and at the end of 2011, staff continued to work with the project independently. The project took up a lot of space in our everyday life and the stories about challenges and successes were enthusiastically shared between staff and management in meetings and on professional development days. The stories created curiosity and an appetite to work together towards the future development and implementation of resilience work in the organisation. The dream was to have all children and adolescents under the age of 18 surrounded by resilient adults who also knew the resilience approach. This kick-started a shared inter-disciplinary development initiative in 2013 that involved club and club-playground staff, pedagogues from the school, and staff from the municipality's pedagogical development department. The interdisciplinary workshop that ensued consisted of a mixture of academic theory and praxis presentations from both internal and external speakers. Between the presentations there were dialogues and group meetings involving staff across the participating institutions. In these meetings, the focus was practical and oriented towards the daily lives of children and adolescents.

In 2010, the staff and management had participated in in-service training about coaching communication. It became clear to us in our interdisciplinary workshops that the coaching communication training we had previously received played a significant role in our work with resilience. Coaching communication creates a foundation for youngsters to reflect and prepares them for decision making later in life. In this way, there was a great synergy between coaching and resilience.

In one of the first group sessions, one of the participants, a 13-year-old boy, had a good deal of challenges. His challenges stemmed from his highly explosive temper, especially on the football field. Often, he ended up fighting on the field and had also been suspended, which he was unhappy about. In working with resilience, he practised different strategies that could help him avoid fighting when he became angry.

He slowly succeeded in gaining control and minimised his physical conflicts on the football field, as well as in school. Some time after his work with resilience ended, the club participated in a big football meeting and he joined as one of the players. The team he was on was standing at the sidelines. They were watching the ongoing match of two other teams, waiting for their turn. One of the players went berserk, kicked the barrier boards and yelled nasty words to the referee and the other players. Our 13-year-old boy saw this scene and said with a big grin, 'Hey, perhaps we should offer him a course in resilience in the clubs!' 'Are you mad?', another boy replied, 'That's only for Pakis!' The players laughed at what was being said between the lines, and the day continued. The 13-year-old boy's statement showed that he could recognise his old behaviour in the other boy. Also through what he said, he acknowledged that working with resilience makes a difference, in his view. Still, the teammate's reply exemplifies what we are up against in one of our greatest challenges in our work with resilience. We experienced that quite a few youngsters refused to participate in the resilience sessions because some among them (and among some of their parents as well) had formulated an understanding that our sessions were only for young people with ADHD or other physical disabilities. None of our youngsters wished to be labelled as psychologically ill or handicapped by their peers. To turn that around and demystify the resilience concept required a lot of informational work in terms of dialogue with parents, at parent meetings and general information to children and adolescents. We experienced progress and held out a little carrot, in the form of a shared tour that we would put on at the end of the sessions. Aside from the reward part of the tour, our pedagogical aim with the tours was to practise what had been learnt throughout the course.

Practising spontaneous resilience

In the youth club we had a group of friends made up of six to eight boys between the ages of 14 and 16. They were often harsh and provoking towards one another and one of them frequently lost his self-control. We made several attempts to motivate the group into participating in the work but had very little success. Through individual conversations with some of them we managed to introduce them to the *Remote Control* and used this to support dialogue about who or what is able to decide/control when we become annoyed, sad, angry, happy, etc., and not least, who or what is in control of an individual's actions. For instance, 'Do I choose to hit, yell, kick or smash somebody or something, or do I choose to laugh, turn my back, take a deep breath or ignore the provocation?'

We had drawn out two remote controls on paper, which we laminated. One of the remote controls had a big button that read, 'THE OTHERS', plus eight small buttons representing emotions. This remote control illustrated the emotions that other people's behaviour may call out in the individual. The other remote control had a big button that read, 'ME', plus eight small buttons representing various possible actions.

In working with this, the group's understanding of violent behaviour shifted from, 'The others made me do it', to understanding and mastering, 'I am the one who's in control!' The result was that in our interactions in situations where troubles were building up, we could just ask, 'Who has the remote control?'

The teaching in resilience not only took place in the club but was combined with physical activity. For instance, walks, where the conversations revolved around the tools that had been introduced and how to listen to ourselves. We spoke about what happens within the body, brain and thoughts while moving. It became obvious that the dimension of moving was beneficial for some of the youngsters. In addition to this, they had been taught about factors that influence the body, thoughts and brain; for example, emotions (anger, happiness, falling in love), sickness, hunger, exercise etc. Again, the important part of the dialogue was to be concrete and visual and to do something practical where the body is involved. What happens to the body and breath when running at the beach? When does the body go back to being relaxed? What happens to the body, thoughts and brain after some rest in a bean-back chair at the beach? Breathing exercises are important to relaxing the brain's *Alarm Centre.* They can take shape in a variety of forms. We emphasised that the participants understood the physiological explanation of why deep and calm breathing matters – that the lungs support the heart to beat more slowly when we breathe deeply, and in turn, that signals to the brain's *Alarm Centre* that there is no danger. In this way, the level of alarm in the body and the brain is automatically tuned down.

Structured teaching sessions

We now work with all aspects of resilience in structured teaching sessions. The sessions are organised along a six-week frame that may be adjusted according to what is required, based on the needs of the participants at any given session. This means that we, the teachers, may have planned sessions but often change strategy because one or several of the participants in the group have something they need time to share. We always work with content that relates to them in the here and now – seen from a resilience perspective. When we make the resilience teaching relevant to our participants' immediate lives in this way, they become motivated and are better able to transfer the teaching into their daily lives. The didactics that underlie the organisation of the sessions are central prerequisites for our success.

We create a concrete framework description around resources, organisation, effort and effects. We work with flexibility in terms of teaching hours contra the number of participants and make sure that collaboration is established between the school and parents.

Session headlines look like this:

1   What are your dreams for the future?

   What is needed to make them come true?
   What is resilience?

2   Presentation of the *Thinking Brain* and the brain's *Alarm Centre*

   Fight, flight and freeze
   Strategies to create peace in a state of alarm

3   Self-control

   Exercising mental strength
   Why is it important to be able to control your impulses and emotions? The Marshmallow test

4   Choosing a *Field of Practice*

   Is there something you would like to become better at?
   Are there situations you may land in, which you would prefer to avoid?

5   Movie about bullying

   Safe and unsafe communities
   Roles – what can we do? Do we have a co-responsibility?
   Dialogue about the oxytocin hormone

6   Evaluation – what made sense to you the most? What do you especially remember? What do you need in order to remember your *Field of Practice*? Are the adults able to help you? Could something have been different?

We offer obligatory as well as voluntary courses with groups and individuals. Participants in the individual courses are often young people with perhaps extensive attention-disturbance or young people who, for one reason or another, may feel socially insecure. They could also be teenagers between the ages of 14 and 15 who are in a period of their lives where they are trying to find their footing and are therefore vulnerable to others' assessment. The group sessions have a fixed group from the beginning. Participants can drop out, but no new participant can join. This is upheld as a way to ensure a feeling of safety in the group. We also have an agreement from day one that what is being discussed within the group, stays in the group. With 10-year-olds, we use the term 'secret club'. This is again a way to lay down a framework that supports safety, community and respect towards one another.

Obligatory courses

Anyone who wants to participate in the club's camps must go through resilience sessions before participating. The learning from a resilience course is designed to be useful in situations that the participants may encounter while they are at camp.

For example, some of the participants were going abroad to visit an art museum. The training before this visit was divided into two stages. In the first stage, they had to role-play in the club. Some of them took on the role of pieces of art, some of them took on the roles of respectable guests and others played guests with indecent behaviour. The exercise focused on seeing our own behaviour from the outside and exercising the ability to sense other people's thoughts and feelings. Subsequently, the group had to practise what they had learnt at the local museum. When the adolescents trained with resilience through role-play, they practised what could take place when somebody crosses someone else's limits. They could also consider consequences that can follow from that, and how these could influence them individually, and on a collective level. It is also helpful to identify appropriate strategies and behaviours in situations where we might think something is extremely boring.

Another example is from a camp where a 13-year-old boy had to voice his needs in relation to his fear of heights. The boy found out how to cope with the feeling of fear by using some of the tools he had learnt in the resilience training. In one of the activities at camp, the group was to visit the Round Tower in Copenhagen. The boy had to confront his fear of heights and became uneasy at the base of the steep staircase when heading back down (the staircase was narrow and there were a lot of people). He sat down with one of the adults. He shared his feelings; that there was a long way down and how, on the previous day, he had fallen down into a cellar. The adult comforted him and explained that others sometimes feel the same way, and then they investigated together which tools he could use in order to handle the signals the boy was getting from his body. They tested the tools together. They took deep breaths and felt the floor under their feet and still the boy was not ready to walk down. The adult waited until the boy was ready, held him under the arm, and they walked down together. The adult had guided the boy into becoming more aware of his body through breathing exercises and, after that, established a connection between him and the ground. Lastly, the adult had used body contact as a sort of anchor for the boy's feelings of safety and calm.

In the all-day school we also carried out class-based resilience teaching for pupils. We do not run the teaching in a full class but in smaller groups of three to eight pupils. It is important to work in smaller groups as a means of creating a space of trust. Also with the aim of strengthening trust, we separate the boys from the girls. For balancing out group dynamics, we try to mix both resourceful and resource-weak pupils, since resourceful participants share more and also help elevate the dynamics of groups.

In addition, we carry out open courses based on need. Some youngsters approach us because they are interested in knowledge about resilience in general, and that may incite one of the open courses to be organised. Their curiosity could be prompted through what they heard from friends who participated in a resilience course. Others come to us looking to refresh the knowledge they had previously acquired about resilience. We even arranged a course for a mother of two youngsters in the club, where the focus was on fear in social contexts.

Reflection and status

Our work with the development and implementation of the concept of resilience and the pedagogics behind it has been, and still is, a priority throughout our entire organisation; that is in both after-school and youth clubs as well as in the youth-school setting. Coaching communication and resilience is the basis for a shared language and shared understanding among children, youth and staff. In the teachings we emphasise relevance, using visual elements which are preferably spiced up with physical activity. In time, awarding course certificates following the completion of a course has been added, together with a sharpened focus on how to work with self-control and impulse-control with our participants. The resilience course is good for young people living in this area, specifically because, by learning about the brain, thoughts, emotions and body, they get to know that they are not so different from anyone else. They can see and hear that they function just as everybody else does. They can practise self-control and thereby act to change problematic patterns of behaviour.

The framework must be in place and basic needs must be met in order to provide the best conditions for participants, and enable them to keep their focus on the teachings. We have, in each department, established a classroom for teaching resilience. These rooms are arranged with the primary goal of creating a peaceful and conducive atmosphere, which includes consideration of the colours of the walls and the furniture chosen for the room. Emphasis is on the atmosphere of the room and possibilities for stimulating the senses. For instance, we decorated the plates with coloured napkins and candles, and have served fruit of various colours. Furthermore, we have posters with photos and quotes from the resilience course pinned at the doors and on the walls, which helps with reinforcing the language and the metaphors to be used in concrete daily life situations. We emphasise very much that our youth learn what it means to be resilient, how the *Thinking Brain* and the brain's *Alarm System* work, how they can be influenced and which accessible tools can be used to care for themselves and one another.

The resilience aspect is both a spontaneous and a planned part of everyday life in the clubs – in the halls, around the animals, in the kitchen, in the swimming hall, on car-rides and walks in the forest, in conflict management, etc. Resilience starts from within, in terms of us being good role models. Resilient adults shape resilient children. We have experienced periods of high conflict and, as a consequence of this, we also have previously had to make use of physical force.[3] The change we have experienced in regard to this is probably attributed to the work of coaching communication and resilience, which has led to a significant decrease in our need to use physical restraint. When we, as staff, change our way of working with our youth and focus on mentalising and thoughtfulness, many conflicts are defused, are nipped in the bud. Also, the conflicts that arise can be talked through without the use of force. Our youngsters practise the tools from our resilience teachings throughout their daily lives – and with practice comes mastery. We plant some seeds and hopefully, in the long run, they will grow into strong resilient trees, which in turn, will plant new seeds in their surroundings.

RESILIENCE FROM A YOUTH PERSPECTIVE

Lotte Dalager

'Young people are more exposed and vulnerable today because society is more complex than it's ever been.' I hear this statement often when I am out speaking to and teaching parents and professionals who work with adolescents. My experience is that the knowledge and the methods we work with, in the context of resilience and mentalising, make good sense when we work with people who are challenged in life in one way or another.

Niels Ulrik Sørensen, from the Centre for Youth Research at Aalborg University, describes some tendencies among today's youth, giving a good description of the complexities in our youths' realities in the world of today (Sørensen & Nielsen, 2014, 2016). According to Niels Ulrik Sørensen, youth research suggests that the idea of normality has become narrower and perfection has become a benchmark, against which young people increasingly measure themselves. The consequence may be that our youth realise that they do not live up to the expectations they have of themselves regarding the future, education, how their body looks and other aspects. Niels Ulrik Sørensen calls attention to the fact that young people are increasingly having to adjust to the logics of competition. They compare their own lives to what they deem perfect and when they do not live up to that, they problematise themselves. They place themselves in the shadow of the idea of perfection, so to speak. This may be a reason why insecurity thrives, and why underestimation of our own abilities comes about, along with more self-destructive forms of behaviour. Niels Ulrik Sørensen also touches upon the youth-challenge he names a double task: to find our self and shape our self at the same time. This may be another reason underlying why our young people feel extra exposed and vulnerable. They must make decisions about a future 'me' who, at the same time, they barely know at all. Niels Ulrik Sørensen points to the need they have for alternatives to the way they imagine themselves and their futures. This could, for instance, entail more possibilities to explore the creative sides of themselves and get a deeper insight into who they are.

I experience that our youth, among other things, can make use of resilience to develop a more accurate image of appropriate challenges and realistic goals for themselves. It is beautiful to have ambitions and dreams for the future, as long as the bar is not set so high that dreams become impossible to reach. We can help, as professionals and adults supporting them, by shining a light on the expectations our young people actually have of themselves, as well as the expectations that are placed upon them by the outside world. They get the opportunity to become better equipped in making choices that consider who they are in the here and now – rather than some phantom version of who they might want to be, based on expectations.

Youth-school course

In this section we will describe a course in resilience at a youth school. It will include who the participants were as well as their reflections about how they have been able to use the course in their everyday lives. I have interviewed four partici-pants – Sophia, Robert, Kate and Ophelia – one year following their participation in a course with me. A local youth school had invited me to arrange a pilot work-shop with a group of especially vulnerable youth. The idea was that the staff themselves would then be able to carry on with resilience courses in the youth school, and in addition award participants a certificate for their learning. Finally, I will engage in some more general reflections about my work with resilience.

The young people's preconditions and their reflections about the course, one year on

The youth who were invited to attend the course had varying needs but they had one thing in common, which was: they wished to be more resilient.

Sophia, grade 8. 'I found it difficult to concentrate, I could not set boundaries for others to respect and I had a hard time sleeping at night.' After the course, she went into grade 9. Sophia expressed that she had gained much more confidence due to the resilience course:

> One of the things I learnt in the first session of the resilience course was that it calmed me down to sit with one of the balls lying on the table. I've had a similar one in my bag since and I take it up into my hand whenever I feel I'm struggling with my concentration. It calms me. I remember to breathe and it becomes easier to listen to what the teacher says.

Beforehand, it was hard for Sophia to speak up in problematic situations, and she regularly ran into conflicts with friends and family. She taught herself to, '. . . go for a walk when I feel I'm starting to stress'. Then, she would listen to music, breathe and take it slow. She became conscious that our bodies produce a hormone called oxytocin, which makes us happy when, for instance, we see smiles, are in love and exchange hugs. She experienced that with this new knowledge, she could also support and calm her friends down when they were stressed.

Sophia ran in the youth town-council election of 2014 and was elected because of her desire to make a difference in the lives of her peers, regarding loneli-ness.

Sophia expressed how she would like to refresh her knowledge about resilience prior to her exams, because she imagined that it would help her. She has decided what she's striving towards, in the future – to be a social worker or psychologist.

Robert is 17 years old and a working trainee in a local enterprise. He had no exams in his public school. He has been diagnosed with ADD, including autistic structures. He was being medicated but, at the same time, was self-medicating with hash. Robert was very preoccupied with the substances our brain produces and widened his understanding of what takes place in his brain when, for instance, he takes his medicine. He very quickly experienced that breathing exercises did him good.

About the resilience course, he expressed that, '. . . it was a nice place to be. It was very relaxing and we dared to utter difficult matters'. Following the course, Robert started an addiction treatment and entered into vocational education. Robert trained and continues to train in martial arts. In the resilience course, he became more aware of how essential it is for his brain that his body exercises and that he eats nutritious food. Robert emphasises that the concepts from the *Thinking Brain* and the brain's *Alarm Centre* have been particularly useful for him. He has signed up for a mindfulness course in combination with his treatment at the addiction centre. He is interested in how difficult it will be for his brain to change habits and set new goals, but he would like to stop smoking hash and is working towards this goal.

Kate was in grade 8 when she entered the course. She was a very vulnerable young girl with huge challenges in her family. She was often uneasy, had difficulties with concentration, ran away from home and was in close contact with the social authorities. Throughout the course, Kate experienced how much she could be helped to find peace through music. It was very difficult for her to sleep, but she found out that listening to tranquil music before sleeping could help her. She could also use music as a way to shift her attention when, 'I am caught up by stupid thoughts,' as she put it. The image of *Attention – the Brain's Spotlight* was particularly useful for her when she attended class and was distracted by thoughts about her problems at home. She used her knowledge from the concepts to remind herself that she was in control of her attention. She expressed that the exercise was difficult. We spoke about how the attention-muscle must be trained just as much as we would train our muscles in a fitness centre. After the beginning of the course, Kate started at a special school and she was enrolled in an individual resilience course that took place once per week, assisting her in finding peace within herself. She was very happy about this. The social authorities also became active in supporting the family.

Ophelia was in grade 9. She was tired of going to school. She was a trainee in a clothes shop, and worked there twice per week. She had dyslexia and a visible disability as well. Owing to her disability, she was struggling with some hesitations in new contexts and she was influenced by what she perceived were other people's thoughts about her. She found meaning in the story of the *House of Thoughts* and used it to shift her attention to a room where she knew there would be people in her life who cared about her, just the way she is. Ophelia started at a boarding school last year and is now attending grade 10.

The four young participants who completed the course had, as can be seen, widely different challenges in terms of age, background and personal trials.

The course in brief

Time frame: The course lasted six weeks and we met once per week for around two hours.

Teaching: Throughout the six weeks, the participants learnt about fundamental concepts and methods from The Resilience Programme and were given the opportunity to work towards a certificate. The participants themselves, their parents, club pedagogues and friends were invited to a festive and somehow ceremonious award presentation at a local enterprise at the end of the course.

Manager: I always make sure to have an internal manager at a resilience course. The manager takes care of all practicalities, sends out reminders for the sessions, knows the participants, knows the area and is generally happy to participate in the course. This creates confidence for the young participants and the teacher can better concentrate on the content. Additionally, this creates a bridge with the participants – also when the course is over.

Side-by-side learning: In this case, both the manager and a pedagogue from the youth club participated in the course. They had both attended a course in The Resilience Programme and were given the opportunity here to further refresh their knowledge on the methods, before initiating a course themselves.

Surroundings: The manager had borrowed a space close by, and had arranged for coffee, tea, milk chocolate, fruits, paper, markers, small cups with Lego, small balls, bean-bag chairs, flip charts, small notebooks, folders, certificate-material, etc. to be provided.

Professional reflections related to the course

When preparing for a resilience course for a group of adolescents, I had initially prepared a plan on how to guide them through the core content. Depending on the target group, and in cooperation with the youths' networks and opportunities at hand, I estimated which subjects should be prioritised. In some contexts, it is vital for the young participants to become more aware of the significance of diet, exercise and sleep before they can connect the rest of the concepts and their ability to improve on learning, concentration and focus, with respect to the parts of their lives they want to focus on. Others have previously expressed their wishes to improve on anger management, to not involve themselves in troublesome relationships and situations, to set boundaries and rid themselves of their low self-esteem.

The youths responded that it was a bit barrier breaking in the beginning to speak about their personal stuff when we spoke about thoughts and emotions. They also expressed that they became more confident in the group, pretty quickly. They told about their discovery that everybody looks the same from the inside, that we all carry thoughts and emotions and that everybody finds that life and the challenges we encounter are difficult. In addition, that this can be useful in finding out what to do with ourselves. They also expressed that the group's small size mattered.

I put a lot of emphasis on the side-by-side-learning of the professionals around the participating youths, because experience shows that the resilient community has decisive importance. We also discovered that once we established a shared meaning through the simple language of the *Thinking Brain* and the brain's *Alarm Centre*, concepts became implicit, so we didn't always have to use language when referring to certain core meanings. In addition, the pedagogues who participated in the course got a better understanding of the needs of young individuals in situations where the brain's *Alarm Centre* takes control. As a consequence, they became more competent at supporting and helping them. In times of peace, we talked about what peace, care and protection might mean to an individual who feels themselves locked in a state of alarm. This created trust for our participants, since they discovered that people could understand what may be going on, as well as what action may be taken. In situations where it was not possible for pedagogues or others from our youths' networks to participate in the courses, they were informed through other channels about the course's content, as they received an introduction to the methods, for example, in the form of an informal lecture for staff and parents.

It made a difference for our young participants to have the possibility of obtaining a course certificate for what they learnt. I have experienced many times that the certificate serves as a kind of reward and that it helps to keep their focus throughout the course. They often put in a bit more effort as they know there is something at stake. Of course, it is important to evaluate whether there could be a counter-effect; that is, for some, certification could remind them of bad experiences from school. Here, it was vital for the teacher to be aware of differentiation between participants and ensure that everybody could follow and access the support and help they needed – all in all, to estimate, in each individual case, whether it is best to aim for a certificate.

We know it may be difficult for young people with special challenges to find motivation. It has therefore, in some contexts, been meaningful to name the courses something other than 'resilience course', and to find a subject that resonates with the group. This could relate to lifestyle, educational pathways, sports or the like. In other contexts, where the institution or the wider community has been working with resilience for a longer period of time, we found that the youths approached us themselves to ask for a course in resilience, often because they had seen and heard about the benefits from their friends or siblings.

In pedagogical work, we are often very aware of using what we call conflict-reducing language. While keeping an overview of the situation, we also work with the internal, the individual's state of mind. We have also practised using alarm-reducing language on an individual level.

Instead of making use of words such as 'conflict' or 'flying into a rage', we would use expressions such as 'alarm situation'. Linguistically, this shifts focus away from the individual, who is able to grasp the new terminology (the brain's *Alarm Centre*). The result is an externalisation of what the individual considers personally dangerous, and of what triggers feelings of alarm. Simultaneously, the language better enables the professionals to deal with what is actually going on.

Resilience makes a lot of sense in relation to supporting our young people in their development of social and personal competences. The methods obviously do not solve all problems, but they provide us all with coping opportunities. Also, the resilience approach provides staff with new tools through which to speak with youth about their needs for coping with some of the alarm situations that arise. Also, *Fields of Practice* are vital because they assist our young people in remembering the new ways of acting they have learnt, so they can help themselves whenever required. They learn to recognise danger signals, such as in, 'Hey, now's the time where it becomes difficult for me to be part of the situation – what is it I can do with myself? What is it that I need?' If they practise such exercises in times of peace, in trusting contexts and communities, the brain becomes better equipped to remember how to go about the process in times where we have to stand on our own two feet and life becomes challenging.

The teachings in resilience and mentalising are based on what is fundamentally human, no matter whether it is for adolescents, pedagogical staff or business leaders. We are on the same level and we are in the same boat. Together we can observe the human mechanisms within each of us with curiosity. These mechanisms cause us to enter states of alarm where we say and do things we can recognise as inappropriate after the fact. They also highlight how it can be difficult to set a goal and reach it or that grief and sadness may overtake us so profoundly that daily life becomes hard to handle. There are circumstances that can impede our adolescents' steps into adulthood. Every youth's and adult's life carries huge professional, personal, social and educational demands. As mentioned earlier, our young people also demand and expect a lot of themselves. The feedback I have often received is that by speaking of resilience as something we all have in common, as humans, we make something otherwise difficult and confusing a bit simpler and normal.

The youngsters have expressed that through this knowledge, they get more opportunities to cope with things they experience internally, and strengthen their resilience. It is the sense that 'I can' that makes us develop resilience as humans, step by step, through useful thoughts, with appropriate challenges.

Notes

1   The results from the evaluation of the projects described in this chapter were published in the summer of 2015 (Lundgaard Bak et al., 2015) and showed that the activities had contributed to the prevention of high-risk conflicts (90 per cent reduction) and sick leave (50 per cent reduction).

2   In principle, this is a simpler version of the Mind Game (see Chapter 1), drawn out on a larger scale using a canvas. The road 'away' is the same as the Mind Game's 'sidetrack'.

3   See also the scientific article which was later published about the project (Bak et al., 2015).

References

Lundgaard Bak, P., Midgley, N., Zhu, J. L., Wistoft, K. & Obel, C. (2015) The Resilience Program: Preliminary evaluation of a mentalization-based education program, *Frontiers in Psychology*, 6:753. doi: 10.3389/fpsyg.2015.00753

Sørensen, N. U. & Nielsen, J. C. (2014) Et helt normalt perfekt selv. Konstruktioner af selvet i unges beretninger om mistrivsel, *Dansk Sociologi*, 25(1):9–30.

Sørensen, N. U. & Nielsen, J. C. (2016) Derailed self-constructions. Marginalization and self-construction in young boys. Accounts of well-being. In T. M. Johannson & C. Haywood (eds.) *Marginalised Masculinities*. Routledge.

Chapter 6

Resilience for teenagers in therapy

Susanna de Lima, and Gritt Graugaard Bonde, with contributions from Lotte Dalager

A COURSE FOR VULNERABLE YOUTHS WITH DRUG ABUSE PROBLEMS

Susanna de Lima, with contributions from Lotte Dalager

In this chapter, I will invite you, the reader, into my niche. I work with drug-treatment programmes for teenagers under the age of 18 in a youth centre in Aarhus, Denmark. The majority of the young people I meet here suffer from complex psycho-social difficulties that involve more than drugs. My experience is that we help them best with a holistic approach, where several efforts come together and support them in more than one area of their lives. In this context, I will describe how we cooperated together with some of the youth undergoing treatment, their parents and contact-pedagogues, who managed share efforts with us in a resilience project.

Project background

The idea of running a group workshop that focused on resilience and thought-fulness/mentalising came from my various experiences with large groups of drug-challenged, vulnerable youth. They often have a hard time understanding and talking about what's going on internally, inside themselves, and they equally have a hard time understanding what others may be experiencing. This was obviously a central theme in our individual treatment sessions. At the same time, I was constantly challenged as a practitioner to keep my focus on thoughtfulness as well as widening the space dialogue about the many crises and the chaos that affect their lives. Their daily crises and chaos often takes up so much time from the individual treatment sessions that our time is spent on their here-and-now frustrations and on support. In the light of these challenges I chose to test, in a non-alarm situation, a workshop format that could provide frames within which we could integrate thoughtfulness/mentalisation and emotional regulation. The starting point was to then invite them to the workshop, where they would simultaneously receive therapy. At the time when I planned the group workshop, I had two teenagers who were ready and motivated to participate in group sessions that would take place alongside their individual therapy. I saw the group as a semi-open one, where more participants could join in after 2–3 months. It became clear, pretty fast, that these two youngsters were too vulnerable at the time to tolerate an expansion of the group. This became evident because it was already challenging enough for them to work together. Both were affected by a burdened background that included abandonment, violence, traumas and common conflicts with others. Both were placed outside their homes. Their contact-persons from the institution where they lived were therefore invited to partake actively in the group workshop. The aim was to support them and their application of resilience and thoughtful-ness in their daily lives. That is helping to transform their knowledge into praxis. The idea is that changes take place in concrete, everyday life, and not within a therapeutic/workshop context.

To participate in the group workshop, they were required to quit using illicit drugs and to come with an open attitude and a willingness to listen to and examine new ways of coping with life challenges, in the form of *Fields of Practice*. Thus, the group was formed with two teenagers, together with their contact-persons. One was a girl of 15 years of age, and the other a young man of 17 years of age. For reasons of anonymity, I will use fictional names and refer to them as Catherine and Max. Their parents also came to be involved.

The group workshop spanned 9 months and consisted of 2-hour sessions each week. We had originally planned for the workshop to last 6 months. Encouraged by the teenaged participants, we extended this by 3 months, as they required more time to practise what was being learnt in their everyday lives. Their wish to spend more time on this was completely in line with my impression that they needed many repetitions and small steps, in succession. The teenagers and their contact-persons had expressed that it was helpful for them to have the support they were receiving while continually refreshing their knowledge and re-examining their *Fields of Practice* plans, collectively.

The course was presented to the teenagers as a workshop in thoughtfulness where the aim was to work with knowledge about thoughts, emotions and experi-ences that occur within ourselves as well as within others, and how they could be inspired to cope with particular challenges such as those posed by anger, anxiety, fear and conflicts with other people. In addition, we had agreed to focus on special factors and events that provoked their desire to use drugs and what other possibilities might exist to replace that addiction with something else. This was part of preventing relapses. Both Catherine and Max expressed their personal desire to be better at coping with anger and conflicts with other people.

Framework and themes in the resilience course

As a way to ensure confidence and predictability in the workshop, I chose to run a fixed programme for each session. The roles of group leader and teacher were clearly defined – who does what, when and how. My colleague and I were very conscious of taking the lead, and at the same time, we had the double role of being the group leader and teacher, staging ourselves as role models who mentalise and ask curiously with positive energy. During the workshop, I experienced that the teenagers became more active, especially in relation to them sharing their own experiences. Later in the workshop they asked to try out a more open agenda. They agreed, for instance, that they would put emphasis on how they managed their individual challenges and *Fields of Practice* between sessions, and that they would share this with each other.

We all agreed that their parents should participate twice throughout the workshop – once in the beginning and once near the end. The aim was to briefly introduce their parents to the workshop and to recap what the teenagers had learnt from the course at the end. The contact-persons had a brief conversation with me prior to the workshop about their role throughout, and then participated in every session. In the sessions, their role was primarily to listen to and support the teenagers in their journeys to defining realistic *Fields of Practice* at home. The contact-persons were willing to support and train these together with the teenagers, between sessions. For our ongoing collection of experiences, we had created small grids we could use to systemise themes, methods and continuing experiences. I chose five overall headlines that were written into each of the teenager's personal grids, as follows:

1   My values, dreams and future goals
2   What are thoughts? Who experiences thoughts? Thoughts about thoughts
3   The helicopter perspective – to see myself from the outside
4   The *Thinking Brain* and the brain's *Alarm Centre*
5   Self-reassuring through breathing exercises.

I will now elaborate each of these headlines in order to provide you with insight into how the themes unfolded and how the teenagers started their journeys of discovery from their own life experiences.

Theme 1: My values, dreams and future goals

Max and Catherine's starting point was their own values and dreams, and they defined, in their own ways, a personal goal for participation in the workshop. They quickly realised that their personal goals actually represented a shared goal as well. Max dreamed about a good life with good and loving relationships. Likewise, Catherine wished to form close relationships and build on honesty. It was a joy to see how they already started to show curiosity towards themselves and one another. I had a good feeling from their initial enthusiasm because they kicked-off well, with them formulating a personal goal related to why they participated in the workshop.

Theme 2: What are thoughts? Who experiences thoughts? Thoughts about thoughts

We introduced the group to a short mindfulness exercise that focused on breathing. The exercise took 2–3 minutes where the participants were instructed to sit, stand or walk silently around the room while they remained attentive to their breathing. Max walked around the room snorting and grunting. Catherine sat still and silently on a chair. After the exercise, the two teenagers were given the opportunity to talk about how they experienced the exercise. Catherine said it was a new and nice experience for her to sit and feel her breathing. Max found it very odd that he could feel his heart hammering away and felt it was one big rumbling heart. I emphasised that the purpose of the exercise wasn't to obtain anything specific but simply to direct their attention to their breath and observe how it felt in the here and now. After this, we shared some of the relevance we could get out of being able to control and direct our attention. We also discussed the meaning of observing the breath and what useful knowledge we could get out of really being present with ourselves in the here and now. Max explained that he often had a fierce unrest inside and often did a lot of destructive things, in order to distract himself from the unrest and uneasiness. A bit later in the conversation, Max mentioned that he had cravings for hash and typically would have smoked a joint just at that very moment. It made good sense to Max that the exercise was an opportunity to become more aware of his own thoughts and feelings in such a situation. I acknowledged Max for being able to stay within the situation, with all its discomfort, without giving in to the urge for a joint. Catherine also expressed recognition of Max's situation, and shared that she also felt the urge for hash whenever she got agitated. Max and Catherine expressed their wish to engage further with mindfulness, and so, throughout the workshop, we worked with thoughts, emotions and the body as a whole.

After the mindfulness exercise, we started learning about thoughts. I began with a description of *Attention – the Brain's Spotlight* and told short stories about thoughts and the existing connections between thoughts, emotions, body and behaviour. My co-teacher and I used ourselves as role models and gave small examples of how our thoughts easily ran on or could take us deep into fantasies that would lock us in. In these examples, we asked about one another's stories with the point of illustrating openness and curiosity towards each other's inner experiences in terms of thoughts, emotions, needs and intentions. While doing so, we encouraged Catherine and Max to contribute their experiences. Max explained that, 'Thoughts can make me go mad, for instance the thought that my girlfriend is cheating on me.' Catherine explained, 'Swarming thoughts give me stress and an urge for hash (. . .) then I start thinking of how the hash calms me down.' Both Catherine and Max immediately grasped that thoughts may cause impulsive actions if we do not learn to be aware of them. After that, we added another step to the activity, namely the possibility for us to choose new ways of reacting instead of blindly reacting to the thoughts. To this, Max told the following story:

> I was visiting a shopping centre together with my pedagogue because I should buy new shoes. Before we entered the shoe shop the pedagogue asked me whether I had considered what kind of shoes I would like. I first considered the question to be a stupid one, because how could I know without having seen shoes on the shelves? I just had to bring a pair of shoes home. Well, I walked around the shop and looked at a lot of shoes but could not really find something I really liked. I honed in on some black ones and a specific brand but the shop didn't have them in my size, which meant I would have to order them or find a new shop. I decided to continue looking in another shop. Normally I would have made a purchase impulsively and I would have just bought any pair of shoes, or worse, I would have stolen a random pair of shoes as I did when I was a criminal.

With his story, Max demonstrated that he had started to reflect. And not just that, he was able to postpone impulses and needs – something that had been a huge issue for him. Max had gained more self-control.

As a part of the teaching and training in between sessions, I encouraged the two to find some *Fields of Practice* where they could train their awareness of the here and now in their daily lives. I provided examples such as becoming aware of the weather, sounds, how it feels to do the dishes, nature, ones' surroundings, etc. A few sessions into the workshop, Catherine eagerly came back with this discovery: 'I suddenly noticed that my boyfriend has the most beautiful blue eyes – well, I know he has blue eyes, but hadn't noticed that they were that deep of a blue.' Later in the workshop I connected their experiences with activities to train their attention in here and now with the idea that we can use our attention to observe our thoughts. I presented the idea that our thoughts can be seen as clouds flying through the sky or as balloons flying up into the sky. The story of the *House of Thoughts* was read to the group. This opened for a dialogue about good thoughts, annoying thoughts, difficult thoughts, uplifting thoughts, funny thoughts and a variety of other thoughts. Max and Catherine showed their excitement about playing with their thoughts in this way. Catherine elaborated with this aha-experience: 'But that's almost as if you're standing there and physically touching your thoughts.' Max commented that it would be, '. . . super nice if you could learn to enter another thought-room when the one you're in becomes too dark'. Our dialogue resulted in a *Field of Practice* that the group felt like practising for the next couple of weeks. The *Field of Practice* had developed from the story of the *House of Thoughts* where the teenagers, along with their contact-pedagogues, would experiment with building the imaginary rooms in which they could practise their awareness of thoughts. I gave them several ideas to help them discover their thoughts: write a diary, draw, paint or similar activities.

A few months into the project, both Catherine and Max expressed that they had become aware of the strength of thoughts in relation to their actions. Catherine shared, for instance, how previously her thoughts about hash could make her smoke impulsively without considering the consequences. In relation to this, they both mentioned how for them, prior to doing the exercises, they felt as though they were melting with whatever thought they'd have and that it would take control over them. They also said that learning to control their thoughts and emotions to a point where they become helpful was new to them. Max told how he was able to sort his thoughts into two boxes inside his head: in either a light and happy box or in an angry and aggressive box. Max named the angry box 'the black box', which was explosive and caused violence against himself or others. Max felt relieved at his new discovery of the existence of various rooms with thoughts, through his work with *Fields of Practice*. This included thoughts about being kind and respectful towards others. He had also discovered that he could spot more thoughts and nuances about himself in moments where he could feel secure and accepted, just the way he is.

Up to this point, our group had worked with values, goals, dreams, wishes, attention training and the connections between thoughts, emotions and behaviour. All these subjects broached new understandings of the self: What occupies me? What are my values, dreams and goals? The next step was to introduce the teenagers to the idea of observing their self from the outside – the helicopter perspective.

Theme 3: The helicopter perspective

The aim with this theme was to provide the teenagers with a mental tool that could help them observe their individual selves, from an outside-in perspective. Observing ourselves from the outsider's point of view prompts us to use our senses in imagining, looking and watching the self. From a mindfulness perspective, we could formulate it as: it is essentially about being with what is, observing thoughts, emotions, experiences and events and learning to accept them as they are. Accepting does not equate to carelessness but rather is the ability to acknowledge ourselves with all the difficult parts as well as the nice ones. It is not about getting out of ourselves but rather about being at home in ourselves. In this context, we focused on observing ourselves: 'How am I doing?', 'What does my life look like?', 'How do I appear when I am quarrelling with somebody?', 'What do I do?', 'I wonder, how I feel?' The point of learning to be at home in ourselves and to watch ourselves from the outside is that when we discover how we act, think and feel in a given situation, our chances of acting more consciously and therefore more appropriately increase. When we work with the helicopter perspective, we may choose to look back into the past, to be in the moment or imagine something in the future by means of our imagination. This could concern how we wish to be or act in a given situation in the future, or to look back in time, observing a given situation from above/from the outside and exploring personal actions, thoughts and feelings.

On the blackboard, I had drawn a helicopter carrying a passenger who could look down at himself and his surroundings. Max and Catherine both went with the idea and said it was a fun scenario to work with. They were given the task of imagining that they were sightseeing from their own helicopter, looking down at their actual young life from above and from the outside. The task was introduced as a mindfulness-visualisation exercise where I first guided them to be present, in the moment, and attentive to their breath. Afterwards, they were asked to imagine themselves sitting in a helicopter, where they could observe their lives from the outside – and they were just supposed to try to be open and curious without looking for anything specific. After the exercise, they were asked to create a collage, depicting what had caught their attention. These turned out to be very exciting collages, which engaged them even further in the exercise. Max and Catherine explained their collages to one another and asked with curiosity about one another's collages. Extending the experience from the presentations of their collages, I introduced them to the idea that we have the capacity to use our thoughts and dreams to play with reality, for instance by creating collages and visualisations. We can watch ourselves from an outsider's perspective in relation to experiences of the here and now, into the past and into the future. As both Max and Catherine had become very keen on establishing good relations with others, especially their closest relatives, we then chose to create various *Fields of Practice* concerning coping with conflict. Max chose to practise simple breathing techniques for when he began to feel worked up. He had become pretty sharp in noticing himself from the outside: 'My body becomes stiff and I start clenching my fists. My upper body bends forward. . . .' Catherine chose to make use of the inner image she had of herself – as someone being relaxed, open and friendly in times of peace. She wanted to use this as a way for her to anchor herself whenever she had to cope with conflicts. She used the helicopter perspective to imagine herself coping and feeling differently in the future. She practised viewing herself from above and from the outside. In this way, she gained a greater insight into how she could cope, feel and think more appropriately in the future.

A few weeks later, when Max came to the session, he proudly announced that he had encountered a conflict where he managed to apply the new principles he had learnt. In an episode where he started yelling at his girlfriend, he suddenly saw himself from the outside and started thinking something like: 'Stop this weirdo.' Max took a couple of deep breaths and walked a bit away from the situation. Later he had apologised to his girlfriend and they managed to talk things through, quietly together. Max shared that this had given him the feeling of being the master of his own house. He was surprised that he was able to be in control. Catherine also shared that she had encountered several good experiences through imagining herself as being more relaxed, open and friendly. One of the other teenagers from Catherine's institution had, for instance, told her that she had become quite sweet. Catherine and Max were surprised that they had succeeded in handling conflicts on their own and also that other people had noticed that they had become more kind and calm. We talked with one another about the significance of our inner imagination in relation to how the outside world responds. We really took the time to examine the impact that stemmed from observing ourselves from the helicopter perspective. We compared it to being two sides of the same coin; that we are capable of understanding ourselves from the inside-out and from the outside-in.

Theme 4: The Thinking Brain and the brain's Alarm Centre

Within this theme we dove deeper into further examining the activities of the brain and what happens during our experiences of different thoughts and emotions. To start, we spoke about six different core emotions (happiness, surprise, anger, sadness, disgust and fear), their function and the expressions they incite. We related this to how thoughts, emotions and actions are connected and influenced by the core emotions, because this made things more recognisable for the teenagers and deepened their insights. I presented different images of the brain that illustrate how the brain looks while in a state of alarm, and also what it looks like when it is at rest (the *Thinking Brain* and the *Alarm Centre*). We looked at the brain's function and how it reacts when we feel threatened, such as in a dangerous situation where the reaction of fight, flight or freeze kicks in. On the other hand, the brain's *Alarm Centre* may react inappropriately if it is activated in situations and contexts that are not actually dangerous for us. I used the following example:

> A woman is alone in her apartment. It is dark and late at night. Suddenly she hears a high-pitched sound coming from the street. The following thought comes to mind: 'Help, someone is shooting in the street.' The woman gets very scared, panics and runs out to ring the neighbour's doorbell. But the neighbour is standing at his window sill, looking out at the beautiful fireworks on display in the street, reassuring his neighbour that all is in order. The woman apologises and then goes back to her home. When she got back, alone in her apartment, she started reflecting upon her fear of the darkness, which makes her so incredibly afraid.

The group discussed in plenum how easily things can get crazy when we get locked in a catastrophic thought. Max mentioned how he experienced his mind going blank when he became angry and exploded in aggressive outbursts. Catherine later added that, 'When I experience adults not understanding me or scolding me, my brain kind of turns off and I am not able to listen to what they say. It feels like being very remote.' One of their contact-persons added that even though this knowledge is commonplace, it cannot be repeated enough and is quite vital to keep in mind when conflicts arise at the institution. In addition to the talk about the *Thinking Brain* and the brain's *Alarm Centre*, I introduced the concept 'self-reassuring', and that we all have a need to be able to calm ourselves down so that we can reflect, and from that point on, act more appropriately.

Theme 5: Self-reassuring

The aim of the self-reassuring theme was to help the teenagers to find out what methods and exercises they would mostly benefit from in relation to regulating themselves in experiences of difficult thoughts, emotions and challenges. We further practised mindfulness exercises with a focus on breath, thoughts, emotions and the body. Max and Catherine were now ready to extend their mindfulness exercises up to 15–20 minutes. At the beginning of the workshop, Max could not even sit still and chose to wander around the room while trying to engage in the exercise for 2 minutes. Now he could sit quietly for periods of 20 minutes and keep his attention on the exercise. Max expressed that he could still sense his inner uneasiness but that he could stand to be present with it without running around or become irritated. He explained, 'It's a new, weird feeling – as if I'm really seeing and sensing myself from the inside.' Catherine expressed something similar. She said it was like coming home to our house and that it was sometimes a pleasant sensation, that at other times, it was still unpleasant, and that some of the time, it kind of felt like an either-or situation. I summarised that mindfulness could be understood as a way to be in the world and as a method of training our attention, for the here and now. The purpose of mindfulness is not relaxation or to reach a feel-good-state, even though these can certainly be nice side-effects. Until now, my focus had been on helping the teenagers train their attention to be within the moment, with their thoughts and emotions, and to make them understand them-selves more clearly, helping them build better relations with others. As a part of this, I added relaxation techniques. The group now explored what they would usually do to relax. Catherine and Max said that they had both been users of hash, especially for relaxation. Max also remembered that he used to calm down by massaging his earlobes when he was little. Catherine shared that she became calm and relaxed when she was lying with her teddy bear, listening to tranquil music. We then spoke about which methods they found worked the best for them and which did not work so well. Both had experienced that hash was not a good solution because it had created more problems for them and added to their stress instead of their peace in the long run.

The group tried out several resting and relaxation techniques, including pro-gressive relaxation where they were guided into tensing the muscles and then relaxing them, as well as a relaxation practice where they could sit or lie still on the floor while listening to tranquil music and exercise with the Wellness Beads.

Catherine and Max both struggled with finding peace and falling asleep and therefore chose to practise relaxation techniques when going to bed. Throughout a few weeks, Max experienced that it was helpful for him to practise relaxation at night. He had shared his experience with other peers at his institution. They had become curious and asked Max whether they could learn what he's learning as well. Max and his contact-person had subsequently bought a relaxation CD for their institution which they could use to practise with the others. This became so popular that also several of the institutional staff wanted to join. When the institution closed for vacation, the staff and the residents decided to put relaxation into the programme as a goodnight ritual.

At the end of the workshop, Max and Catherine had experienced that the many hours of practice had been well invested. They had become so skilled in self-reassurance that they had started to apply the methods automatically in other areas of their lives. Catherine's train-ride is a good example of this process: 'I was sitting on the train and experienced inner restlessness. The thoughts swirled in my head and I was just about to flip out. Then I just started breathing in slowly and deeply into my stomach and breathing out slowly. I put on my headphones and searched for tranquil music on my mobile. And damn! I just sat there and became completely relaxed.'

Closing the workshop

The group workshop was completed with a meeting in which the young people's contact-persons and parents participated. The two teenagers took part in the planning of the closing activities; with respect to selecting the space, what kind of cosy activities should be included and what the content should be. Max and Catherine were very engaged in the planning and beautifully demonstrated their competence to transfer their knowledge and training into reality. They exhibited thoughtfulness towards one another and asked for one another's ideas. They reflected upon interesting topics that their parents would appreciate, and asked for guidance in selecting these. During the planning process, I overheard the following dialogue between them:

Max: 'My girlfriend's birthday's in a few weeks and I'm thinking about what I should buy for her.'
Catherine: 'What's your girlfriend like? What are her interests?'
Max: 'She's the sporty-type.'
Catherine: 'What about a tank top?'

The beauty in this very down-to-earth exchange is how Max and Catherine show that they have become more open, curious and competent in relation to being interested in their own and others' thoughts and feelings and that they are able to look at things from the inside as well as from the outside. They had achieved a higher degree of resilience and ability to mentalise in connection to understanding their own and others' thoughts, emotions, intentions, needs, goals and motives.

Catherine and Max chose to present their collages at the closing session and shared a bit about the journey they had each begun and what they had taken away from it. Catherine's father spontaneously said that he wished he had had some of that knowledge as a young man, especially about the brain's *Alarm Centre*. Max and Catherine answered together that he was welcome to get a copy of the course-material. All in all, Max and Catherine's behaviour seemed to reflect that they had attained greater insight into the connection between thoughts, emotions, behaviour and the brain's *Alarm Centre*, and what occurs on the inside when they become afraid, angry, happy or excited. It was also clear that they had become more open and curious towards others, including other people's thoughts, emotions, needs and desires. Likewise, Max and Catherine had integrated constructive ways of calming themselves down into their lives, and had exemplified that practice leads to mastery.

During the workshop, we decided to maintain a focus on the same models and methods for a long period of time so that the teenagers could take the time to integrate, experiment with and build their own experiences. Repetitions were important in order to ensure an effective learning process where knowledge and skills were being built, step by step. Repetitions do not have to be boring. My experience was that nuances were added continuously along the way.

Working with vulnerable teenagers who have complex psycho-social challenges requires time and patience as well as a very well-orchestrated team of adults and initiatives that come together to make it happen. It was a gift to have the teenagers' contact-persons participating in the workshop because they got experience with the same knowledge as their dependants, and got to engage in building experiments and *Fields of Practice* together with them in between sessions. The collaboration between the teenagers and their contact-persons had a rub-off effect in their institutions. As the teenagers were closely monitored by their contact-persons, there was just about full attendance throughout the workshop, which obviously contributed to the good flow.

The intention underlying the workshop was to create a safe space with a community feeling, play and thoughtfulness. We additionally had the hope that it could awaken their curiosity about themselves and others as well as inspire them to find new and constructive skills. The teenagers got to experience being in a small, safe community, which gave them the courage to open themselves up to one another. They built a new relationship with their own thoughts, emotions and behaviour. Each in their own way, they moved from a psychologically locked position into increased flexibility, from being out of control with respect to thought processes and emotional life, to being able to relate to their own thoughts and emotions and harness the capacity to regulate themselves.

COOPERATING WHEN IT'S DIFFICULT

Gritt Graugaard Bonde

Background

Young people with depression are often scared by negative thought or behaviour patterns which are difficult to change. It is as though they wear dark sunglasses and automatically perceive themselves and the world as being dark and gloomy. They have lost hope and belief in a better life and a brighter way to view the world. I often find that our youth are far harsher in their judgement of themselves than others and they set unrealistic demands for themselves. They find it easy to recognise the unrealistic parts of depressive thinking and high demands when looking at a friend, an acquaintance or a stranger who is locked into these patterns.

Only then are they able to perhaps get a glimpse into their own negative patterns. Without the external examples, they seem to lack the ability to recognise negative patterns within themselves. When I worked as a psychologist in a project with children and youth in psychiatry, I met many of these young people, especially girls, in treatment. I was well grounded from my previous experience of working with stressed and depressed groups of adults, where I combined mindfulness and cognitive therapy. I wanted to try this out with the youth I was now treating. At the time, I took part in an interest group with physician Poul Lundgaard, who was in the midst of developing the material we now know as The Resilience Programme. It was in line with what I wanted to do with my group. Mindfulness can appear somehow long-haired and mystical, and I have reflected quite a lot on how I could present mindfulness to the young people I was working with in a way that would make sense to them. The tools and the entire content of The Resilience Programme were the answers to my troubles. The stories and tools are so simple and easy to access. They speak using language and images that cut to the core and cut out all the noise and mystics. What is left are the distinct points.

In this section, I will describe a course that I put on for young people that combined mindfulness, cognitive therapy and The Resilience Programme. The paragraphs are arranged in accordance with the different exercises we went through in the group. Individual paragraphs present a mixture of experiences from the group, thoughts and the theoretical reasons for my choosing the exercises I did. At the end of each paragraph is a 'do-it-yourself' part with inspiration for how to start practising the exercises described.

The group

Everybody who has arranged group treatment for young people knows that it is difficult to find a suitable number of participants, inside the target group, motivated enough, and with enough time to participate. I had decided to invite up to eight participants. We ended up being a girls-only group with five girls between the ages of 15 and 17. One of them quit after the first meeting. All participants had been or were engaged in individual therapy, either with me or with one of my colleagues. We met as a group six times for two hours each time. In the group, we aimed to investigate the role that our thoughts and emotions had in our lives, when they were helpful and when they were not. When we become wiser about who we are, we become better equipped to make good choices. In the group, the girls practised and became better at discovering when they allowed their thoughts and emotions to control them in negative ways and, thus, they enabled themselves to start categorising. I really wanted to see the group try to work in a playful and experimental way. They were not supposed simply to swallow my words without question. I wanted to provide them with experiences that would urge them to question their depressive attitudes towards the world or at least give them the opportunity to experience themselves and the world in another light. We did not speak about the rights or wrongs but experimented with the ways in which different approaches to the world lead to different experiences. The aim was for these girls to exit the group with the knowledge that they had a choice – that they were in charge of the direction they each wanted to give to their lives, that they controlled the depression and it didn't control them. I deliberately aimed towards this, in this group. I wanted to exploit the fact that, for them, it might be easier to recognise a depressive state of mind in others, and then relate it back to themselves, than to use themselves as the starting point. It was my hope that by mirroring themselves in like-minded people, they could straightforwardly realise their own depressive distortions.

How does the brain work?

The brain reacts automatically in most circumstances. This is practical and resource saving. However, in some cases, it can create problems. If we understand how the brain works, we have better opportunities to react appropriately to tricks of the mind. Most of us consider our experiences to be real. We are sure that what we experience is true. This is not always the case, though. In the group, we began by looking at different examples of visual depictions that show us how the brain sometimes plays tricks on us. I had several reasons behind my choices of explanations for something so very complicated as the brain. We avoid the eventual stimulation of negative associations in those who carry bad experiences from school. The illustrations I had chosen for the purpose were amusing. In this way, they could be more closely associated with free time and fun than with school work. Another reason I used the illustrations as I did was to promote experience-based learning, since for many, it is more effective than lectures. By actively relating to the learning, we engage, which positively affects our capacity to learn.

Simons and Chabris' gorilla experiment illustrated how transient and context-dependent our attention is (Most et al., 2001). A video of the experiment is on YouTube.com, where a group of basketball players dressed in white and black t-shirts pass a ball among themselves while moving around a court. Observers are asked to count the number of times the white team, specifically, passes the ball from one of its players to another – very simple. Most people get the right answer but only a few notice that a dancing gorilla enters the court and dances about as the ball is being passed between players. Seventy-three per cent of those who watch the video do not notice the gorilla. This is called 'inattentional blindness' (Most et al., 2001). If we are too focused on one element, we invariably overlook or become blind to other elements. In many situations, this is a strength. The ability to be blind to disturbing elements in our surroundings is useful. For instance, when we need to focus on solving a task, it is of great use that we are able to tune-out from most things are taking place around us so that we can focus on what is important for solving the task. For the depressed brain, however, this is not the case. When we are depressed we are often over-attentive to negative reactions in the surroundings. As illustrated through the gorilla experiment, this means that we can easily overlook positive reactions even though they are in plain sight.

We do not see them because depressed people's attention is simply not directed towards positive reactions. In this way, depression becomes self-perpetuating. We end up being locked into an incomplete understanding of ourselves or the surrounding world because attention is limited. We will not naturally seek or notice positive experiences but, rather, focus will be on the negative. If we expect something, the likelihood of experiencing what we expect increases. Our attention is drawn towards the elements that confirm our basic understanding of coherences in the world. This is central to most depressed people, who, as mentioned earlier, have a negative expectation of themselves and of the world around them. Their negative expectations not only cause them to have so-called 'inattentional blindness', but they are also at risk of believing in more negative fallacies.

The *Thinking Brain* and the brain's *Alarm Centre*

Different emotional reactions activate different parts of the brain. When we feel threatened, the brain's *Alarm Centre* is activated. A threat towards the self can be activated by various circumstances. People react differently. This means that the same circumstances may elicit different emotional reactions, depending on who you are. When we feel threatened we react with fear, sadness or anger. When these emotions are present, the primitive parts of the brain are activated. Our behaviour becomes more automatic, that is, we react without thinking about our actions. The more intense the emotion, the less reflection about how we react. The part of the brain we use for reflection shuts down and the primitive parts of the brain take over. The primitive parts of the brain that are activated in this context are known as the brain's *Alarm Centre*. When we meet people who are unrealistic in their thought patterns, for instance with fear or depression, a natural response is to try to speak to their common sense. In theory, it makes good sense that irrationality or distortion must be countered with common sense. It is a problem, though, if someone is influenced by intense emotions. A common way of referring to this is to say that they are 'choked-up' with emotion. If we are very scared, angry or sad, it may hinder our access to the *Thinking Brain*. This was eye-opening for the girls. At various times, they had all experienced feeling stupid when they could not think clearly or could not follow their lessons in class. We spoke about ways in which they could calm down the brain's *Alarm Centre*. They were given the task of going back home and discussing with family and friends the best ways they could help the brain's *Alarm Centre* calm down in situations where it was being activated by intense emotions. In my work as a psychologist, I constantly use illustrations of the *Thinking Brain* and the brain's *Alarm Centre*, not only with youths but also with their network, family and professionals. In this way, they get a deeper understanding of why they react the way they do. To parents and networks, it not only provides a better understanding of the reactions they witness, but also serves as a good foundation for talking about how they can best support their young people.

The brain's pharmacy

Brain scans reveal differences in the brains of people with depression, which can be moderated with medicine. Several of the girls in the group were acquainted with the effectiveness of medicine in its capacity to influence state of mind and ease depressive symptoms, but they had no idea that we each possess our own pharmacy, which can be operated through our behaviour. The body has its own happy pills, consisting of various hormones and neurotransmitters. Through activity and being together with others, we can activate the brain to release neurotransmitters that can help calm the brain and produce happiness. We also know that exercise can have a positive influence on the brain. Similarly, we can avoid certain activities that have a negative influence on the brain and increase the brain's stress level. The girls in the group had all felt a tendency to isolate themselves when they felt low. They would lose the inclination to be with others and pulled away from family and friends. In the group, we spoke about ways in which they could each use the knowledge we have about the brain to plan their activities, and thus activate the brain's own pharmacy. When we are in a state of depression, we often lose both the inclination and the initiative to do things. At the same time, we are influenced by a distorted thought pattern. When we spoke about the chemical processes in the brain, the girls found it easy to relate to the arguments. They, and their depression, did not distort the information they were receiving about the brain's processes – nothing personal is at stake when discussing the mechanics of the situation and there is no question of right or wrong, but rather, a number of facts that may be useful. These facts are so useful that we have come to learn how we can avoid the activation of states such as shame and guilt. Those states are characterised by strong emotions and automatic negative thinking about the self. As previously mentioned, we know that strong emotional states activate the brain's *Alarm Centre*, which hinders us in reaching new insights. When we teach about the brain, it is important to adjust the information for the audience. There is a difference in the language that is suitable for a young person versus that for a parent, who may have an academic background. When I teach about the brain it is always with purpose. The brain is very complicated and I have to take care that the point I wish to emphasise does not drown in academic jargon and complicated connections. I usually say as little as possible, in order not to patronise parents. For example, I sometimes say that the brain is very complicated and that the explanation I give is a simplification of the brain's functions. My experience is that keeping explanations fairly simple works best for most people, and I use professional terms only if absolutely necessary.

When thoughts take over

We have thoughts pretty much all the time. Sometimes thoughts dominate a lot and sometimes less. We all know the condition of having thoughts that do not completely match objective reality. We know it, for instance, from superstition.

If a black cat crosses the road, we may consider whether or not to spit over our shoulder. Most of us are able to push superstitious thought to one side. We adjust our thoughts in accord with reality and question the truth-value of our thinking. Our thoughts and emotions are closely connected. The intensity of the emotion that is connected to our thoughts has a great influence on how effortlessly, or not, we are able to adjust our thoughts. It is obviously not only the emotion connected to the thinking that influences how easily we adjust our thinking. Our brains function in different ways, and, according to our cognitive levels, we can be more or less rigid in our ways of thinking. If very strong emotions are connected to a particular thought, we will experience it as something more real and important, no matter whether it is positive or negative. We are simply wired to believe in the thought. The danger of this is that we may start to mistake thoughts for facts. When this happens, we typically allow our thoughts to control us, and even if we wished for it, there would be no easy way for us to push the thoughts away or shift our mindset. When someone has depression, their thinking is very negative. Depression is simultaneously characterised by strong negative emotions that cause us to experience thoughts as more real, which, in turn, governs our behaviour and mood.

In the group, we practised many different exercises that could make us wiser with regard to our thoughts. We read *The story of a mind train*, which brilliantly depicts how we can be consumed by our thoughts. We spoke about how this can be experienced in depression as an engine driver that drives us away. We become one with the depression and cannot see the opportunities open to us to get off the train. In the group, we played with thoughts about moving the engine driver out of his seat, letting the girls drive the train themselves instead. The depressive thoughts were noisy passengers, irritatingly noisy, but still not the ones in charge. We spoke about practising ignoring the noisy passengers and perhaps even throwing them out of the train because of their bad behaviour. This seemed to be an engaging way for the girls to talk about their depressive thoughts, enabling them to observe the thoughts from the outside. When externalising their thoughts in this way, it became easier to speak about them without engaging emotionally with the thoughts.

In another exercise, we read the story of the *House of Thoughts* as a starting point. First, the story was read aloud to the girls and then they were asked to draw their own Thought-Houses. For the exercise, they were each provided with a sheet of white paper, pencils and a lot of magazines from which they could cut out images that appealed to them. Most of them found it difficult to get started, but as soon as they did they became very engaged. Everybody managed to create a house. The houses were very different and very personal. When the girls had finished their houses, they presented them to the others in the group. It was striking that even though the girls were affected by their depressive negative thinking, all of them also had positive rooms represented in their houses. During the presentation of the houses, it became clear to many of the girls that entering a room was connected to a choice. They could control in which room they wanted to be. Some rooms were easier to enter than others. Some rooms were difficult to leave, but there was a choice.

Realising the possibility of choice is an important step towards creating change in our lives – for the girls, this was to get out of depression.

To be present and accept what is

In each session, we conducted different meditation exercises (mindfulness exercises). We tried body-scan exercises and various guided meditations of differing lengths of time. The aim of the formal meditations was to become attentive towards internal activity in the here and now – and become aware of what we are doing. By focusing on a single element, for instance the breath, thoughts or bodily sensations, we increase our awareness of what takes place within us. At the same time, we become increasingly aware of how often our attention slips away from what we are determined to focus on. We are easily seduced by a thought, a sensation in the body, a sound or something completely different. Sometimes a long time passes before we even realise that we are not paying attention where we thought we would. It is exactly when we are no longer conscious of our actions that we run into the danger of turning on the autopilot. In principle, there is nothing wrong with being on autopilot. In some cases, it is quite practical to act without spending too much mental energy on it. The purpose of mindfulness exercises is not to take us permanently away from the autopilot. Still, in mindfulness we practise discovering when we are there and we make it a conscious choice. When we act automatically, the risk of unconsciously repeating unfortunate thought and behaviour patterns increases. This, we would like to avoid.

In the group, we began each session with a mindfulness exercise. Often it was a short five-minute meditation with the purpose of becoming present in the room and mentally preparing ourselves to be there. This was a good way to silence the list of duties rumbling in our heads or the thoughts about what we did earlier in the day or about what we were going to do later on. We spoke about the exercises afterwards. This gave me clues as to who would need a little extra attention. We also ended the session with a short meditation each time. In this way, what we had been speaking about came to a close as the session ended. In sessions where we worked exclusively with mindfulness, we meditated for a longer period of time. I was guiding all meditations, that is, I instructed the girls in what to do throughout the meditations. We would meditate on breath, thoughts and bodily sensations. We also sat in meditations with visualisations that were designed to create a sense of strength and safety. After each meditation, we spoke about the group's experience of the exercise. Some found it very difficult. They struggled to keep their focus on the guidance. If they felt like it, they shared what had caught their attention, but this was not the most important part for them. Rather, it was important that their insights into what was taking place internally were strengthened.

A theme that is always part of feedback from meditations is acceptance. Many tend to express how they feel that they have not adequately meditated if they encountered struggles with their focus or fell sleep. This may create irritation and self-reproach. A central point in mindfulness is to accept what is, no matter the cause. This is not to be confused with having to like what is, or passively leaning back and not caring. Mindfulness is an active form of acceptance where we become aware of what is at play, accept it and thereafter decide on the most appropriate reaction. If we do not accept what is, we will often try to work against it or try to repress it or forget it. In the group, we worked on accepting depression. If we do not accept that we have depression, we will very likely not be taking good care of ourselves. None of the girls had accepted that their depression was setting up limitations for them. When we are depressed, we have to adjust the expectations we have of ourselves. If we do not do this, we will often end up with unrealistic expectations. This may lead to self-reproach, and thus depressive symptoms are maintained or reinforced. In their return to healthy capability levels of meeting expectations, the girls had to accept taking things more easily for a period of time. This was difficult for the girls when they were self-reflecting, but easy when they had to give good advice to others in the group. The mirroring they gave each other made it easier for most of them eventually to take on the same good advice.

I am the light master – the attention as a baton

A great part of mindfulness involves the conscious control of intention. To illustrate the nature of our attention, we used the image *Attention – the Brain's Spotlight*. In the theatre or at concerts spotlights are used to guide the audience's eyes towards the centre of attention. Most of the time, we focus on the activity in the spotlight's circle and we don't take much notice of what goes on elsewhere. In our own lives, our attention decides our point of focus. When we focus on something specific, there will be other elements we do not notice. Our focus is consequently determining our experience and then our experience influences how we are feeling.

To illustrate what happens when we narrow our awareness, we undertook the *Thought Bubbles* exercise. The girls were each given three sheets of paper with *Thought Bubbles* on them, and they were requested to write down a positive, a negative and a neutral thought in each of the bubbles. It could be, for example, 'I have many friends (positive thought)', 'Nobody likes me (negative thought)', 'I ate a bun and an apple for lunch (neutral thought)'. We then pinned the *Thought Bubbles* on the walls in a completely dark room. Each girl was handed a torch or a forehead light. They were then asked to place themselves in front of someone else's *Thought Bubble* – I wanted to avoid them being caught in their own negative thoughts. At the same time, I wished them to hear what others were saying about their thoughts. While the girls stood in front of a *Thought Bubble* with a torch, they were guided to notice the thoughts, emotions and bodily sensations that the *Thought Bubble* provoked in them. We shared the group's experiences afterwards. Everybody tried to stand in front of a positive, a negative and a neutral *Thought Bubble*. The difference became very visible to them.

For homework, the group were invited to look in a different direction than usual. They were to create a positive-experience calendar with which they practised becoming aware of the good things in their lives. They were supposed to write down three positive experiences every day, in a grid they had been given. Positive experiences are not necessarily big events and could just be the joy of listening to a bird singing, the delight of eating a cheese sandwich or similar. They were to relate it to their simultaneous experience of their thoughts and body. At our next meeting, we spoke about the occurrences they noted. Not everybody had found three things in their day. Some had struggled to remember about it during the day and did not look back at the day's experiences before going to bed. It became very clear that in order to notice the positive elements in their lives, they had to be very conscious. For the following week, they were once again given the task of filling out the positive-experience calendar. Through practice, it slowly became easier for the girls to become aware of the rays of comfort that a day would offer them.

Reflections concerning the group course

When I look back at the group course I find it both meaningful and fun. The group course could not stand alone as the girls' only treatment for depression. It was not designed for that. There were elements I would change and some that worked very well. Both the girls and I felt that our time together was too short. It would have been appropriate to have a bit more time in the individual sessions. We could hardly keep up with the programme I had planned for each session while also squeezing in a decent break. We could easily have spent half an hour or an hour extra per session. A long break would have allowed the girls to get to know each other better, in an informal way.

The group's size of four turned out to be just right. It would have worked with one or two more, but the number of participants made it possible to create an intimate atmosphere at the same time, as there were enough of them to form a group. My initial reason for creating a group was to introduce mindfulness to young people. I believe that adding mindfulness to a framework where it was combined with other approaches worked very well. The exercises supplemented one another nicely. The combination of learning about the brain and the more experience-oriented meditations and exercises was very valuable. In this way, learning occurred on many different levels and we engaged many different senses throughout our exercises together. It was a helpful supplement to the traditional conversation-therapeutic approach that the group-members experienced in their individual therapy sessions. There was certainly repetition of therapeutic principles about the coherence between thoughts and emotions, but we dealt with it differently. The positive effect on the girls' depression was noticeable, due to the creativity that we all contributed to in the group. The creativity made the material from The Resilience Programme and from mindfulness more alive and personal, which positively influenced the learning. We had fun and we were serious.

We used our bodies and our brains. We were challenged on many different levels, and we did it all together. We were facing the difficult moments together – and we worked together in finding strategies to make things better.

Reference

Most SB, Simons DJ, Scholl BJ, Jimenez R, Clifford E & Chabris CF (2001) How not to be seen: the contribution of similarity and selective ignoring to sustained inattentional blindness. *Psychological Science.* 12(1):9–17.

Chapter 7

Appropriate challenges in a special needs school

Joan Dammeyer

The class, which is my starting point in this chapter, consists of a group of intellectually disabled pupils in a special needs school. The school operates using a broad concept of learning so as to ensure that all the school's pupils are provided with possibilities to develop in relation to their diverse competences and challenges. If, for a moment, we reflect on the term intellectual disability, we will find that it covers a group of people with widely distinct diagnoses and a very high spread across the cognitive, linguistic and academic spectrums. Common to all is the fact that they are constantly developing and are far from merely being disabled. I was teaching this special needs class and, in the class, I worked over a long period of time with thoughts, emotions and attention. I have built a shared language in the class about something that can be highly abstract, especially for this group of pupils. When I chose to put resilience on the agenda it was, among other things, because I wanted a deeper insight into how much the pupils would be able to learn to mentalise; that is, understand their own and others' thoughts and emotions. For instance:

- What are thoughts, emotions and attention?
- What happens in my brain when I become happy, angry, annoyed or sad?
- What do other people think about me when my emotions totally take over?
- Can I become better at regulating my emotions?
- Can I use strategies when emotions take over?
- Can I become better at understanding and give space to my classmates' challenges and differences?
- Can I become a bit more resilient?

The Thought-Tree

In class, we drew big *Thought Bubbles* on paper and held them over our heads – as we see in comic strips. In this way, the pupils tried to guess each other's thoughts through short role-plays: 'When Jeremy acts as if he is tired, what is he most likely thinking about?', 'When Jeremy has not eaten breakfast before school, what thoughts could you guess he has?', 'When a new chauffeur, whom Jeremy does not know, is driving him to school, which thoughts do you think come to his mind?'

We hung a masonite board on one of the walls in class and painted a huge tree on it. Every time we talked about a new subject, we used the tree as a board on which the pupils would place word-cards. One of the pupils quickly named the tree the 'Thought-Tree'. On the table we had *Thought Bubbles*, cardboard pieces of various sizes, forms and colours, ready to be placed on the tree. While we worked on discovering our invisible thoughts, the pupils were lying on big mattresses with pillows and blankets and listening to tranquil classical music. After this, everybody sat at the table and took turns telling us about a thought they had encountered while listening to the music. Each found a cardboard *Thought Bubble* that best fitted their thought. I was very conscious that, for some, their selection was random, and that for others, it was carefully considered. Some were able to write out their thoughts on their own and others received help with spelling. From there, their *Thought Bubbles* were placed on the Thought-Tree: happiness, my cat, mom and dad, confirmation, swinging high, a good friend, lovers, movies, football, weekend-cosiness in pyjamas, a day without conflict, etc. Finally, I pointed to one thought at a time and asked, 'Who thought this thought?', thereby finding an author for each thought.

The next day, the class repeated the session, now with more dramatic classical music. Big emotions were activated and some even became a bit scared. They were reminded of different instances, such as: when a ram once ran after some of them at a camp; when a helper fell into the water with his clothes on; missing mom and dad; grandfather dying; a busy morning without breakfast. We pinned the thoughts onto the Thought-Tree again and gave them the same attention as we did the day before. I told a simple version of the story of the *House of Thoughts*. The story illustrates through imagery that it is possible to practise shifting our attention from one room to another. At the table, we had cardboard and a small illustration of how they could draw a house, and everybody started drawing their personal *House of Thoughts*. Some houses had many tiny rooms, others only a few, some houses had several floors and some had a balcony and flower-boxes.

Thoughts with door plaques

The pupils came up with the idea that several thoughts could like one room in the *House of Thoughts* and quickly became preoccupied with creating door plaques for all the rooms. One of the pupils called one of her rooms the Music Room. In there, many *Thought Bubbles* lived, bearing the names of different music idols. Each day, when she came home from school, music was the first thing she thought about. Another pupil asked for help in spelling the Missing Room, because she always missed her mom and dad when she went to respite care. She then moved these *Thought Bubbles* into that room: 'mom and dad', 'grandmother', 'grandfather', 'Fido, her dog'. Many of the children made space for a big Family

Room because family means a great deal to them. Others drew a Friend Room, Lovers' Room, Fashion Room, McDonald's Room and Candy Room. When the pupils named their thought-rooms, they thought about their own thoughts, that is, they trained themselves in what it is to mentalise. When the pupils then presented their thought-rooms to one another, they became aware not only of their own thoughts, but of each other's, which is crucial in gaining insight and compassion towards one another in class. If a pupil, for instance, missed her mom and dad, a classmate would come to meet her and say, 'I guess you're in the Missing Room now. Will you join us for a game of Uno, then you might come over to the Friend Room and be happy again?' The pupils mentalised by reflecting on their classmates' thoughts and emotions, and empathy arose, giving rise to possibilities for action.

Sixteen years externally and 3 years internally

To think thoughts about thoughts requires a certain level of cognition. All children 3–4 years of age have brains that are not yet sufficiently developed for them to realise that something invisible and of great significance is going on inside their brain and in their peers' brains.

In line with the brain developing, it becomes possible to talk about invisible thought processes. It becomes possible to practise feelings and observing thoughts and emotions without having to act upon them as soon as they arise. We can organise and choose to act upon specific thoughts, while others drift by like clouds. In the long term, this can help us become less impulsive and more resilient.

At this school, all pupils are challenged by the fact that their physical age does not equate to their cognitive level. It can be very challenging to be 16 years old physically and 3 years old intellectually. The ability to mentalise is an extremely advanced cognitive function, and people with limited cognitive capacity therefore find it harder to mentalise. Some researchers presume that the delayed and reduced development of our capacity to mentalise is related to the fundamental disability in autism spectrum disorders (Fonagy et al., 2005). Children with these types of disorders have difficulties reading other people and are therefore challenged in communication and relations. Pupils with ADHD are often in a state of high alert and stress, and have similar difficulties in mentalising even though their ability to mentalise can be completely normal. No matter the disability, everybody will be challenged to mentalise when thrown out of balance emotionally. Therefore, it is also critical that the people around these children, including the professionals, have the ability to mentalise. The pupils must be presented with appropriate challenges, requirements and expectations. The requirements should not be too big, as this would not support resilience but rather may create vulnerability and weakness. The requirements should not be too small either, because development could halt. The bigger the disproportion between the pupils' capacity and what is required from them, the bigger the risk for unfortunate behaviour patterns.

Where is the torch pointing?

In class, we had spoken a lot about ADHD as a state where it can be extra challenging to control the *Attention – the Brain's Spotlight*. We can use a huge amount of energy trying to focus, which has the consequential effect of feeling overworked. In this case, the spotlight swings uncontrollably in the air with its cone of light and catches all inputs without any kind of filter. When a pupil, for example, requested to pull down the curtains, it was a clear signal for me, as a teacher, that there was a need for me to help control the attention (the torch) better for a moment.

As a means of making the attention challenge more visual and developing a language around it, we came up with an exercise where each pupil was provided with a forehead lamp and challenged to walk down into the school's cellar, where it is pitch-dark. The cellar room was filled with old furniture, boxes and various materials. It was cold, smelly and mouldy. On one side, there was a small passage where the pupils could walk hand-in-hand, one after the other. What the pupils did not know was that I had asked the class assistant to hide in one of the rooms in the cellar. The moment the class entered the dark room, lights were swirling from the pupils' head-lamps. The light cones directly revealed what caught their attention. Some had their head-lamp turned down towards their feet in order not to bump into anything along the way. Others had their head-lamp turned towards strange things in the dark. Others again were busy with their breath and the sounds being uttered, and sometimes suddenly the light cones would point directly to a classmate's head.

Just as we moved around, and just as everybody became highly engrossed in what they were focusing on, something happened. Suddenly the assistant started yelling out loud, a high-pitched sound of alarm. Everybody was startled. Some were excited, while others jumped into one another's arms. The interesting part was to observe the light cones, which suddenly were all pointing in the same direction. The ceiling-light was then quickly turned on and we laughed and shrieked and cheered. Then, we realised that there were no ghosts in the cellar. Right then, an expression popped up, baptising our 'attention' as: 'Torch'. There is no doubt that this is a story the pupils have recounted many times. At one of the walks with the class, a long time after this activity, I was asked what actually happens if a girl from the class doesn't take her ADHD medicine. While I was still considering my answer, another pupil said straight away, 'Then, she cannot control her torch!'

Mindfulness

One of the activities we can engage in to create peace in the body, thoughts and emotions is to put mindfulness on the agenda. We did this for an entire year. The pupils would sit or lie down with blankets in the classroom and everybody would be offered a warm stone to hold in their hands, while we explored mindfulness for about 20 minutes. The pupils would place their stone on their stomachs, on their cheeks, over their eyes or pat it around their bodies. This helped some to feel safe enough to close their eyes, while others couldn't stand it. Everything was okay. I would guide them through a body scan, asking them to focus and move their attention around their bodies. For some, this was too difficult and then it just became a quiet moment for them in the midst of a long school day. For others, the exercise became easier, step by step: how they could practise feeling a knee, for example, the warmth in a hand, the beating of their heart, lungs that pumped air through their bodies, etc. Several of them also came to realise that our attention is disturbed again and again by car noises in the parking lot, a stomach that rumbles, a creaking door, etc. I would always reassure them that it was fine if their attention happened to shift, and that they could just shift their attention back to their breathing if that happened. I would explain that our breath is like an anchor that is always there to give peace to the body, especially in moments when we experience something difficult.

Often, we have the experience of handling epileptic attacks in class. But once, there was a girl who experienced it for the first time. She got scared and we had to comfort her, care for and protect her, and we helped her by having her lie down on a couch in a quiet room. I then started doing what we as adults often end up trying to do: I was talking her back into a state of peace. It did not help her, though. She cried, hyperventilated and was miserable. Suddenly I realised what I had forgotten – to focus on deep breathing. I took her hand, placed it on her stomach and asked her to breathe deeply with her belly while I did the same. I mirrored her without speaking. After a minute or so, she became calm. Now she knew, and the staff discovered, what would work for her, in the future.

The *Thinking Brain* and the brain's *Alarm Centre*

We have spoken in class about situations where pupils become angry, annoyed, disappointed or feel left out from the community. We all knew that in these moments, the brain's *Alarm Centre* takes over and that the *Thinking Brain* simultaneously shuts down, preventing us from being able to reflect, or listen, or cooperate. In these moments, we all need peace. The whole concept is quite simple to grasp, in fact, because when the intensity of emotions rises, the ability to think is tuned down. When the brain's *Alarm Centre* calms, the *Thinking Brain* can be turned on again. When our children experience the brain's *Alarm Centre* taking over, they do not sense anything but their emotions. It is only when they can find peace, care and protection that they slowly begin to calm down. And, after a while, this opens the *Thinking Brain* again. I experienced many variations of this process, and how long it can take. For some, it may even take most of a day, while others calm down faster.

Once, I bought a snow globe for the class as a means to help explain how things are when chaos reigns in the brain (the snow in the glass ball takes time to hit the ground). I used it to explain to the pupils that when the brain's *Alarm Centre* fully takes over, things in the brain become like the snow moving about wildly and fast inside the snow globe. After some time, just as in the brain, the snow gently falls and finds its peaceful resting place. Then, the *Thinking Brain* fires up again. This had an eye-opening effect on them, and especially on one of the pupils diagnosed with ADHD. Her reaction was, 'Now I understand why it becomes so difficult for me. It's my brain that really has a hard time, it's not me at all who's wrong or stupid!'

What is the easiest way to return to the *Thinking Brain*?

All pupils had been interviewed about how they experience things when the brain's *Alarm Centre* takes over, and what the best way for them to get back to the *Thinking Brain* might be. Their answers were compiled visually in an image with the *Thinking Brain* and the brain's *Alarm Centre*. This has become a central piece of our work with the children and is continuously updated. Often, pupils have added new strategies to help them in difficult moments. The pupils also received a copy of the image that they could take home as a kind of eye-opener for parents and supporters. A boy who faces many complicated challenges had been inter-viewed for this activity. He was having a really hard time when relocating between the school and the after-school club, because the shift often stressed him. In these periods, he would react violently, and he was unfortunately rather familiar with forceful intervention. At times, he almost couldn't stand any type of unpredict-ability or demands, which could come in the form of a very small comment or a shift in regular procedure. I asked him what he was experiencing when the brain's *Alarm Centre* took over. He answered, 'My brain switches off and my body takes over. My body stings on the outside. I don't bother. I say: "go away". I smash things when I'm really angry and I start screaming and swearing really loud. I can hit myself and run away, but I don't touch other people as long as they keep their hands off me.' Then, I asked him how he returns to the *Thinking Brain*. He answered, 'Adults must listen the first time when I say that "my head doesn't work" and then the others know I need some peace. I like to get away from everything and just go for a bit of a drive, as long as there's good radio music. I like to go to the playground or to visit the sports centre. I become calmer when I drink a cup of coffee. Adults should not touch me when I'm angry, but afterwards, when I feel a bit better it's okay that someone special gives me a hug.' The boy was very immediate in his formulations. This is an example of how our pupils often hold the key to what can help them.

Another example is with one of the other pupils who has a wider emotional registry. She can feel stressed, for instance, by the unpredictability of when people come together, even in a small gathering. She regresses when something confuses her. She can suddenly pull out from a lesson because the brain's *Alarm Centre* shuts down the *Thinking Brain*, causing her to stop participating in any class activity, often refusing to rejoin. One day she shared that she had found a smart way to control her emotions. When she started struggling, she said that she would imagine a box in her belly. In the box, she explained that there is a nice carpet, a red sofa, a beautiful chandelier, nice paintings on the side, etc., and that it is warm and cosy, with a very nice atmosphere: 'When I feel bad, I practise putting all the bad thoughts into the box and close the lid. After a while, my thoughts start to feel better – but I have to practise, because it's difficult. My dad says I must practise many, many times.'

Fields of Practice

One Friday, in the first module, the timetable specified 'calendar' and 'new *Fields of Practice*'. Everybody was offered a green *Thought Bubble* on an A5 sheet, with two questions on it: 'What have I become better at this week?' and 'What should be my *Field of Practice* for the coming week?'

Every Friday we would evaluate the week, individually – all nine pupils, talking about what had worked better for them from the previous week. Anything could be counted, for instance writing letters correctly on a line, working with a specific reading app, practising numbers from 15 to 20, remembering to put the lunch boxes in the fridge, retreating to the playground instead of getting into conflicts with a friend, etc. At the bottom of the *Thought Bubble*, a new *Field of Practice* for the week ahead would be formulated, and evaluated on the following Friday. Often, the pupils came up with their own ideas for their next practice, or, for those who needed a bit of help, staff always had good suggestions at hand. For example, this could include learning to use a new app, practising the donkey-game or working with academic content. With their individual iPads, every student took a photo of their *Thought Bubble* which they then inserted in their digital diaries – an alternative contact-book that allows for pictures, video or sound tracks to be recorded.[1]

The *Thought Bubbles* make the learning processes visible and they function as a portfolio for each pupil's development. At the same time, they give pupils a sense of pride and ownership. All *Fields of Practice* are written on an A4 sheet and are then compiled into a shared reading sheet on the class's smartboard. When a pupil has presented her/his *Field of Practice*, the classmates snap their fingers in acknowledgement and thereby show that they recognise the practice it takes to reach the goal. This supports them to keep focusing over a longer time span. Exactly this shared awareness is very powerful. The pupils often comment on each other's *Field of Practice*. They do this in cases where they succeed as well as in cases where someone has forgotten their *Field of Practice*. The exercises must be fun, and it is said that it is necessary to practise for 10,000 hours in order to become really good at something – this amounts to practising four hours per day, for seven years. Still, less than that will do.

When the pupils are challenged appropriately, that is, with requirements they can master accurately, they develop the most. We should, as staff and parents, make an effort to offer appropriate requirements – neither too big nor too small

– and, at the same time, closely watch the individual's daily state of mind. Even though a *Field of Practice* may have been a bit difficult and demanding for a longer period of time, it is a victory to learn something new. It is crucial for pupils to be motivated and to feel acknowledged when they keep practising towards reaching their goal. It gives them confidence and an urge to learn – also the difficult stuff. Over time, the pupils build resilience when they are aware that it is necessary to practise many times in order to master something. I usually tell the class's parents at the school–home conversations that their children must be pushed towards 'standing on their toes' in the sense that they are just able to see their learning objective faintly over the horizon. At the same time, it is just as important that they do not have to 'jump' all the time in order to see their learning objective, as this would impede their motivation and their wish to learn. It is important that those around each child become aware of the child's accelerator and brakes. It is also crucial that the practice takes place within safe relationships and that this is supported by communication that is acknowledging; then the children are able to find appropriate challenges on a personal, academic and social level. The bigger the mismatch between what we can handle and what is demanded, the faster unfortunate behavioural patterns develop. If pupils are repeatedly exposed to situations they cannot cope with, they do not become resilient but rather vulnerable and alarmed.

Resilience has its limits, and the limits vary individually. It is vital to know the individual pupil and notice the circumstances at play, each day. Even a forgotten lunch box may turn the day around for one pupil, while another may not care. Simultaneously, it is central for me to learn about the class's pupils and their parents so as to be able to handle any uneasiness or insecurities, because this is the state in which we can actually develop resilience. If life is never challenging because parents or staff are overprotective or require too little, a child will not become resilient but will remain vulnerable. Resilience is developed only because we discover that we can handle something that we could almost not handle before we practised doing it.

I have no doubt that it has meant a lot to the pupils that they tried feeling, physically, what attention is, by entering a dark cellar with forehead-lamps. They felt and experienced in their own bodies how hard it may be to be in control of their attention. They felt that something was constantly trying to grip and pull their attention: elements from outside stimuli, such as sounds, smells and friends, as well as internal signals from their bodies in the form of a beating heart or breath, as well as from inside their heads, in the form of thoughts and emotions. Something difficult became very concrete and understandable. When the experience is strong, it becomes easy to translate into imagery. The intellectually disabled pupils have, to varying degrees, developed ways of acting and have gained insight into how they can take care of themselves. They have also become wiser as to what they can do when a classmate is struggling. All these pupils have reduced abilities to mentalise. The simple language and the simple images in regard to the mechanisms of the brain have had a huge impact on our pupils when they have had to understand what takes place when somebody enters a state of affect. In addition, the imagery has also supported the development of empathy and curiosity towards differences that exist among others – no matter how different others can be: nerdy, straight, kooky or outlandish. Through this, resilient communities are developed.

Example of an individual case

Kim is a young man who finished the 10th grade in the special needs school. He has been severely challenged due to complicated diagnoses and fierce emotional outbursts. The consequences have been critical, resulting in an interrupted boarding-school year, followed by an interrupted so-called 'specially arranged education' (SAE). In this same period, Kim's parents divorced. It was around this time as well that Kim was also a member of a youth club, frequented by other young people who have general learning disabilities. Being a member of this club was a part of his SAE, and when he was not allowed to finish his SAE education, this offer was also cancelled. He and his family felt pressured, to an extreme level. The club's leader asked me whether I could offer four one-hour sessions to Kim, where I could teach him about mentalising, in order to help better equip him mentally, prior to him leaving the club and moving to another activity centre with new staff and new members. We agreed on one hour per week, which would give Kim time to practise and work with all the challenges he was facing in this period. The aim was to prepare Kim for a good start in the new places he would have to switch to, and at the same time provide his new activity centre with information the staff could use to support him. Upon completion of the sessions, I decided there should be a meeting with the club's leader, a contact pedagogue, Kim's parents and the activity centre. Kim and I could then pass on what we had been working with.

Kim had looked forward to the sessions. In the first hour, I presented him with the *Thinking Brain* and the brain's *Alarm Centre*, showing him laminated images in an A3 format. Kim told me that he experienced being in the *Thinking Brain* most of the time. I chose to add small yellow Post-Its at the brain's *Alarm Centre* every time Kim came up with an example where he had been angry, worried or insecure and had been shouting. By doing this, my hope was that I could make Kim slowly realise that his brain's *Alarm Centre* was particularly sensitive. With time, more and more Post-Its were attached to the brain's *Alarm Centre*, for example in relation to relocation, change of timetable, duties, etc. At some point, Kim had suddenly exclaimed: 'My brain has cheated on me! I believed I was mostly in the *Thinking Brain* but I am indeed in the brain's *Alarm Centre* often.' I showed Kim the snow globe, told him about it and asked him what could be done in order to help him back to his *Thinking Brain*. I wrote all statements down on a piece of paper. Every time Kim came up with new examples throughout our four sessions, we updated the paper, making it into a kind of script for the new activity centre. I told him about the importance of letting 'the snow fall to the ground' and finding control of his volume button as a means of practising tuning things down himself when his emotions started running away with him. I designed a *Field of Practice* for Kim as an exercise for the next session; he was to learn to breathe deeply with the support of a mindfulness app. Together, we listened to one of the short meditations the app offers. He then promised to practise the exercise throughout the next week. The day after that session, I received a text message that he had already practised five times that same day.

In our second session, Kim explained that he had not used the app for the previous couple of days because, 'Now I know all the lines. I have actually been breathing deep into my stomach all the way here, in the car with my mother.' I told him that what he had done was fantastic, because there could come a day when he might lose his mobile phone, or it runs out of battery, but that even if this were to happen, on his own, he could do the exercise. So he could just do it anytime and anywhere. Kim was happy that he had found a smart way to practise breathing. I told him that there is a kind of broadband connection between the brain's *Alarm System* and the heart, and that's when Kim declared, 'It is like the brain's *Alarm System* sends a text message to the heart: we have problems, I am angry now, and then the heart starts beating wildly. Then, when I breathe deeply several times, the heart sends a text message back: just take it easy.' There was no doubt, in this situation, that he was actually thinking thoughts about thoughts. I read the story of the *House of Thoughts* to him and explained that we have many useful thoughts as well as some thoughts we cannot use, and even some that may be damaging to us. I asked Kim whether he could recall days where he might have been mostly thinking sad thoughts. He knew that very well. I told him about *Attention – the Brain's Spotlight* while he was sitting with a torch and a green and a grey *Thought Bubble* in front of him. I clarified that the torch is like a theatre's lighting director who controls where a spotlight should point to and how everything outside the spotlight stays in darkness. I gave Kim a *Field of Practice* for the following session, which was that he should practise smiling at one of the members of staff in the club he had been angry with for a week and try to focus on everything positive he could possibly think of about this person.

In our third session, Kim happily told me that he had smiled and even spoken to the person he had been angry with for a long time. Kim excitedly expressed that he was very happy they had chatted because this person was fun to be with and he would be missing that if they never got to speak again. I explained that when we smile at others and show kindness, they are urged to smile back. Smiles are infectious, and it is beneficial to get better at saying 'it's not all that important after all'. Kim figured that he essentially always has a choice – a choice between remaining in the *Thinking Brain* or the brain's *Alarm Centre*. This prompted me to draw a volume button on a red piece of cardboard, which I cut out. Around the volume button I wrote some of the opportunities for action we had been through: mindfulness, breathing deeply, letting the snow fall, using the app, saying 'it's not all that important after all' and 'I have a choice'. The *Field of Practice* Kim was assigned for the following week entailed practising using the volume button in regulating his emotions and also that he should continue with his breathing exercises. This time, I asked him to keep his focus on his finger, to place it under his nose so as to make him aware of the air's cold temperature while inhaling, then placing his hand over his mouth when exhaling, thus becoming aware of how the air became warm. He was given an additional *Field of Practice* where, at bedtime, he should listen to a meditation that focused on breathing and thinking nice thoughts before sleeping. Kim was also provided with three green *Thought Bubbles* that he could place beside his bed.

Just prior to our last session, Kim was experiencing a day of struggle. He was in the brain's *Alarm Centre* because he had become confused about the day's programmed activities, at the new activity centre where he had also started an internship. A 'rhino-piece' was placed on the programme board, indicating that something entirely different (unplanned) was to take place – in this case, an external visitor was to come. Kim was not familiar with the use of the 'rhino-piece' and he had not been able to control the volume button. He had become both annoyed and enraged and the torch had only shed light onto his dark thoughts. In this moment, Kim had not managed to breathe deeply, and instead, he had run out into the hall, in search of one of the staff members he liked. It was not until he had spoken to this adult that Kim was able to sit down, in a good chair, and start to breathe calmly. We reflected upon the fact that it was a positive thing that he knew there was help to be found from a specific adult, and that he should just keep practising and eventually, next time, he would manage to catch himself at the point just before being triggered, and would start inhaling deeply, keeping a focus on sensing the cold and warm air travelling in and out. We spoke about how long it takes to practise something difficult and also that it takes time to learn to wash your hands, for instance, to brush your teeth, ride a bike and read. We have to practise a long time when something is difficult.

At the final meeting with Kim's network, Kim presented a kind of script and explained, 'What makes me go from the *Thinking Brain* to the brain's *Alarm Centre*?':

- When the day is tiresome
- When I get confused
- When something does not work
- When somebody says something that is not true
- When somebody interferes
- To-do's and duties that I do not like
- When I become angry at my mom and dad
- When mom and dad disagree
- When somebody scolds me.

And, 'What can bring me back to the *Thinking Brain*?':

- I can breathe deeply 20 times
- I can listen to my app

- I can turn down the volume button and wait for the snow to fall
- I can lower my voice
- I can think, 'I have a choice'
- I can say, 'it's not all that important after all'
- I can practise turning the spotlight
- I can go to my room
- I can speak to an adult
- It's okay for mom to ask, 'What's the matter?'
- I can make a cup of coffee after a little while
- I can call my dad
- I can practise smiling at the one I have been angry with and get on with life.

Reflections about Kim's sessions

The praxis story about Kim is an example of the work we can do in regard to thinking about our own thoughts as well as other people's thoughts. Because of my experience with Kim, I have often thought that since he was able to get so far in his capacity to mentalise with just four hours of session time together, there is tremendous hope for many others who are in a much better position to mentalise. Kim learnt that there are several resilience buttons we can turn and that it is crucial to practise our control of the volume button, first and foremost, by breathing deeply with the stomach. He learnt that breathing always opens up an opportunity for him to use, like an anchor, to grip whatever moment he finds himself in. Kim learnt how to make his heart send a 'text message' to his brain's *Alarm Centre* and activate the volume button.

I gained insight into the effectiveness of creating a script for a person's emotional regulation as a tool, and not to waste valuable time – in this case, for whenever a young person is relocated in the system and new staff must hastily learn what works in times of rising conflict. There is no doubt that our knowledge about resilience and mentalisation, communicated in everyday language, is very effective. It immediately points precisely to all that takes place inside the brain. It is a way to integrate acknowledgement into developmental work, when we talk about the images of the brain and *Thought Bubbles* as a kind of shared objectivity that is externalised. The method has given Kim a lot of hope and belief that moving on will be okay.

A course for siblings

In the following praxis stories, focus is turned towards another target group – still involving the disability perspective; this time, within families. The Resilience Programme becomes the point of reference in a case where our school offers courses to siblings of the disabled, where they are provided with an opportunity to meet, in an inclusive community, and feel that they are not alone. There is a lot of value in people belonging to a community where they are being seen, heard and acknowledged. Many siblings of the disabled feel that their needs and emotions go unnoticed in the family because the parents do not have the extra energy required to go to the cinema or football matches when a sibling has gone through his fourth convulsive fit that day, for example. Siblings of the disabled easily end up in the shadows of their disabled brothers or sisters. Sibling courses are offered to children aged 7–14, serving as a safe space for reflection where they can express dilemmas and where it is okay to have any type of thought: loving, but also angry thoughts, thoughts about jealousy and heavy thoughts about wishing our brother to be far away.

For these siblings, it is vital to find different ways to cope with challenges. The course lasts for three sessions and is arranged by an external special needs pedagogical consultant, and me. After the course, we have a one-hour evaluation meeting with each pair of parents as well as a follow-up session with all siblings, about six weeks later. We start every session at a nicely set table with a white tablecloth and candles. We eat together and ensure that all siblings get the feeling of being the centre of the 'party'. At some point in the course, we are visited by a big sister, 22 years old, who has three brothers with varying degrees of autism. She shares her experiences of growing up with brothers who are all diagnosed, and her focus is to share the thoughts and feelings she had as a child, and reflect on them as a grown-up. What helped her at that time and what could have helped her? She is an important role model for everybody on the sibling course.

Resilience and vulnerability

During the three sessions of the course, we worked within the same framework as described for the intellectually disabled pupils in the form of games, stories and small inputs concerning resilience. On the sibling course, we have more opportunities to start essential reflections and go deeper into them, and supplement them with further games and exercises, because the children come with different preconditions in their abilities to mentalise.

With the aim of making these siblings focus on how they, using their attention, can practise thinking less about what burdens them and more about what creates joy, we placed a huge layout of *Thought Bubbles* on the floor. They were cut out from canvas and were so big you that you could stand on them. There was a green *Thought Bubble* representing the happy thoughts that do us good. A grey *Thought Bubble* represented miserable thoughts that make us worried or sad. A white *Thought Bubble* represented the thoughts that are fundamental conditions in life: to go to school to learn something, to go to work to earn money, that when it rains, things get wet, etc. The children took turns to stand on the white *Thought Bubble*, where we verbalised that despite everything, it is a fundamental condition that they have a disabled brother or sister. We explained that this fundamental condition may trigger a variety of emotions depending on the thoughts they called attention to. Siblings can practise the fact that they have a choice in relation to how they paint their emotions and thoughts. Here they all tried to sense the difference when they stood on the green *Thought Bubble*, in contrast to the grey *Thought Bubble*, when they thought about the thoughts they had regarding their family.

Another way we started a reflection was with a game we call 'Fishing a Thought'. We placed laminated photos, which depicted faces showing a variety of different emotional expressions, face down on the floor. The children stood in a circle around the photos and took turns 'fishing' for an expression from the floor. This then became our starting point for conversations about when each of them last experienced the emotion they 'fished' from the floor – how the emotion felt in the body: 'When were you last angry (irritated, worried, disappointed, frustrated, scared, lonely, happy), in relation to your disabled brother/sister?' On one of the sibling courses a little boy picked a happy face and said: 'When I came to this course for the first time I thought to myself, tell me, is this paradise or what?' A girl fished a feeling with a worried face and said: 'I miss my brother since he moved to a care-home because now I am alone with my mother and before that we were three. I am also thinking about whether he is well and whether he misses me.'

'Viewed from my shoes' is a game about shifting perspectives and changing thoughts by means of a big pair of men's shoes and a pair of red high heels. The game can be used to discover how mom and dad, for instance, think about a little brother with Down's syndrome. The photos from 'Fishing a Thought' can be used in this new context. When we stand in a big pair of men's shoes, we are supposed to imagine what our father is thinking, causing some to discover new thoughts. A 10-year-old boy stood in a big pair of men's shoes and 'fished' a facial expression of a person who is frustrated. The 'father' answered after a while: 'I am so tired that my disabled boy is so fond of food because he begs for McDonald's all the time.'

How do you make a 7-year-old child understand what resilience is? As an answer, we have chosen vulnerability – the opposite of resilience – as a starting point. To evoke images in the brain, we invented a small story about sending two packages by post. One package to be sent out into the world was of a stuffed toy cat – always a fun activity on the sibling course. The stuffed cat was a tiny 'hippie cat' with peace signs on it, flowers, and its name, Curt, embroidered on its back. The other thing to be sent was a Royal Porcelain figure of a small boy sitting on a stone looking a bit lonely. We called him Edward. The two similar cardboard boxes were placed on the table and we spoke about how to send Curt in a way that would make sure he is safely transported to grandma. Curt was thrown into the box, the address was written on it and then we did not worry any longer about whether he would crack on the way. We knew he could handle anything; even if the postman sat on the box, we could say, 'go ahead, sit on the box'. In the case of Edward, things were quite different. We could not just throw him into a box. First, he had to be rolled in bubble wrap and extra-thick paper and finally we had to put a lot of flamingo pieces around him in the box so as to ensure that Edward would be able to survive bumps along the way to grandma's. On the outside of the box we wrote 'Fragile'. Still, we worried because he could still be crushed if the postman dropped the package. Not until getting a call from grandma to say thank you for the gift could we stop worrying.

This exercise led us to talk about whether we mostly feel like a Curt – resilient – or mostly like an Edward – vulnerable. The game where we stood on either the green, grey or white *Thought Bubble* was deployed again: 'Place yourself on the thought you are thinking right *now* and consider whether it is a resilient or a vulnerable thought.' Different occasions can provoke a feeling of vulnerability or resilience. We talked about how it is good to be able to allow ourselves to be both. In this way, vulnerability also becomes okay, as long as it does not stick. A boy on the course thought a bit about that and then responded, 'I actually feel quite resilient. I am often the one who is able to calm my sister down when she becomes totally unmanageable.' A girl also said, 'Resilience is when I can experience more of the fun side,' and she added, 'Resilience is about saying something in class with more ease and not caring if anybody laughs.' A bit later, when we took a tour around the school, she suddenly needed the washroom. Many doors were locked and alarmed, and she therefore had to wait until we were back in our space. But suddenly, she couldn't hold it in any longer, 'Now I really need to pee.' My colleague sensed the urgency and hurried to unlock a toilet without thinking that it turned on the school's alarm system. The girl ran into the toilet while the alarm was ringing and came out shortly afterwards with a grin, saying, 'You're resilient if you have to wildly pee and can stand an alarm without panicking.'

Resilience buttons

If you, as a sibling, have the feeling of being mostly vulnerable and sad, you can practise the activation of different resilience buttons. You can try to be more direct and commanding by uttering sentences such as: 'I would like to spend more time with mom and dad'; 'I don't feel like being with my brother every time you pick me up from football.' A resilience button can also be taking the initiative to speak with mom and dad, a grandparent, a teacher, or to text a classmate when you are stuck in some grey and miserable thoughts and find it difficult to express what you feel. Another resilience button is to state clearly what you need or wish for, without feeling bad about it, even though mom and dad are stressed and do not have the time. Likewise, a resilience button could be lowering the activity level, resting more, being more or less at home, etc. Finally, a resilience button could be a breathing exercise where you learn to breathe deeply into your stomach and focus on calm and peaceful breathing. Instead of becoming angry, you can learn to give yourself some peace, care and protection and moderate your emotions instead of allowing frustration, which may lead to outbursts.

When I explain how deep and calm breathing comforts the heart into beating slowly, because the brain's *Alarm Centre* is calmed, I also add that when I breathe deeply into my stomach, my lungs are completely filled with air before I empty them again. In this way, the lungs give the heart a hug – and calm it. After a short while, the heart is able to message back to the brain's *Alarm Centre*, 'Just take it easy, there's no reason to worry.' Some laugh at the image that the lungs give the heart a hug, but the story still gets told quite often when the children recall what they have learnt on the course.

House of Thoughts with an emergency exit

Everybody was given a torch to hold while I told the story of the *Brain's Spotlight* and how people experience the world differently through their attention. The torch was turned off and then back on, turned and rotated around, and they quickly realised that the attention was like the light from the torch. I explained to them that everybody has an '*I*' inside and that this '*I*', by means of its attention, can direct light towards a thought and rapidly move the light to another spot – another thought. The *Thought Bubbles* were lying on the floor and could be included again into this activity – 'What thoughts do I choose to shed light on? The green, grey or white thoughts?', 'I am just tired of how my brother is always noisy. He is autistic and doesn't care to listen to what my parents say. I have learnt that it doesn't make sense to take space at home when he rages.' Everybody knew the feeling of their brother or sister taking up space, both physically and mentally. This opened up a conversation about how each of them, with help from their torches, could move from a miserable thought and, instead, shed light on a happy or neutral thought.

We spent time reflecting on how we could train ourselves to control our attention and ensure that it would be our '*I*' who would more often decide what we would be thinking about. We compared it to exercising muscles in a fitness centre. Now we just had to train the '*I*'-muscle instead. Once in a while we would lose this ability because so many things can pull our attention. Still, we each could continue practising and that is how resilience would develop, because we can learn that we have a choice: 'Now I enter that worrying room again where I become uncertain whether dad and I will make it to the cinema on Saturday. But that's where I can learn to say, no thank you, worrying room, I will exit again and go into the cinema room. Then I tell my dad that he's going to the cinema no matter what, because he promised me. And if my little brother happens to get an attack that day he must come up with a plan B.'

When the story of the *House of Thoughts* was read aloud and everybody started drawing their own Thought-House filled with important stories, we emphasised that the house should always have a hall so that there could be a neutral space to enter from and into all other rooms. This point is about always creating an emergency exit. It must be possible to close the door into a thought-room and say, 'No, thank you, not today,' and then you can practise entering other thought-rooms that do you good. The spot from the torch should always be movable from one thought-room to another, and this is why the emergency exit is crucial – symbolic of having a choice. On the sibling course, the emerging thought-rooms are of a different kind from those described earlier in the chapter. For a 7-year-old girl, her Thought-House had two floors where her little sister, who has autism, occupied the entire ground floor because she takes up so much space. She demands attention and sometimes reacts physically when she is angry and stressed. The girl wrote words on the door to the little-sister-room: 'sick', 'evil', 'boring', 'curious'. On the first floor of her Thought-House, she drew a number of rooms with the following signs: 'Scared Room', 'Sad Room', 'Embarrassed Room', 'Stressed Room', 'Alone Room', 'Happy Room', and the last one she named the 'Relaxing Room'. She shares that she sometimes takes care of her little sister for half an hour while her mom and dad hurry with the shopping. She turns on the TV and makes sure her little sister is downstairs watching her favourite movie and then she goes back upstairs. Still, she is afraid that her sister will become angry with her, but doesn't tell her mom and dad. For this reason, she had both a 'Scared Room' and a 'Stressed Room' in her Thought-House. The 'Relaxing Room' meant a lot to her because as soon as mom and dad return home, she relaxes and becomes happy and relieved. When we, at the evaluation meeting with her parents, showed them the Thought-House and told them how their daughter is afraid when she is alone with her little sister, both parents were deeply touched. They had no idea their daughter felt like this, exactly because she always seems to be a strong and positive girl who likes her disabled little sister.

An 11-year-old boy drew his Thought-House as one big room and called it 'The Strange Room'. He was a somewhat immature boy who was struggling massively to navigate in a home with a brother who has ADHD and autism, and he was convinced that everything was cheating him and was unfair. His mother and father had divorced and he lived mostly with his father. He was seriously challenged in regard to controlling his own torch, and every time he got the chance, at home, he would eat or drink sodas and feel that a great injustice was being done when he was not allowed to do what he wanted. After we talked to him about his Thought-House, he drew a fridge in 'The Strange Room'. Little by little, he added more and more rooms with names such as 'Puffing Myself Up', 'I Am Bored', 'I Hit', the 'Cheating Room', the 'Game Room', and a 'Fantasy Room'. When we told his father about his Thought-House at the evaluation meeting, it opened up a very honest conversation about needs and wellbeing at home and at school. We reflected on how dad could work with the boy's experience, that his boy felt how everything was cheating him and was unfair. That became a focus, also that it is important for the two brothers no longer to continue sharing a room. The father expressed that what we had discovered made a lot of sense and he was grateful for this help to gain insight into the needs of his boy.

Going for a walk in the street

When siblings of a disabled family member try to understand everything that is going on within the family dynamics, it is helpful to know about the *Thinking Brain* and the brain's *Alarm Centre*. A 14-year-old girl who has a little sister with a general development disorder presented the following story: 'My sister became really angry when she was supposed to help me set the table. She was frustrated because of the napkins I had chosen. When my sister gets angry, it's often me who's good at calming and helping her. When it happens, I'm a bit alarmed inside while I try to act. When I've found a solution, and tell her find some other napkins or decorate the table with Duplo bricks, I can feel myself returning to the *Thinking Brain*.' This clear knowledge of the infectious qualities of the brain's *Alarm Centre* is important to explore in our work with children. In the same way, it is important to discover when the brain's *Alarm Centre* starts closing again and the *Thinking Brain* takes over. There is great significance in analysing the workings of this with others, because it opens possibilities to see what mentalising is.

A happy but quiet guy on one of our sibling courses hadn't shared so much. Suddenly, though, he said, 'My brain's *Alarm Centre* is often turned on at my mother's place. Last time I was scolded because I fell and hit myself. I found it strange to scold me for this because it hurt. But when my mother's boyfriend and his son are there, I'm not scolded so much.' This prompted another of the siblings on the course to say, 'It's probably because your mother would like to show her best side to her boyfriend and his son.' On the floor, there was a white 3-metre-long canvas that we called 'Going for a Walk in the Street'. It was an enlarged version of the Mind Game. First, a circle was drawn in which we could stand. From the circle and three metres out, a broad street was drawn out, leading towards a goal, symbolised by another circle. A 14-year-old girl suggested the following goal: 'I would like to become better at expressing what I need, guilt-free.' This goal was written down and placed in the goal-circle. When the girl stood at the street and looked at her goal, there was a great deal of work to be done and she therefore needed to think of a *Field of Practice* where she could rehearse at an appropriate pace. She decided the first step should be telling her mom and dad that she practises 'walking down the street' because of being enrolled on the sibling course. After that, she planned to say that she wanted to go shopping, including a visit to a café, together with her mom, the following weekend.

If the challenge is fitting and the motivation to create change is real, the conditions for development are set. Practice must be continued. There is no *Field of Practice* without challenges, and that is exactly how it should be with *Fields of Practice*. They are supposed to be a bit difficult in the sense that we can just about see a chance of reaching a goal that is set, by persistently practising and making efforts. When we are on a real highway, driving too close to the edge of the road, the car hits the rumble strip and we get a very loud warning to get back into the lane. Things are similar on our metaphorical road, but if the challenges become so big that we lose grip and are side-tracked, the *Thinking Brain* will close down. There was a sign at the exit of our road: 'What is able to side-track me?' This side-track was drawn on the canvas as an exit lane and a blinking brain-alarm. At the side-track there were signs that read: 'What do I do when I am side-tracked?', 'What do I think and feel?' Participants from the course will be challenged, because old habits are hard to break. When we have to put ourselves aside for a long period of time, it takes persistent focus to break the pattern. The brain has memory lanes that require a lot of endurance to change. The next sign on our road read: 'What can get me back on the street again?' Here it was sometimes necessary to adjust the *Field of Practice* and make it slightly easier to reach a given goal, because no one develops resilience by being side-tracked again and again. In that scenario, the *Field of Practice* may be too difficult, the bar must be slightly lowered and the goal should perhaps be adjusted. When we are back on the street again, attention is fixed towards the goal once again, and we have re-created the conditions to mentalise.

A very sensitive boy stood on the street and looked towards his goal. He said that he had a burning desire to go to school every day. The goal was written down and placed in the goal-circle. Due to massive problems with his little brother's disability, he had developed some fear, and had a long period where it was a challenge for him to go to school every day. He was often hit by stomach aches when leaving the house, while at other times, he was happy about the thought of school and his classmates. He showed with his body that when he walked the street and the urge to stay at home arose, he would become side-tracked. While he was turning towards the side-track, I asked him what would help him get back on the street again. Without hesitation he said, 'Dad talks to me and we go for a walk when I feel bad. It's good to walk while we're talking.' I asked him whether there was a thought that might help him keep his focus on the street. Some time passed before he answered, 'My dad usually says to only think one hour ahead at a time.' The example illustrates that obviously all the resilience work, thoughtfulness and practice is happening to a great extent in normal life, and that our contributions as professionals is perhaps the elucidation of all the important things we already do.

Siblings measure their own resilience

The follow-up session that took place six weeks following the completion of the course clearly showed what the participants had become more aware of and what they had practised since starting the course.

A 9-year-old girl recounted that when she now visits her brother at his care-home, she experiences much more happiness in her visits. Before, she did not like to be there, was bored and played on her iPad, and now she learnt to move the torch in her Thought-House and be happier while she visits him. She focuses on the fact that the visit will be over in one hour's time and then she focuses on having a good time with her brother, and thereafter being able to go home and enjoy the time with her mother, guilt-free. A 14-year-old boy shared that he now has much more time for himself and hangs out with his buddies because he has become good at saying 'yes' and 'no' guilt-free. He has given himself permission to fill his day with all that makes him happy because his focus is no longer on being the third 'adult' at home. He also expressed that it has been helpful for him to discover that a thought is just a thought. With his ability to mentalise, he is able to categorise the thoughts he will act upon versus the thoughts he will passively let go of. One of the girls had just celebrated her confirmation. She spoke of the joy she felt on her special day, where everything went well. A master-plan was devised for the day about who would be in charge of her little brother, who is scared of organ music due to his autism. She did not need to worry about any mishaps in her day because an adult was responsible for him for the entire day and her little brother only attended part of the party. It had been a nice feeling to know that mom and dad would be present, because everything was planned to succeed.

Reflections about the development of resilience on sibling courses

Siblings of the disabled must be very, very resilient and also need support in learning how to say 'no' once in a while, guilt-free, especially since they are quite used to saying 'yes' to everything. If we design a *Field of Practice* about staying true to a 'no', and become skilled at carrying it out, guilt-free, then it also becomes nice to stay true to a 'yes'. Stories, tools and exercises have, on a very visual level, opened up the stories that have somehow been embedded in the siblings' bodies and thoughts. These have provided the siblings with a shared language that strengthens their belief in knowing it is okay to be resilient in some areas and vulnerable in others. They have also obtained insight into the good reasons to voice their own needs, thoughts and emotions so that they are not left in the shadows of a disabled brother or sister who always seems to take up most of mom's and dad's energy. Silence does not make us resilient.

Course for parents

The aim of the school's courses about resilience for parents is to provide the parents with knowledge and tools they can use in their relationship with their children in building a shared understanding and a shared language to talk about brains, thoughts, wellbeing, health, conflict prevention and conflict management. With a mixture of lecturing and praxis exercises we deal with the fact that it can be pretty hard to be together with a child who has difficulties with mentalising, and that such continuous strain may influence their own ability to mentalise. The brain's *Alarm System* can be hyper-sensitive and activated by almost nothing. Here, the dilemma arises: there can be a difference between the way we wish to react as a parent and the way we actually act because the ability to be thoughtful and mentalise can be affected by the many years of hard work the parent of a disabled child puts in.

Knowledge about the activities in the brain helps parents understand a child's situation and a child's reactions as well as the impact they have on the conditions for a relationship. A father once said, 'I've understood why I shouldn't scold my child when I become impatient. It doesn't help indeed'. And a mother added, 'I've realised that when I set demands for my daughter it's often too big a demand which she cannot fulfil. I've really had my attention turned towards dividing a goal into many small parts, thus making the challenge more appropriate.' There was also another father who shared, 'I've put too many high demands on my daughter and thought she should be pushed as much as possible in order to develop. I often find that my wife is being too tender around her and I therefore counter that by going even more in the opposite direction. As I have come to learn that appropriate challenges create resilience, I have something to think about now. I've been driving at 100 miles an hour and my daughter's maximum is 12. I have to slow down the pace and carefully consider what may be an appropriate challenge for her in accordance with her mood and state of the day.'

Final reflections

The responsibility for the development of a relationship between the professional and the pupil rests on the professional, as does the success or failure of that relationship. Our knowledge about resilience, thoughtfulness and the brain points out some fundamental human mechanisms in relation to ourselves and our relationships with other people. The Resilience Programme is imbued with simplicity, everyday language and imagery. It is very effective when we have to pass on difficult knowledge to children, young people and adults. The same language can be applied in all arenas. This allows more energy to focus on the relationships and the communication. The knowledge is not just a toolbox we can bring out of the closet in emergencies; rather, knowledge is a vitamin that contributes to a fundamental way of being healthy in the world.

There is no doubt that it is hard to control thoughts and emotions. The good part is that we can all practise as long as we remain aware that everybody brings widely different preconditions to their ability to mentalise. Pupils with reduced mentalising abilities, due to inborn disabilities, are struggling more to understand the world they live in. They become apprehensive and insecure a lot faster. For most of these pupils, the bridge between the *Thinking Brain* and the brain's *Alarm Centre* is rather short. For that reason, knowledge about the brain's functions is very helpful when we are planning an everyday scheme in which they can learn and develop. This applies to the teaching as well as in meetings with pupils.

Note

1   'Moment Diary' is a simple version of an electronic calendar. The pupils/staff add tasks or *Fields of Practice* that the pupils are working on at a given moment. This may include pictures from the teaching, or, for instance, when a pupil has just learnt to tie his shoelaces, or has learnt to differentiate between p and b, etc.

Reference

Fonagy P, Gergely G, Jurist E, Taget M (2005) *Affect regulation, Mentalization and the Development of the Self.* Karnac Books.

Chapter 8

'Will you help me?'

Experiences from a children's home

Louise Lundgaard and Mette Haahr

Background

We worked at a children's home in Greenland in a city that was isolated, in a vulnerable community that was hard-hit by unemployment, social problems and abuse. The children in the home had suffered from neglect and had a very hard time coping with their emotions and dealing with life's smaller and bigger challenges. The Greenlandic and Danish understandings of pedagogical work are divergent and the professionalisation of staff in East Greenland can be characterised as low. At the same time, there exist fundamental cultural differences, and all in all, this posed some special professional and managerial challenges with regard to our aim of creating a resilient environment for Greenlandic individuals and for the community.

Michael is a boy who had experienced major challenges in life, and it was difficult for staff to handle him in daily pedagogical work. We presented The Resilience Programme's knowledge frame to the staff. As a result, an immediate change in the staff's approach and mode of relating to Michael took place. This was a success story and we decided that, based on this experience, we were going to implement resilience in the children's home's pedagogical work. The aim was to provide the children with deeper insight into their inner worlds so that they would be able to act more appropriately in relation to themselves and the surrounding world, and be better equipped to cope with life's challenges.

The pedagogical tools

As an entry point to the work, we introduced two posters with images of the *Thinking Brain* and the brain's *Alarm Centre*, as well as a wide selection of pictograms. The pictograms symbolised safe and unsafe everyday situations and the care needs that seemed applicable to most of the children. For instance, it is vital for the kids to have a friend and that they be able to rely on the knowledge that there is an adult to take care of them. At the same time, it was generally difficult for the children to cope with the fact that they were missing their parents, but also it was difficult for them to cope with parental neglect: that they felt alone and were scolded. The symbols were chosen based on the criterion that everyone should be able to mirror themselves in the symbols, visually and through dialogue. In addition, we focused on supplementing the individual child's choice of symbols with the child's own drawings. The material was used to support the children's attempts to voice what made them feel safe and unsafe.

The story of the *House of Thoughts* describes in a simple way how our thoughts live in different rooms and how our attention can shift between thoughts. Inspired by this story, we built a two-dimensional, wooden, eight-roomed version of a Thought-House, with a small touch-lamp that could be turned on and off in each of the rooms. The lamps functioned as visual artefacts of *Attention – the Brain's Spotlight* and helped children keep their focus on what was inside a room they chose to be in. The house was hung on the wall and, underneath it, each child had two drawers for saving their symbols and pictograms that referred to the *Thinking Brain* and the brain's *Alarm Centre*. In the following, we refer to this house as the Thought-House.

Pedagogical days

We arranged pedagogical days about resilience and we started each day by talking about which dimensions of life could influence someone's resilience. Staff members also created their own posters and images of the *Thinking Brain* and *Alarm Centre*. Subsequently, staff had the choice of whether they wished to share the posters with colleagues. Then, we presented the Thought-House and the pedagogical work involving the house.

We performed a role-play about the work, where staff took on the roles of their children as well as those of adults. In the role-play, along with some grown-ups, the children chose the pictograms of the *Thinking Brain* and the brain's *Alarm Centre* that had some significance for them. First, this gave staff members a greater understanding of their own responsibility and their influence on the dialogue and processes they undertake with the children. Second, the role-play gave insight into the children's thoughts and reactions. It was fun at the same time and thus loosened up the atmosphere, in light of the serious talks we were having about the difficult elements of life there; challenges that several staff members recognised from their own lives. The aim was that the contact-persons in the pedagogical praxis should start working, along with their contact-children, with the symbols from the *Thinking Brain* and the brain's *Alarm Centre*. The children should actively select their own pictograms showing thoughts and emotions, in order to make more visible their own thoughts and emotions, through words and visualisations. Simultaneously, the contact-person should pass on knowledge, through play and dialogue, about the attention's influence on what we think about. The Thought-House and the chosen pictograms were meant to create a framework for the contact-persons' conversations with the children. In relation to this, we discussed whether such conversations between contact-person and contact-child required a special professionalism which some of the contact-persons did not have. We found, though, that the safe and confidential setting where an adult sat alone with her/his contact-child was emotionally significant enough to ensure that the conversation would always be a qualitative experience for the child, no matter the adult's background.

In the following, we will describe two cases where we worked in a goal-oriented way with the pedagogical tools mentioned.

Michael

Michael was 3½ years old when he moved into the children's home. He was a tiny, skinny boy with big, scared eyes. His eyes were seeking ours, but it was difficult to keep eye contact with him. As far as personal belongings were concerned, he brought only a small, creased bag containing a few pieces of shabby clothing. Not much was said, but suddenly Michael screamed – short, scared screams. We took him by the hand and managed to calm him with soft words. Michael's screams changed for a brief moment to low whimpers while he held the hand that was holding his and squeezed hard.

Michael's face tensed and a furrow appeared between his uneasy eyes, and then he shut his eyes really tight in order to protect himself from further external stimuli. Michael's movements were uneasy and stressed. He was tripping on his toes without moving an inch and his arms were entangled anxiously around his body in an attempt to protect himself from sensory impressions that could potentially be alarm provoking.

Michael was approximately 5 years old when we started working with resilience at the children's home. He was sensory sensitive and was affected by all stimuli from the inner and outer worlds. He was often in a state of alarm and it was difficult for him to have positive experiences in his interactions with other people that he could eventually bring into new interpersonal contexts. The form of contact with Michael consisted of touch and gesticulation, followed by limited vocabulary and sounds. When he had the energy, and was not in a state of crisis, it was possible to make eye contact with him. Michael's emotional outbursts were primarily out of happiness, frustration, powerlessness and fear. He did not express any feelings of missing something or someone, rejection or physical pain, neither through words, body language nor tears. He could register other children's emotions if they were sad, but their emotional expressions had no impact. Michael had almost no safe relations with his family, network or with the children at the children's home. Still, he had established a safe relationship with his two contact-persons, who managed to develop a sphere of security in which his alarm-state was curbed and in which he was able to achieve and get a sense of small experiences of success.

Michael performed rituals; for instance, he arranged physical things in rows or followed an object's form with his finger. His rituals seemed like an attempt to create balance and peace. The rituals changed in form and character in different situations and over time. They were often triggered when Michael was experiencing some sort of emotional shortage and was in a state of extreme stress. Michael had not been checked by a psychologist or a child psychiatrist.

Pedagogical work prior to the introduction of resilience work

Michael's internal alarm-system influenced the children around him, causing them to feel constantly on high alert as well. They took care of themselves and their playtime by rejecting him. It was a pedagogical challenge to support each child in her/his need to take care and, at the same time, support Michael into appropriate social challenges. Michael seemed quite fearful and he often retreated, as described, into his own world, through rituals and repetition. When these were interrupted by another child, a grown-up or by his own impulsive behaviour, his world would collapse, and this created insecurity and fear. He would scream and could be self-destructive and destructive at the same time. Some of his rituals were invisible and it was therefore complicated to foresee how best to guide Michael.

It was time for lunch, one day, and Michael and the other children sat down at the table. Michael guided the assisting adult by saying what should be put on his piece of bread. The adult found a piece of salami and put it on the bread. But then, Michael started screaming and his eyes enlarged while his face made harassing grimaces. He became physically uneasy and his arms overturned everything within reach. The shape of the salami did not fit the shape of the rye bread. Michael retreated into himself and he became unreachable – no one could make contact with him. He crawled down his chair and, with his fingers, traced the edge of the chair. If the assisting adult tried to reach for him, he would scream and everything would start over again. He would again start tracing the edges of the chair with one of his fingers while he kept the other finger in his mouth. The adult told him, 'This is the last time,' and so Michael panicked and his finger quickly sought out the edges of the chair while his brows deepened the furrow between his eyes. He tried to use his finger as an escape, but the adult stopped him. Everything seemed difficult for Michael and he screamed aloud and kept being anxious. The assisting adult took Michael to his room. After a while, they came back and Michael was ready to eat. The adult cut the rye bread into a shape that fitted the salami and Michael ate his food. The staff members struggled to cope with Michael, both personally and professionally. They did not understand his reactions and had no clue as to how best to help him. We spoke a lot about the challenges and about how we could support Michael, but it was difficult to keep up with the effort.

The pedagogical work with resilience

At a staff meeting, we introduced The Resilience Programme's conceptual framework. The aim was to foster greater insight into Michael's world through the staff members' insight into their own alarm-systems (the brain's *Alarm Centre*). In our introduction, we visualised the alarm-system through storytelling. We wanted the staff members to feel the fear their own alarm-systems could activate. A simple visualisation exercise provided crucial insight into, and understanding of, Michael's behavioural patterns. The staff members understood the background to his violent emotional outbursts to a higher degree following the exercise, and that 'danger' activated his alarm-system, which he needed help in moving on from. The dangers Michael encountered and reacted to were subjective and connected to his previous experiences. At first, they could be hard for those around him to understand, but it was vital to acknowledge Michael's feelings. We introduced posters with the *Thinking Brain* and the brain's *Alarm Centre* in combination with photos of Michael in various situations and states of mind. The staff members chose pictograms that showed when Michael was resilient and when he was vulnerable. At the same time, a preventive pedagogical action plan was developed and agreements were made on how we could act when Michael was in a panic. At first, the posters were meant to be a professional tool in the meeting room. One of the images on Michael's *Thinking Brain* poster was of an adult's hand holding a child's hand. This was showing symbolically that it was the adult's responsibility to care for him. While working on the posters we talked about sharing with Michael that we wanted to take care of him and wanted to help him, both when in difficult times and when he felt good. It was a matter of activating his *Thinking Brain*, mostly through a sense of safety. One day, Michael entered the meeting room in which the posters were hanging on the wall. He looked at them for a while and touched the symbols with his fingers while mumbling to himself. Michael caught sight of a staff member, pointed to the pictogram of the two hands and said, 'Helping me' – that just came out of him in the most natural of ways. We decided that, from that point onwards, Michael was to collaborate with his contact-person in becoming active in choosing pictograms for his posters.

Michael sat with his contact-person in the resilience-room on a mattress by the Thought-House. The contact-person showed him one image at a time. Michael was able to mirror himself through some of the images and then choose some of them for himself. He chose, for instance, the dangerous polar bear, bathing, an image of an angry adult and one of helping hands. His contact-person choose to show him how to put words to what was largely still invisible for him, image per image. She expressed, for example, that it is sometimes difficult for him to play with the other children. Based on that, he would smile and choose a pictogram that could symbolise the feeling he associated with her statements. They sat like this and talked for more than half an hour. Michael was peaceful, as was his body relaxed. He was concentrated and took the initiative to hold eye contact, after which they worked together to find pictograms he could choose. He cut them out and glued them to his poster with the *Thinking Brain* and the brain's *Alarm Centre*. When they were done with the poster, it was laminated and put on the wall, while copies of the pictograms were placed in his personal drawers.

For Michael and his contact-person this process was a successful experience. He was curious about every single pictogram and wanted to understand the meaning before he choosing or dropping each pictogram. His contact-person was good at verbalising and was aware of the pictograms in which Michael did not see himself. Going forward, his contact-person planned time with him and continued with Thought-House conversations.

The staff members had practised some routines that supported Michael in moving on from his moments of struggle. For instance, they helped him sit with some Lego or go to his room in order to regain some peace. Some time afterwards, however, Michael started taking the initiative himself to go through these routines whenever he started feeling stressed. Michael opened himself up to his surroundings and became more interested in his peers. He joined in their role-playing games and was once invited to be a 'dog' in the game. He was happy to be cast a role and joined in without a deeper understanding of the other children's intentions. When he was rejected by the other children, though, in contrast to his previously extreme and hysterical outbursts, he became very sad and could cry.

Summarising

The pedagogical effort meant a lot to Michael's development and wellbeing, and at the same time staff members were professionally enriched. It was a great experience to see how Michael and the staff members, through a dialogical process, developed by mirroring one another. The staff members managed to see Michael and adjust the challenges, ensuring that they were within his zone of proximal development. They mirrored his daily successes and voiced what was invisible to him. Through the staff members' more authentic relation with Michael, his safety zone expanded and his alarm-state threshold strengthened. The mirroring of one another's experiences of success also resulted in a more professional approach to the relationship. We experienced Michael showing his need to see himself as a human being, separate from all the others. He would initiate contact with children and adults by laying his hands on the person and saying, 'You . . . Louise,' then placing his hands on himself and saying, 'Me . . . Michael.' Michael seemed to be able to be aware of himself to a higher degree and, therefore, act on his feelings.

By working with their own self-insight, the other children became more open and gave space to Michael in their play. We simultaneously experienced how the influence of the pedagogical work for some children resulted in their rejection of him, in a way they had not done before, while others opened up to him more and took care of him. This depended on the individual child's resources and showed the group's increase in self-insight and self-care. They were learning about their own limits far better than any of us could, and were able to estimate whether they could handle a relationship with Michael or not.

The staff members became generally more open in terms of verbalising their everyday life challenges. Earlier, this had been difficult because many of them had felt that it was them, personally, who could not manage the job and they therefore avoided mentioning challenges. Now they had acquired insight and a professional understanding of the dynamics and could verbalise the difficult situations, also reflecting upon them together. They had formed a shared professional language, which made it easier to communicate personal and professional experiences.

Elisa

At the time we started working with resilience, Elisa was 7 years old. She was an intelligent and mature girl who had great insight into her complex inner and outer worlds. She was vulnerable and resilient at the same time, which complemented and strengthened her perception of herself. Elisa understood much of what happened in society around her, including that her parents could not take care of her because of their alcohol abuse, though she could not grasp why her parents' need for alcohol was greater than their need to be with her. Elisa had taken care of and worried about her family throughout her childhood. She was one of the grown-up children who, far too early, had been given a lot of responsibility. This motherly feeling of responsibility towards others was a huge part of Elisa's identity and gave her a feeling of strength. It happened, though, that she encountered a conflict with herself because, on the one hand, she identified with being a 'mother' and, on the other, she was a little girl with her own needs. It was difficult for Elisa to allow herself to be a child. Thus, Elisa experienced many contradictory emotions, and when these emotions became too much for her to cope with, she often found herself in a state of alarm. She cried and could react physically towards other children and adults, and she could also destroy personal things that she cared about. When her body's energy became depleted, she would pull her emotions back inside herself and would break down crying in a foetal position with her arms wrapped around herself.

Pedagogical work prior to the introduction of resilience work

It was a weekend and several children had been picked up by their parents, but Elisa had not been picked up. She asked the adults around her a lot of questions, seeking hope. She asked whether we knew if her parents were okay. She imitated what happens when we drink alcohol and become drunk. She told stories about her parents, who had been injured while drinking, and spoke about how this all scared her. She asked again whether they were okay, but no amount of answering her question could reassure her. When Elisa's eyes turned to tears, she breathed in deeply and, on exhaling, she let go of her vulnerability and straightened her body, smothering the 'little, vulnerable girl' inside her, until she vanished, giving way to the 'strong girl'. Time passed and Elisa's eyes stayed on the clock, where time disappeared into nothingness. Elisa was not picked up that weekend.

That Sunday evening, a child returned from having spent time at home and he happily shared all the things he had experienced with his family. In a split second, Elisa's nails had torn three red stripes down his cheek. She was completely out of herself and could not control her body. She screamed and cried, and the boy's defensiveness raised her hysteria. Elisa was helped by an adult and led away from him. The photos in her room that showed her happy being together with her family and all her happy drawings were torn into pieces. Her shrieks accompanied a stream of words and the air filled with: 'Nobody loves me, nobody likes me.'

Suddenly everything was quiet and Elisa put herself back into a foetal position on her bed and cried. She received comfort from the assisting adult but still held herself in her own embrace. It was hard for staff members to support Elisa when she was let down by her parents and expressed herself in such emotional and verbal outbursts. It was at the same time that a challenge arose for her to set boundaries for her 'motherly' instinct, which would organise and arrange matters for the other children. It was difficult for staff members to understand her reactions and her need to be seen as a child.

The pedagogical work with resilience

It was interesting to see Elisa work with the posters of the *Thinking Brain* and the brain's *Alarm Centre*. She picked one pictogram at a time and shared her thoughts, reflecting on her emotional life. Elisa could not stop talking. It seemed as if all the thoughts and emotions she had had throughout her life had found a place to be heard. In the end, she had to fill out two extra posters in order to make space for the whole of who 'Elisa' is.

We chose to work with resilience at a children's meeting with the aim of having the children present their personal posters to one another. In the beginning, it was the adults who took the initiative and spoke, but as the children started to recognise their own symbols in one another's posters, they started opening up to each other.

All the children's posters had been shown and only Elisa's was left. Elisa excitedly jumped up from the floor. Everybody's eyes rested on her and she turned halfway round and made eye contact with all the gazes. Her contact-adult sat down with the children and Elisa giggled while she straightened her back and took a deep breath. Her fingers chose one image at a time. She told her audience about the difficult parts and about the parts that made her happy. She shared that when she was missing her family, her heart became sad. The other children joined the dialogue and their different stories combined, forming a feeling of community. When she finished, she placed her hands behind her back, and did not know what to do with herself. The short silence was suddenly interrupted by applause from her friends, and the adults followed. Elisa giggled as she curtsied in front of her audience.

Afterwards, the children created some personal symbols for their drawer in the Thought-House. A variety of symbols were shaped with putty while they mirrored one another, and throughout the process, spoke about their parents' neglect, for instance. A lot of different hearts were made in this activity – some of the hearts were cut in half. A kind of community had been built, with a space for the children and their individual stories.

Elisa lay in her bed crying. An adult passed by and they went to the Thought-House together. That was when Elisa opened the drawer that contained her personal pictograms. Elisa chose the pictogram showing a scolding grown-up, placed it in a room in the Thought-House and turned the room's lamp on. The adult asked about the pictogram and Elisa started explaining that the adults did not understand her and that she felt that nobody liked her. Elisa and the adult talked silently together. Their eyes met and they smiled at each other. The grown-up asked Elisa how she could become happy again and Elisa put the pictogram with 'children playing outside' into the house and turned that room's lamp on. They then went to the playground together.

Summarising

Elisa was a great inspiration to the other children in the group, who became more open and interested in one another's emotions throughout our work with resilience. She had, by voicing her emotions, given the other children a vocabulary which resulted in the children having, to a higher degree, the possibility of expressing themselves from a child's perspective. Elisa had experienced that the vulnerability she did not know where to place before, had now become a part of her resilience, as something special. It made a huge impact on her and her relationships with the other children and adults. At the same time, it looked as if her need to make a difference to others had been supplemented with a healthy development-promoting function of her as role model. It was still difficult for Elisa when she became overwhelmed by emotions. However, through resilience work, she had gained a deeper understanding for what did her good and what gave her pain, and she could, with help and support from an adult, shift her attention, act and get better.

During the process, it also became evident that the staff members' pedagogical challenge of embracing Elisa's emotional outbursts stemmed from the fact that her emotional expressions reflected their own personal vulnerability. Then, Elisa's clear need to achieve more self-insight and her approach to coping with her own emotions and conflicts, as well as her experiences of success, influenced staff and she somehow showed them a way into the implementation of the pedagogical tools.

Elisa became more embracing of her relations with other children in the group. The fact that the children's group had been together in their work with resilience had made a huge difference for her. She could see herself in the other children's life stories and, consequently, did not feel so alone in her own story. At the same time, Elisa could more easily handle the other children's emotional outbursts. Her state of alarm was not being triggered in the same manner as it had previously been, when other kids were struggling. Elisa became aware that the strength of the children's group could be found in the community they had created, and it was important for her that they continued to get along well. Elisa's wider awareness of her own vulnerability had influenced the children, staff members and their mutual relations with one another.

Conclusion

The work with resilience was a successful experience for the children. Together with their contact-persons, each child opened up to voicing and visualising their thoughts and emotions in a way that fitted their individual development and age.

The children gained a deeper self-insight and became better at feeling and verbalising their own needs. They became better at adjusting their actions in accordance with themselves and their surroundings, and also at asking adults for help. By talking about one another's posters, they gained a greater understanding of each person in the group and became more embracing and empathic. A community developed where the children could speak together about difficult things.

The materials (posters and the Thought-House) were pivotal throughout our work. They were significant in a major way because they were concrete, they appealed to the senses and they helped make thoughts and emotions visual. A child's thoughts and emotions were therefore externalised – moved out of the child's inner chaos and into 'out there'. As a result, they became visible and manageable; less abstract.

In the process, where the child sat with her/his contact-person and chose her/his own pictograms, the materials seemed to have had the function of 'a shared third' (Husen 1996). This is characterised by a goal shared by the adult and the child that they work towards, together. The shared goal moves attention away from the relationship and the child experiences the adult as a collaborator rather than as a caretaker. The adult plays a motivating part in the process and, thus, becomes a role model to the child. It was crucial to the pedagogical work that knowledge was disseminated in everyday language and that imagery was supported by the materials we produced. All in all, this created a shared scheme of things between children and adults, formally educated or not, as well as between management and staff members. It was at the same time important that we focus on some fundamental knowledge and aspects about being human – with ourselves and with others. The general human challenges, which transcended age, education and culture, were part of forming a connectedness.

The staff members showed trust and openness towards one another. This was despite the fact that many of them were hugely challenged in life and therefore vulnerable themselves. Many projections and reflections came to the surface and it was difficult at times, for several of the staff members, to embrace the children and each other. During their work with resilience, they became more skilled at handling the vulnerability that came up via the children's reflections. The vulnerability transformed into personal strength, which, for instance, meant that they could identify with a child and be more authentic. They experienced success through the children's experiences of success, and a resilient community developed and gave individuals a personal and professional boost. The staff members became better at reflecting and being present and sensing the children. Overall, the pedagogical work has strengthened the staff members' ability to mentalise, which can be defined as 'minding your mind'. The staff members gained a deeper insight into their own thoughts and emotions throughout the process and could embrace the children and themselves to a higher degree than before. The self-insight seemed to have strengthened their self-control. They also improved their ability to comprehend the children's reactions and to acknowledge and support the children, whatever their stage of development. They were, in general, more empathic and we sensed that they experienced a professional challenge and humility in terms of verbalising and understanding the children's emotions and reactions. They showed professional dignity, alone and in cooperation, and we fully respected their great effort.

In the positive process of the resilience work, the shared frame of understanding became core to the overall developmental work at the children's home. It supplemented the children's perspective and the development plans with a new perspective. Moreover, the staff members' experiences and knowledge about the children's thoughts and emotions became central in the writing of reports and developmental plans. The pictogram of the adult hand holding the child's hand became a symbol for the children–adult relationship at the children's home. Michael's 'Help me', while he grabbed onto an adult's hand, and Elisa, who reached out when she needed the presence of an adult, became influential images. They showed that the resilience work had united the child and adult worlds through a shared language based on security and care.

Reference

Husen M (1996) Det fælles tredje. In Benedicta Pécseli (ed.) *Kultur & pædagogik*. Hans Reitzels Forlag: Koebenhavn, 218–232.

Chapter 9

A municipal perspective on resilience

Johanne Cecilie Andersen and
Morten Lysdahlgaard

A MUNICIPAL PERSPECTIVE ON RESILIENCE I

Johanne Cecilie Andersen

This is how it started

In the municipality of Guldborgsund we work with 'effect': What is the actual effect of what we do in daily life? Does it make sense? Does it influence our citizens in the ways we imagine? Working with effect creates an awareness of what works. At the same time, it creates an awareness of how complex it is to work with helping other people to cope with their own existence and to diffuse that awareness out into communities. We know there is evidence showing that working with the resilience perspective can help people in various situations handle challenges. As you can read in other chapters of the book, many easily accessible pedagogical tools and ways of working with resilience are available. We also know that when we are to engage with something, it is important to be motivated by experiencing an effect of that work, which then creates excitement.

The choice of working with resilience in a municipality will often be a decision made at the management level. In our case, the idea was nevertheless to initiate a wave of engagement and motivation to work with The Resilience Programme and then let this wave roll out – if it made sense. We hoped that if a leader or an employee, through experience and reflection, found it meaningful to work with the method, it would spread. That is, we did not want to force anyone to work with the programme, but we hoped that individual experiences would show that the approach worked and that thereafter it would be passed on through inspired dialogue, based on trustworthy, experiential engagement. The idea behind this is, among other things, built upon the organisational theorist Ralph Stacey's (2010) approach to organisational development. Informal relations and dialogue are seen here as an important, but still often overlooked, resource in institutions. When we communicate with each other, on a human level, it influences our individual development, one another's development and an organisation's development. Changes thus take place in the organisation due to the relationships between employees and leaders. This way of thinking challenges the prevailing understanding that we are able to design changes and beliefs by completing a particular process. It is typical to set goals, plan processes and design frameworks of cooperation. There may be a need to do this, to a great extent, as a means to making us feel safe and creating a shared understanding of a common direction. It is also important, though, to know that we cannot control relationships, nor opinions. Instead, we can work with relationships as a resource, which is exactly what we attempted in our process here.

Course in resilience

It all started in a delimited area in the autumn of 2014. At that time, I was the leader of the teaching department. The leading health visitor and I were contacted by parents who were looking for options for their children who suffered from anxiety. Together with a leader from day-care, health visiting and community healthcare, I met with the committee for health information in order to hear about their experiences with a particular group of children. After an introduction to chief physician Poul Lundgaard and manager Charan Nelander, we saw some possibilities for working with resilience and how it could be implemented. What started as our intention of dealing with lighter anxiety neuroses in children rapidly turned into reflections about dealing with, and prevention strategies for, children and adults who live with various challenges. Following this, we involved more leaders who were curious to know about the approach's applicability. Still, our first emphasis was put on inclusion in schools, in cooperation with all the transversal collaborators within this area.

The first step was an invitation to an introductory meeting about resilience for managers, children's social workers, behavioural counsellors from the schools, psychologists, the day-care institutional section and the family section. Poul Lundgaard introduced The Resilience Programme, and shortly thereafter we noted our intention to initiate a course for resilience-supervision. There was great interest and several leaders signed up for the course. We wrote to other leaders in order to get them to consider whether they had employees who could also join.

The following criteria were set as requirements for participation:

- Teaching experience
- Health professional or pedagogical educational background
- Possibility for and wish to teach others
- Time priority to teach in our own centre or in the wider organisation
- Participation in follow-up meetings.

The course had 17 participants who were leaders and employees from areas such as community healthcare, health care, day-care, day-care centres, job centres, psychologists, school departments and administration, public schools, special needs schools and the family-consultant sector. In addition, we had invited some external collaborators with the aim of strengthening cooperation with them and thereby the all-inclusive-oriented work with children and youth. A leader from a production school participated, as well as a pedagogue from the children's ward of the local hospital. To Jeanette, the hospital pedagogue, it meant a lot to participate in the course. She said, 'Probably the most significant part was to share experiences and knowledge with professionals from the children and youth sectors across the public systems. Also, to build a network and achieve a shared conceptual understanding we could work and communicate from. A coherence is growing and a recognisability that you can elaborate further, from an individual starting point and in various directions. Just imagine that you can communicate from a shared referential framework across municipalities and regions, benefitting and creating happiness for children, youths and parents. That gives energy!'

Resilience and the work environment

Resilience as a concept has gradually also included considerations of the work environment, and the idea of resilience has been in the media quite a lot. In regard to individual work environments and recruiting, the concept has different connotations and many people are on their guard. It can therefore be a challenge to start working with resilience in relation to work environments. Reactions can be positive and favourable, but they can be reserved as well – What is the intention behind introducing resilience? Why is it suddenly necessary to introduce resilience, as an employer? Where is the responsibility placed? What kind of culture are we fostering when we suddenly speak so much about resilience? Are we now to be considered as electroplated and able to stand up to anything?

When we first started working with resilience, we were introduced to the indirect effects it could have on the work environment when employees learnt to apply the tools in relation to the user groups with whom they were in contact. This caused us, in the management group, to widen our perspective instead of just focusing on the effects at the citizen level. We could picture some valuable synergy effects taking place when focusing at one level, while at the same time keeping an eye on other areas. Thus, there has been work with resilience both directly and indirectly in relation to work environments through the various individual efforts we have initiated.

In the following, Lene Stillund, day-care manager, provides us with an example:

> I am Head of the day-care section and have, over some years, become aware that the reasons for sick leave have changed. In recent years, we have seen a great deal of wellbeing challenges in individual day-care groups. There have, for instance, been employees who felt bullied or who have felt left out by their respective communities. We therefore decided to focus on the theme 'a good colleague', and when Poul Lundgaard Bak was visiting the municipality in relation to this he spoke about how we can work with children's and young

people's resilience. I was very inspired by the thought that the staff who work with children and youths should be resilient as well if they are to support children and young people in their development of resilience. At the same time, I knew of experiences from the day-care staff that precisely confirmed this. After many discussions with my colleagues, I decided to sign up for some further education, together with many other interested colleagues from our municipality. Throughout the course, it became evident to me that we, in day-care, should work especially with resilient communities. We were three resilience-supervisors who came together and discussed my reflections and ideas. We introduced sessions in which all employees should participate through a staff meeting, and in which one of the resilience instructors would present resilience tools to all. Afterwards, everybody continued with the work in their respective day-care groups. Each group was keen to describe what offers them peace in the brain's *Alarm Centre* and energy as well as what drains energy in relation to the community.

The next step was to introduce this to the group managers. There was some consideration as to what extent it mattered who would introduce The Resilience Programme to employees; what barriers, advantages or disadvantages would be implied if it was the leader versus an external person? We decided that I, being the manager of the entire day-care provision, should offer a lecture, including discussion time and exercises. This session lasted three hours. All group managers were very interested and were attentive throughout the exercises and discussions. All exercises had their starting point in the challenges of everyday life and in the resilient – or less resilient – communities. In addition, we chose to offer a lecture on communication to supplement the content of The Resilience Programme. The group managers all said that the day's content had provided them with plenty of material for further work to support the process we had initiated.

Gossip, negative energy, unspoken expectations, experience of too many tasks and mistrust in the community were some of the subjects that the groups described as draining. The groups worked with identifying the core of matters and with listening and continuously building upon other expressions and ideas. When the groups identified the core of a problem, they moved on to clarifying a goal they wished to reach as well as how to achieve it. During the entire work, they used *Thought Bubbles* as a shared concept in all discussions. Our next step at the group meetings was to initiate an activity in which the participants could choose from several solutions to the challenges they worked with in their groups. In particular, we introduced *The story of a mind train* as a tool to create awareness around the possibility of moving between and controlling our thoughts. We worked a great deal with the process and spent time on reflection and learning. We did not know, within the moment, which step would be next. It was an extraordinarily exciting process, full of learning that challenges all familiar thought patterns to a high degree. Since we launched this work we have, in the management group, not heard about incidences of bullying or enmity among colleagues – there is a sense that we are all a part of creating an organisation comprised of good colleagues.

This example from Lene is a good one that helps highlight how we can work in both ways. If we work with resilient communities, this will also affect relations with citizens (here, children and their parents) – and vice versa. In a collaboration between the municipality's Department for Human Resources and Work Environment and the Department for Community Health, we have tried various initiatives and have worked either with the citizens or within the work environments. We have offered thematic days about resilient communities in which managers, work environment representatives and employee representatives gathered for one-day lectures and discussions about resilience, with special attention to the work environment. Here they also had time to work with the concept in relation to their own daily life.

Wellbeing in the municipality of Guldborgsund

Concerning resilience and the work environment, it is my experience that it is important to paint a picture of the correlation between individual resilience, resilience at group level, management-related resilience and organisational resilience. When we work with resilience and with other areas relevant to work environments in the Department for Human Resources and Work Environment, our starting point is our so-called IGLO model, in which the various levels of an organisation are taken into consideration. When we speak about resilience we explain it like this:

I: Individual resilience.
G: Resilience in relation to the Group – resilient communities.
L: Resilience and wellbeing of Leaders. The point is that when the brain's *Alarm System* is triggered in a leader, it is far more infectious than when it happens among colleagues, and it directly influences employees, and ultimately the citizens as well.
O: At the Organisational level, resilience is explained as involving a stable economy and a common direction that do not change so much over time. It is mentioned that changes, new legislation and technological systems also influence organisational resilience.

Each level involves an opportunity as well as a responsibility. All levels co-influence one another and may strengthen and weaken the other levels. The effect diminishes, however, the more resilience we can build at each level.

The Department for Human Resources and Work Environment has launched a larger holistically oriented effort to increase wellbeing. This is an effort that takes all levels of the IGLO model into account and is fundamentally based on the understanding of the brain's *Alarm Centre* and the *Thinking Brain*. Parts of this effort involve explicitly working with The Resilience Programme; at other times, only particular elements are picked and utilised, without specifically referencing the programme. The holistically oriented effort to increase wellbeing has, for example, a sub-offer that targets manager-wellbeing. This includes concrete leadership tools, individual sparring sessions about personal challenges, personal planning and many other things, including the development of effective and meaningful management groups, all with the point of strengthening wellbeing for the individual leader. Resilience is typically not mentioned in this context. However, knowledge that is embedded in The Resilience Programme is added when relevant.

Recruiting

If we speak to a group of employees and managers about resilience, the question of whether we can write anything about resilience in a job advertisement naturally pops into the discussion. It is often in the media and concerns staff and job-seekers, but what is resilience for, and what would be the consequences if someone says at a job interview that they are 'resilient' and then falls sick soon afterwards?

As a consequence of the different and very individual definitions of resilience and the consequentially derived insecurity, in the Department for Human Resources and Work Environment we have decided to offer special counselling in regard to using the concept in job advertisements. Instead of writing about the concept, we encourage management to reflect on their understanding of it. Are they referring to physical resilience or mental resilience? Is the point to be able to manage deadlines or handle difficult cases? By describing the kind of resilience that is needed, the job-seeker is much better informed about the requirements of a specific job. It is key for us that we do not use the concept of resilience as a cliché in the municipality. The consequence of this could be superficiality or perhaps abdication of responsibility. We wish to work with resilience and its concepts where it is relevant and makes sense. It would be in direct opposition to our intentions if we applied the concept without, at the same time, explaining what we mean by it. We have to acknowledge that certain interpretations and stories align with our use of the concept, and it is therefore vital to ensure that a shared understanding of the concept emerges, in order to avoid guilt, shame, abdication of responsibility and resistance.

A MUNICIPAL PERSPECTIVE ON RESILIENCE II

Morten Lysdahlgaard

The Department for Community Health in the municipality of Guldborgsund is in charge of many undertakings, various in nature. The tasks assigned to me and my three closest colleagues are related to paragraph 119 in the Danish Health Act, in which it is stated that the municipal board is responsible for managing the creation of a framework for citizens' healthy life. My colleagues and I primarily work with citizen-related prevention, with the aim of minimising occurrences of illness, psycho-social problems or accidents. Citizen-related prevention targets citizens of all ages – including healthy citizens, the disabled, the psychologically ill, citizens with early signs of illness and citizens at risk of illness.

Why the Department for Community Health adopted The Resilience Programme

In 2014, our manager of the Department for Community Health participated in the development of ideas regarding the eventual use of The Resilience Programme in the municipality of Guldborgsund. It was natural, therefore, that she sent several of her consultants to a workshop concerning the application of the programme's perspectives. Shortly after our attendance at the resilience workshop, we had a discussion in the Department for Community Health about the department's priorities in regard to our focus on mental health. We were aware that resilience made sense in relation to many aspects:

- In 2012, the Danish Department of Health published a prevention package about mental health. The package included recommendations for the promotion of mental health in the population. It specifically focused on the environmental influences on mental health and what exactly contributes to the quality of such environments. In the municipality of Guldborgsund, it is the Department for Community Health that is in charge of implementing all prevention packages, including the prevention package 'Mental Health'.
- From research, we know that it is hard for many to change their unsuitable lifestyle. In this case, lifestyle should be understood as encompassing the health-related choices we make in life. Our personal lifestyle is affected by internal factors (motivation, knowledge and inspiration) as well as external factors (family, economy, work conditions, etc.). Changing our lifestyle is a challenge; for instance, quitting cigarettes, eating healthily, making healthy lunch packs for the kids, stimulating their exercising habits, etc. This all gets especially challenging if we do not have the necessary mental energy and understanding of the mechanisms of our thoughts and emotions. The Resilience Programme was a concrete tool for us in this respect, and opened up the possibility that we could also offer a focus on the mental aspects of lifestyle changes, alongside our focus on the 'classical' health factors.
- The amount of national, regional and municipal data about decreasing mental health in the population is vast. Besides, there is increasing national and municipal focus on the factors that influence mental health in a negative way; factors that are simultaneously responsible for the social imbalance of health.
- The Department for Community Health has increasingly received enquiries from different municipal institutions and employees in the municipalities who

have encountered challenges concerning citizens' mental health. Among other things, the institutions asked for tools they could apply to such challenges and help alleviate the consequences of acute, emerging challenges, as well as inspire the promotion of mental health for all.

My colleagues and I from the Department for Community Health are dependent on cooperation with the rest of the municipality. We cannot lift an entire segment of people's health on our own. We are therefore dependent on the scope we have to support employee competence development for those who are on the front lines of health promotion and health prevention with different target groups (children, youth, families, vulnerable citizens, etc.). Similarly, we want to develop transversal cooperation between different areas around the implementation of evidence-based methods or best practices that promote mental health.

Still, we have experienced difficulties in mobilising things, stepping out and cooperating around the promotion of mental health – in relation to both employees and citizens. Cooperation explicitly implies a shared language around mental health as a means to support our understanding of the challenges and needs experienced by citizens and employees. Our meetings about resilience with other people within the municipality, where we can discuss the challenges we all face and wish to solve, were something that gave many of us the drive and energy to cooperate more and to come up with ideas and transversal solutions. As evidenced from Jeanette's and Lene's statements presented above, these new perspectives and a shared language were exactly what made a huge difference.

The Resilience Programme is a validated programme and therefore an obvious launching pad for creating a system that spans various professional sectors. This is especially the case since The Resilience Programme builds on common human competences, imagery and everyday language and because it is research based. The last point is often of special importance to management and at the political level. It creates success when we, as employees, can present research-based tools that are able to support structural changes within organisations and among citizens. A tool that:

- is connected with an implementation that requires relatively few resources;
- can be viewed in relation to other projects/focus areas.

Dilemmas concerning the organisation of competences

It had not been our initial purpose to have the resilience work centrally decided upon or managed, but rather to let it flow, due to the energy and interest it created, and produce a ripple effect. However, we must admit that an employee's position made a huge difference to how much resilience was taken up – whether someone was an employee or a manager at the time of implementation – as did the framework and opportunities they had to manage their own time.

The municipality's 17 resilience instructors come from very different sectors and cover, for instance, pedagogical preventive work, day-care, public schools, social services, etc. It is a strength, of course, that competences are spread throughout the organisations. At the same time, the challenge is that the instructors may feel professionally isolated, may lack some daily sparring sessions, and may not be able to allocate enough resources to support cross-organisational resilience work. Equally, several employees and managers were, and are, participating in other further education and developmental activities, and have to prioritise which methods to work with. The idea was, and still is, that instructors should be available as a resource to other departments. In this way, the instructors could, for instance, arrange inspirational meetings and introductions to The Resilience Programme, as well as supervision for those interested in further work with the approach. The experience has been, however, that it is hard for these instructors to find the time to work cross-organisationally with The Resilience Programme, to help ensure an optimal spreading of competences. One worry is that we do not have a resilience instructor in the municipality who possesses the competence to educate future instructors. This means that we have to find the money for external education and training.

At the same time, the Department for Community Health has experience with several competence development training courses for front-line employees or ambassadors that point to specific challenges worth considering. Some time ago, when the municipalities had taken the tasks of public health away from what was previously known as counties, the Department for Community Health offered a lifestyle course (diet, smoking, alcohol, exercise) for municipal employees. The purpose of the course was to encourage health in the workplace. It has also been a challenge to maintain the ambassador network, because different attitudes were in place regarding the roles and tasks. Today, this exists in some parts of the organisation while in others, it has disappeared.

Now, 17 resilience instructors have been educated and the idea was to have them educating the front-line staff; but how to move on from here? How do we move from a good idea to having the tools implemented and used within a municipal organisation? When an organisation works with general competence development, that is, the development of general competences which can be applied throughout the organisation, several challenges are probable. For instance, through our work with lifestyle, the Department for Community Health had realised the importance of:

- Ensuring and upholding of the continuous development of the applied competences
- Ensuring that the applied competences are realised in action towards changes that create wellbeing for citizens
- Ensuring a constant ownership across the organisation: employees, groups (teams) and management
- Ensuring that the competences support existing strategies and/or policies.

What is the next step for us to keep the pot boiling?

How do we ensure that the work is spreading from ongoing interest and that the initiative does not fade? The way things look now, we have organised the approach through the Department of Human Resources and Work Environment, which manages resilience and the work environment, as well as through the Department for Community Health, which manages citizen-related endeavours. The Department of Human Resources and Work Environment takes a goal-oriented outlook on resilience, which is a well-defined area, whereas the citizen-related initiatives are broader. One idea could be to divide the management functions out into the centres and have one project manager within each department who would be responsible for opening up something easier, accessible and closer to praxis. Additionally, we are about to arrange some after-work meetings as practice for the resilience instructors' dissemination competences, where colleagues can be inspired to work with resilience. Several centres and departments have already incorporated the concept of resilience in their descriptions of effect-objectives. In this way, resilience instruction will possibly become more goal oriented, closer to praxis and easier to work with in a concrete and guiding manner. We are also lucky that a community health project, 'The Bridge to Better Health', a huge transversal health and research initiative in our region, is also showing interest in resilience work. This will support some of what we have already launched. Prioritising the time to disseminate resilience principles and methods will still be a challenge that requires management's decisions on time allocation. However, this is an ongoing challenge related to all areas.

Our next steps in the process concern maintaining the instructors' network, thus enabling them to continue sparring and exchanging ideas. At our next meeting with the resilience instructors, we plan on preparing a presentation for managers and leaders about resilience. As part of this, each of us will introduce how we are working with resilience in praxis.

Through the municipality of Guldborgsund's employee intranet, a link will be added to a site about resilience. This is meant to create:

- Visibility of resilience.
- Awareness of the imbalance in health issues, especially regarding the lack of mental health focus among groups of citizens.
- Awareness of the concept of resilience, what it means and how it may be applied.
- Visibility regarding the results created by instructors and employees within the organisation. The results will be presented as stories about successes, short movies from real events, interviews, etc. We are planning, among other things, to film short sequences of ideas about combining resilience with whatever praxis we may be using, stories from instructors, comments from citizens, actual work-sessions that involve elements from the programme, etc.

We have the courage to move on

As mentioned, the municipality of Guldborgsund puts great emphasis on effect. Where work with resilience contributes to young people's ability to cope in life, it may still not be possible to measure the direct effect that resilience has, as it is part of a whole. It is not a concern to us to document this effect as a research endeavour, but rather that you, as a leader, employee, pupil or parent, experience it as meaningful. We know that the work with resilience has an impact, but it is just as important that we, as leaders and employees, feel within ourselves that the work makes sense before we integrate it and start disseminating it. The idea behind working with resilience in the municipality was never to force anyone to apply the method, but rather to initiate something we knew worked and have people become motivated to continue using it by trying it out themselves.

Ralph Stacey (2010) has made the point about how local interactions (for instance, conversations and actions) create patterns and new tendencies over time. It is our hope that small pushes, here and there, will initiate informal conversations and reflections about how we build the language and knowledge of resilience together.

Reference

Stacey, R. (2010) *Complexity and Organizational Reality*. Routledge.

Index

For Product Safety Concerns and Information please contact our EU
representative GPSR@taylorandfrancis.com
Taylor & Francis Verlag GmbH, Kaufingerstraße 24, 80331 München, Germany

www.ingramcontent.com/pod-product-compliance
Lightning Source LLC
Chambersburg PA
CBHW070339270326
41926CB00017B/3916